The Future of Knowledge
& Culture

The Future of Knowledge & Culture

A Dictionary for the 21st Century

Edited by

VINAY LAL

ASHIS NANDY

PENGUIN
VIKING

VIKING
Published by the Penguin Group
Penguin Books India Pvt Ltd, 11 Community Centre, Panchsheel Park, New
Delhi 110 017, India
Penguin Group (USA) Inc., 375 Hudson Street, New York, New York 10014,
USA
Penguin Group (Canada), 90 Eglinton Avenue, Suite 700, Toronto, Ontario,
M4P 2Y3, Canada (a division of Pearson Penguin Canada Inc.)
Penguin Books Ltd, 80 Strand, London WC2R 0RL, England
Penguin Ireland, 25 St Stephen's Green, Dublin 2, Ireland (a division of Penguin
Books Ltd)
Penguin Group (Australia), 250 Camberwell Road, Camberwell, Victoria
3124, Australia (a division of Pearson Australia Group Pty Ltd)
Penguin Group (NZ), cnr Airborne and Rosedale Road, Albany, Auckland
1310, New Zealand (a division of Pearson New Zealand Ltd)
Penguin Group (South Africa) (Pty) Ltd, 24 Sturdee Avenue, Rosebank,
Johannesburg 2196, South Africa

Penguin Books Ltd, Registered Offices: 80 Strand, London WC2R 0RL,
England

First published in Viking by Penguin Books India 2005

Copyright © Vinay Lal and Ashis Nandy 2005

10 9 8 7 6 5 4 3 2

Typeset in Sabon by SURYA, New Delhi
Printed at Saurabh Printers Pvt. Ltd, Noida

To the memory of Ivan Illich who has not contributed to this book but whose invisible signature adorns many of its pages

Contents

Preface

Vinay Lal and Ashis Nandy

The twentieth century, for most part, was an unfolding of the nineteenth century and the social evolutionist theories of sociocultural and political change typically associated with that moment in history. Only in 1989 did the twentieth century finally emerge from the cocoon of its predecessor by demolishing the last great institutional symbol of its captivity to the earlier century: the Soviet system, which had become a perfect symbol of a form of dissent that pays homage to its opponent by being its mirror image in violence, oppression and attempts to ensure epistemic hegemony. The twentieth century never had much time or opportunity to establish itself as an entity. The break with the various forms of nineteenth-century social reformism is not yet complete—there are doubts whether even colonialism with its developed theories of the civilizing mission is truly dead or has found rebirth in the mainstream ideas of development and globalization—but signs of transition are now everywhere. These persist despite the continuity in global patterns of dominance.

This dictionary for the twenty-first century tries to capture something of that sense of transition and the open-ended nature of human sensitivities at the beginning of the new millennium. Its editors know that, in this exercise, a crucial component is the diverse construction of time itself. For some, time moves through history—connecting the past to the future, the old to the new and the possible. For others, time is an impersonal betrayer: it not only ensures the mortality of social and political institutions but also of the categories that give meaning to them. For still others, time is a relentlessly playful entity: it can resurrect the old, revivify the familiar and ensure that the new is not stillborn.

Unfortunately, in the presently dominant global common sense—the one with which the global middle class lives—time is primarily interpreted as history, and negotiating time is the process of negotiating history. It is true that hard-boiled historical determinism constitutes a small part of public consciousness, even in the heart of the so-called historical societies. Few feel that history has closed all except a few options, except probably for the widespread conviction that all societies are moving inexorably towards resembling the modern, liberal-democratic West—with the same kind of material prosperity, unfettered right to consumerism and exorbitant levels of wastefulness. Nonetheless, such societies also love to believe that history shapes us much more than we can hope to shape history.

There is also a moral dimension to this belief. History is supposed to supply the values by which we should be guided in our collective choices and, indeed, in defining the social and political options available to us. In this respect, history is the unacknowledged scripture of the moderns; we choose according to the parameters of history not because we are immersed in history but because history is the last recourse of those rendered socially and politically rudderless and looking for something authoritative or canonical. As a result, our concept of time binds us to the past—a past that is first historicized and, thus, objectified and sometimes rendered absolute—in a way that few 'primitive' or 'savage' societies have ever been tied to the past through their traditions. Today, in society after society, the open-ended past, the legendary mythic or fabulous past transmitted through rituals and folk memory, has something of the nature of village churches and temples. People take them seriously but do not find them awe-inspiring, overwhelming, outside the domain of human review. History, on the other hand, is like a cathedral. Its formidable presence shapes the life of the agnostic and the non-believer much more seriously.

The other possible way of engaging time today is enshrined in a discipline that serves as esoterica in the world of discursive knowledge: future studies. It has a marginal presence in what we have called the dominant structure of global common sense except in two areas: fiction, where utopias and futuristic vision have a natural place, and forecasting in areas like economics, environmental studies and climatology. The former is seen as an area that covers feats of imagination rather than interventions in the real world. The latter is seen as a cluster of knowledge systems that covers quick, informed projections of the present into the future. Both are seen as empirical, pragmatic and, therefore, very comforting— liable to endow one with a sense of control over the immediate future. Apart from these, other areas and other kinds of future studies always verge on the lowbrow, if not the disreputable. For such studies do not truly give us a sense of having control and are seen as partly outside the domain of empirical testing. Even when a prediction turns out to be correct, one is never quite sure about what to make of the role of the researcher in it. His or her success too often looks like a product of intuition rather than that of scientific deliberation.

Likewise, the concept of space to many in the dominant global middle-class culture is entirely a geographical entity; its coordinates are given and measurable. In any case, it is difficult for the moderns to accept that all space could be defined as intrinsically psychogeographical, that one of the means of creating space for the imaginary has traditionally been, in many cultures, constructing an imaginary space.[1] As a result, space is increasingly becoming a matter of latitudes and longitudes—a form of territoriality that diplomats, businesspersons and tourists have to negotiate. Constructs such as home, which were even a few generations ago psychogeographical by definition, have been now almost totally discredited, as amply evidenced by the gory record of the twentieth century during which the slogans of homelands and living spaces (lebensraum) killed millions, destroyed thousands of communities and brutalized entire societies. Perhaps, understandably, there is

---

[1]See, for example, Ashis Nandy, 'Time travel to a possible self: Searching for the alternative cosmopolitanism of Cochin', in Ashis Nandy, *Time Warps: The Insistent Politics of Silent and Evasive Pasts* (New Delhi: Permanent Black, 2001), 157–209.

now a tendency to say or imply that the idea of a psychogeographical home is itself an anachronism. The new cosmopolitanism that is sweeping the globe has no need for it.

A good example of this trend is the idea of hybridism that has become salient in cultural studies in Western universities. For thinkers like Homi K. Bhabha, hybridism is primarily a cultural category, even though implicitly it has increasingly acquired a hard spatial dimension. The first criterion of hybridity that is celebrated is spatial uprooting, voluntary or otherwise. In the popular culture of cultural studies, if we may use the expression, it is increasingly a marker of the expatriate scholar. The formerly colonized countries from which many of the leading postcolonial scholars have emerged always experienced 'mixing', but the theorists of hybridity have always insisted that relying on this phenomenon is a rather embarrassing, unreflective and unsophisticated way of thinking about the pasts and presents of these societies.

In this new world of globalization where the manifest expansion of space and time is accompanied by a covert shrinkage of the meanings of space and time, the first casualty is the form of utopian thinking that encrypts alternative visions of desirable societies. For utopias may lie neither in the future—in the projections of a desirable society and in the foresight of seers—nor in a golden past, as in many Chinese and Indic cultures. They may lie in human minds as explorations in human potentialities, as the ability to envision and play with alternatives. Such mechanisms of ability and play are now threatened species in the mainstream culture of knowledge; the only kind of games that modernity can countenance are those with clear 'winners' and 'losers', the operative terms in much of public discourse.[2] However, we suspect that, outside and at the margins of the known world of knowledge, the concepts of time and space today have begun to acquire more jagged as well as more fuzzy contours. After decades of hard-eyed

---

[2]For further elaboration, see Vinay Lal, *Empire of Knowledge: Culture and Plurality in the Global Economy* (London: Pluto Press, 2002), and James Carse, *Finite and Infinite Games: A Vision of Life as Play and Possibility* (New York: Ballantine Books, 1986).

political realism and flirtation with the positivist sciences, many are learning to confront situations where time and space are inter-translatable by default, as for instance in the Southern world's pathetic effort at different times to emulate, first, the colonial powers, then the socialist states and now the sole surviving superpower. At least in some sections of the intellectual world, ideas of the future now intersect with our capacity to look at the past and the present from the vantage ground of the future. It will be our aim in this book to introduce the more academically minded reader to this emerging world of knowledge and imagination.

Do these processes have anything to do with the pattern of human violence we have seen during the last hundred years? Do the attempts to consolidate nation-states and nationalist sentiments, following the European and North American patterns, explain the mix of venom, jealousy and scapegoating that characterize Hindu or Jewish nationalism? Are nation-states and ideas of nationality intrinsically violent categories? Is the Southern world's attempt to duplicate the Western experiences of the nineteenth and twentieth centuries an essentially self-destructive exercise? Do yesterday's victims tomorrow make good killers?

It is our belief that responses to such questions vary not with the nature of one's access to empirical realities but with the way one chooses to conceptualize the world and the categories one deploys to exercise that choice. As we leave the twentieth century behind—a century of total wars and exterminationist mentalities—it is clear to us that dominance and oppression have increasingly become the functions of categories of knowledge, often of categories that have at one time been emancipatory. It is true that the military-industrial complex is not entirely a thing of the past and brute force continues to be a part of our daily diet. The incineration of Iraq, the carpet-bombing of Yugoslavia and the pulverization of Afghanistan are vivid demonstrations of the continuing place of naked power in international politics. The twentieth century was ushered in by the Boer War, which lovingly gifted us the idea and the practice of concentration camps, and we bid the century farewell with a war at Europe's eastern frontiers that combined the primitivism of death camps with awesome technical marvels like 'stealth' fighters and 'smart' bombs. Yet, dominance can no longer be justified the way the colonial states justified their domination so effortlessly some decades ago, with the rhetoric of a crude 'civilizing mission', or in unabashed defence of the 'white man's burden'.

The 'new world order' is no longer framed by explicit contrasts— between the colonizers and the colonized, superior and inferior races, not even perhaps the developed and the underdeveloped— though residues of these distinctions, as well as claims about the moral responsibilities of the advanced countries, are still encountered in the pronouncements of the leaders of the 'free world'. The new world order is defined by a more nebulous set of contrasts— between those who speak the language of laws and the language of universal human rights, and whose lexicon has found new uses for 'caring', and those who would not or cannot subscribe to the new ground rules of universal political conduct. As a consequence, the rights to punish and kill are now drawn from the re-identification and nomination of entire states as 'rogues' or 'outlaws', who invite retribution by allegedly stepping outside the pale of the law or by disowning what the North American and West European politicians define as the 'international community'. These days, the only superpower in the world seeks nominal agreement from other 'civilized' nations for its own oftentimes barbarous conduct, and the 'international community' remains a sanitized fiction that suggests to recalcitrant 'rogues' and 'outlaws' that defiance against what is putatively the collective will of humankind will be justly punished.

In this new world order massive populations of the primitive, the backward and the rebellious continue to be oppressed by the rhetoric of kindness. They struggle towards their graves or funeral pyres listening to the lofty verbiage promising poverty alleviation, the right to work, development, progress, human rights and democracy. Such offers are made at grand international summits, targets are set and the unfed and underfed segments of the world are led to believe that 'leaders' went sleepless for a night or two in the interest of procuring greater amenities for their suffering subjects. However, neither the conventional grammar of political science nor the dictionaries produced by lexical specialists can help us understand the language of selective misanthropy disguised as philanthropy. Such dictionaries are often part of the immunization and numbing, indeed of the massive structure of denial, that the fin de siècle imperium of knowledge has produced.

For instance, few in the aftermath of 11 September 2001 have cared to investigate the systematic fashion in which terror has been institutionalized over the last 200 years as an integral part of modern statecraft and public policy. From the time of the French Revolution, when terror was declared as the handmaiden of virtue by Robespierre, to recent times, when terror was systematically and constantly deployed as an instrument of state policy by the two superpowers, the picture has not changed radically. The greater bulk of what passes for 'terrorism' in state discourses is the handiwork of those employed as counter-terrorism experts. Similarly, in its incarnation as counter-terror, terror has had the blessings of personages such as General William Sherman, Winston Churchill and Sir Arthur Harris. Sherman held, Wendell Berry tells us, 'that the civilian population could be declared guilty and rightly subjected to military punishment'. The United States, Berry adds, has never repudiated that doctrine.[3] Churchill and Harris systematically justified the idea of area bombing as opposed to that of strategic bombing directed at militarily significant targets; and though the American high command professed to have some qualms about the indiscriminate bombing of German cities, which were seen as part of the glorious legacy of Western civilization, no such restraint was ever contemplated when the extermination of the 'yellow vermin' was in question. The bombing of Tokyo killed in a few hours many more than the nuclear weapon did at

---

[3] Wendell Berry, *In the Presence of Fear: Three Essays for a Changed World* (Great Barrington, Massachusetts: Orion Society, 2001), 5–6.

Nagasaki.[4] And, as is well known, Hiroshima never qualified as a military target, not even in the eyes of the Americans who, judging from the air assaults on Iraq, Serbia and Afghanistan, have a rather capricious understanding of the term 'military targets'. So ample was the notion of 'dual-use' technologies deployed in the American regime's sanctions policy against Iraq that thousands of items were on the list of forbidden imports to Iraq—these, too, were military targets. Technically, the justifications for such terrorism against civilian populations have varied from case to case, but all of them have had as their underside a common tacit theory of retributive justice.

This legitimization and institutionalization of terror as an instrument of state policy might have prompted Madeleine Albright, then the American Secretary of State, to declare that she considered the lives of about 500,000 Iraqi children expendable as a price for the containment of the Iraqi President Saddam Hussein. Against the background of such powerful defenders of the right to use terror as a part of normal politics, the terrorists who attacked the World Trade Center towers, in retrospect, seem to have only apparently produced the wrong reasons for killing nearly 3000 innocent human beings. Their implicit genocidal self-justification does not differ significantly from that of their sworn enemies. Only, they appear to have poor control—an unpardonable error these days—of the media and an even poorer understanding of global public opinion and the language of the kinds of self-justification that such opinion finds sensible and rational. One of our major efforts in this dictionary has been to give an idea of how this genocidal world of violence might appear if different prescription lenses are worn.

Simultaneously, in countries such as India, Indonesia, Pakistan and Sri Lanka, the state sector and the public sphere are becoming arenas of increasing violence, intolerance and, sometimes, blatant incitement to human slaughter. As if to prove the theories of

---

[4]Michael S. Sherry, *The Rise of American Air Power: The Creation of Armageddon* (New Haven: Yale University Press, 1987), Chapter 9, makes for grim but instructive reading.

progress and stages of history correct, Europe's past is being acted out in the backwaters of Asia. Indeed, it appears as if the political and cultural categories that were imported into these countries by their earlier generations of elites as emancipatory devices have been helping reproduce the same patterns of violence that had plagued Europe during the last two centuries. While mass violence for Europe and North America now mostly takes place at a distance—on TV, in newspapers, enquiry committee reports, in histories and in films—in Asia, Africa and South America such violence has become normative, assimilated into daily life.

Meanwhile, the globalizing impulse carries the categories of knowledge of the global middle-class culture to even the remotest destinations. The traditional cultural and political repertoires of Afro-Asian societies are often proving themselves inadequate and inaccessible. The inadequacy is largely on account of the way traditions have been sealed off from the public sphere and political institutions. The inaccessibility is due to the way dominant global culture has begun to screen traditions for safe-keeping and judicious consumption in the dominant culture of public life.

With the global middle class becoming increasingly central and global commerce demanding cultural transparency and common norms, the vernacular and the regional literati are getting systematically and progressively marginalized all over the world. Yet, simultaneously, at no time has the global middle class been so hospitable towards multiculturalism, at least as part of an overt official position and intellectual conviction. This is probably because multiculturalism has come to mean a form of cultivated or acquired culture in which the ethnic, the vernacular and the local are represented in accessible, housebroken forms. Salman Rushdie unwittingly articulated an important canon of such multiculturalism when he said a few years ago, as the best-known face of Indian literature in the English-speaking world, that nothing worthwhile has been written in contemporary times in any of the hundreds of living languages that survive in India. The author thinks he is simultaneously serving Indian and global literatures by demanding translatability and common axioms of aesthetic judgement. By accommodating and defending Salman Rushdie against the Iranian fatwa, on the other hand, the votaries of the new globalism obviously feel that they protect not merely intellectual freedom and the literary creativity of one billion Indians, but contribute to international understanding and to the flourishing new trade that goes by the name of 'dialogue of civilizations'. A small set of simplistic categories have become the markers of civilization and cosmopolitanism—among them an unconditional commitment to the rationality of modern science and technology, a cultivated mediagenic optimism and the ideas of unending progress and ever-expanding consumer choices.

Nothing probably illustrates the contours of the new cosmopolitanism better than two concepts and institutional processes that have acquired global currency: the nation-state and development. Even self-declared Islamic states, sworn to the notion of the ummah, the worldwide community of Muslims, have borrowed, adapted and appropriated the format of a modern nation-state. The oligarchic elites of Saudi Arabia, Algerian fundamentalists and Kurd secessionists alike have been reduced to agitating in, or using, the language of a political science which recognizes the nation-state and its various appendages, such as a full-fledged army and security apparatus, as the only authentic expressions of political intent or cultural longing. So compelling is the idea of the nation-state that even entities such as India—which was a civilization long before it was anything else, and an empire before it was a nation-state—have forsaken their more complex civilizational identities for the dubious advantages of modern political engineering within the contemporary global nation-state system. As the recent expressions of India's nuclear ambitions show, even an ancient country, in its haste to arrive on the world stage as a great nation-state, can forget that as a civilization it might have been poised, in the long run, to be a far greater player.

The story is similar with respect to all the other principal orthodoxies of the day. To question 'development', for instance, is to virtually declare oneself mentally ill, for today nothing is considered more heretical than the supposition that 'underdeveloped' countries should not mechanically trudge the paths hacked out, often at the expense of the 'underdeveloped', by the 'developed' countries. Culturally, these terms constitute an evaluative scale, which in substance is part of the imperial logic, disseminated as a paradigm, that the colonized countries, by virtue of being colonized, had to be culturally inferior to the colonizing powers, whose superiority in material attainments, morality and intellectual capacities endorsed their right to dominate and evangelize in both spiritual and material domains. According to the dogma of development, no people could reasonably wish to remain underdeveloped, even if all data show that a fully developed world living according to the standards customary in North America and West Europe is fully unsustainable; it would mean a dead world and signal the annihilation of humankind as well as of all living species. If a small island nation, Mohandas Karamchand Gandhi was insane enough to ask, had to bleed the world to satiate the needs of its people, how much exploitation would the millions inhabiting India require to reach the same level of comfort and affluence? That levels of personal consumption in the United States are at least forty times that of the developing world is one of the central verities of our times, and no amount of American philanthropy can even remotely compensate for this gross phantasmagoria of excess.

Yet, even this may not be the most chilling part of the narrative of 'development'. The six million Jews who perished at the hands of the Nazis and their collaborators are recognized—even honoured—as victims of a genocide, but the twenty-five million Chinese who perished during Mao's Cultural Revolution between 1958 and 1961 or the millions of Russians who were exterminated in Stalin's gulags are still largely invisible. It is seldom admitted that they were victims not only of a sadistic theory of revolutionary social change but also of developed ideologies of scientific history and socialist 'development'. Development has claimed more lives than outright war or race-based genocides in the twentieth century; indeed, even good liberals can afford to agree that the victims of development are the 'necessary' price to be paid to move upwards on the scale of progress. A hidden component of the idea of development that was exported from the centres of the world in 1940s and 1950s was exactly this message—the rest of the world should learn to do to its peoples what the developed world had done to its own. Only such blood sacrifice, the argument went, would ensure the emancipation of the underdeveloped world.

That message has never been retracted. The World Bank, the International Monetary Fund and the WTO have merely made minor editorial changes. The rest of the world—or at least its elites—are all too eager to pay the price. Indeed, their commitment to the myth of development is often more unconditional and unequivocal. Their own peoples often seem to them redundant or obsolete, and the massive populations of the underprivileged, who cannot be wished away, are a threat to elite notions of a decent life, with modern amenities being the benchmark of 'progress'.

At the threshold of a new millennium, the only thing that is turning out to be truly 'new' is a form of social engineering that seeks to obliterate the remnants of the knowledge systems and cultural practices that have not yet been assimilated into the world view of globalizing modernity. In this world view, nothing is as much global as the knowledge systems that perform the interpretative, political, cultural and managerial work for the dominant global structures of political economy, and which constitute the dreamwork of the dominant contemporary ideal of cosmopolitanism. This ideal is expected not merely to consolidate the long-term gains of the Enlightenment vision and cement its global hegemony but also to supply the ideological accoutrement for negotiating the new century.

To see through this dreamwork, it becomes imperative to provide a cartography of the global framework of knowledge and culture, as well as of those paths that open up possible alternative frameworks for a more pluralistic future. This dictionary is a preface to such an enterprise.

A dictionary of 'ideas' is no longer an absolute novelty; there have been some recent efforts to furnish roadmaps to the global public culture in the new century. The most notable of these efforts is the *Encyclopaedia of Global Culture* (1995), edited by

Henry Louis Gates, Jr. While it has a political edge, on closer examination this text turns out to be an improved version of numerous listings—such as those previously furnished by Harold Bloom and E.D. Hirsch—that, according to the editors, should be part of the intellectual inventory of every educated person. While Bloom and Hirsch are comfortably and unapologetically Eurocentric, Gates makes a concerted and genuine attempt to be 'multicultural'; he has furnished African oral epics, Indian texts, elements of Japanese culture and American Indian religious practices—alongside Bach, Miles Davis, Jane Austen, Toni Morrison, Shakespeare, Flaubert, Picasso, Giotto and Leonardo da Vinci—as the pharmacopoeia for the educated, largely white, middle classes wanting to be ecumenical without spending too much intellectual energy on civilizations that may be at radical variance with received ideas of 'civilization' in the West. Indeed, Gates's *Encyclopaedia*, with about 1000 entries, can be appreciated primarily against the backdrop of serious debates on multiculturalism, and its preferred form of intervention is to allow a multiplicity of voices that might render the world more plural and, in the jargon of the newly initiated, 'fascinating'. (In the West, particularly the United States, the Holocaust can be no better sold, for instance to university students shopping at the beginning of term for courses, than by describing it as 'fascinating'. The oppression of others holds an endless store of surprises for all of us.)

One might reflect on the fact that Gates, like many academics similarly disposed—some of the subaltern school of historians have been particularly creative in this respect—has elegantly demonstrated that history must be made more complex and its practices rethought. Yet, neither Gates nor indeed the most radical historians of the day are prepared to concede that history, as the binding principle of the dreamwork of modernity, may itself be a 'totalizing' form of discourse. Better histories—whether of women or of the marginalized and the oppressed or even, for that matter, history from below—are still histories, and more nuanced critiques will have to point to the way in which numerous ahistorical modes of comprehension can fruitfully be brought to confront dominant discourses and to serve as correctives and radical critiques of such dominance. The modern world is in agreement that a sense of history is an inescapable element of freedom, but it has sometimes turned out to be the inescapable condition of a freedom that is controlled, monitored and ultimately packaged.

We hope *The Future of Knowledge and Culture* will contribute to a different, self-reflexive and perhaps more self-doubting cultural politics of knowledge. It does not have any pretension to be comprehensive, nor does it aspire to furnish all the 'keywords', to use Raymond Williams's expression, that might demand our attention in the coming century. It only hopes to allow the reader a glimpse into the transient world of ideas where the familiar is shown to be not so familiar and the unfamiliar turns out to be not so unfamiliar after all. Many of the book's contributors have, in their own fashion, sought to enlarge the scope of our understanding, question the dominant frameworks of knowledge, bring the 'local' to engage with the 'global', render the 'global' 'local' and construe many purported localisms as competing or alternative forms of globalism. They create conditions for the flowering of creative dissent and pave the way for a plural ecology of practices, beliefs and forms of reasoning.

We have also tried, successfully or otherwise, to build this dictionary on the premise that politically informed, intellectual work need not be always insufferably self-righteous or animated by the fervent belief that it would help the academic disciplines to implode. Nor need the sense of play be merely an adjunct of narcissistic intellectual ecstasy and linguistic excesses that go under the name of jouissance. This dictionary is 'beholden' to conventional notions of academic disciplines, which have often disciplined our knowledge and made it serviceable. The editors, however, hope that the contributors, to whom they are immensely grateful, will not be judged by the extent to which they have demonstrated academic responsibility, awareness and accountability, but by the extent to which they have moved us to a greater sensitivity regarding the conditions of freedom and oppression, human resilience, compassion and creativity under conditions of violence and stress.

Apologies

Vinay Lal

Scarcely a month goes by these days before one hears of an apology, usually by one nation-state to another, or from one nation-state to one of its minority communities, for grievous harm committed in the past. When an American submarine split a Japanese fishing boat into pieces as it surfaced in February 2001, everyone must have noticed the grave reluctance with which the American leadership apologized to the Japanese, and the anguish experienced by the Japanese at the failure of the submarine's commander to appear immediately in person before the bereaved families to tender his apologies. One article in the *Los Angles Times* referred to the culture of apologies widely prevalent in Japan, but another commentator in the *Washington Post* found anomalous the Japanese desire for an apology while Japan itself has been less than forthcoming with a full apology for its conduct in the Second World War. In recent years, however, the Japanese, who doubtless have much work to do by way of appeasing their former enemies and victims, among them hundreds of thousands of 'comfort women', POWs and slave labourers in concentration camps, have taken their culture of apologies to a new international level. In 1995, the then Japanese prime minister, Tomiichi Murayama, admitted that Japanese 'colonial rule and aggression' caused 'tremendous damage and suffering' to many people, especially Asians; he expressed 'feelings of deep remorse' and stated his 'heartfelt apology'. Formal expressions of contrition for the Japanese occupation of Korea and for the inhumane treatment of British POWs in Japanese camps have since been offered by other Japanese prime ministers.

It is not amiss to speak of the epidemic of apologies that now engulfs us. The modern trend—leaving aside the apology tendered by the US government in the 1980s to Japanese-Americans for their illegal incarceration in concentration camps during the Second World War—can be said to have begun when in 1993 the United States, on the hundredth anniversary of the annexation of Hawaii, tendered an 'apology to Native Hawaiians' for 'the overthrow' of their kingdom. This appears to have been a signal to other Western powers and institutions to act likewise: soon Germany was to follow suit, appearing contrite for its invasion of Czechoslovakia in 1938, while the Czechs reciprocated for having, in the aftermath of the Second World War, expelled Germans from what was then Czechoslovakia. President Chirac of France apologized to the Jewish community for the wartime French government's complicity in sending Jews to their graves. Even Canada, which must appear to many people as a benign nation, considering the gross and loud abuser of human rights that sits on its border, has expressed remorse for oppressing its native people, suppressing their languages and culture, and rendering nearly extinct their modes of religious worship. Thus the minister for Indian affairs stated: 'The government of Canada today [7 January 1998] formally expresses to all aboriginal people in Canada our profound regret for past actions of the federal government.' Much has also been made of the Pope's apology, offered at the cusp of the new millennium, for the sins of the Catholic Church in its persecution of Jews, 'heretics', women and native peoples.

Shortly after gaining the office of the prime minister, Tony Blair offered an apology to the Irish people for the cruel potato famine of 1845–49 that decimated the population of Ireland and eventually drove the survivors, as William Butler Yeats was to suggest, into madness and poetry—and more immediately into exodus and migration. From 8.2 million in the early 1840s, the Irish population had shrunk by 1911 to 4.4 million. The Great Potato Famine of

1845–49 is, however, scarcely the only enterprise to which the English lent their rapacity. British rule in India in the mid eighteenth century was inaugurated with a famine: as many as ten million Indians succumbed to starvation in the territories under the East India Company's rule. Two hundred years later, at nearly the end of their rule, which had been heralded with the pompous declaration that they were engaged in a 'civilizing mission', the British were again crucially instrumental in creating conditions of mass death in India while they were purportedly saving the world for democracy. However, this has not generally been considered worthy of comment in Britain. No apology has ever been tendered to the Indians by the English for the 1943 Bengal famine, which left behind three million dead and owed everything to the callousness of the British administration: perhaps the English are still inclined to consider the Irish, even the popish Irish, as more worthy of an apology than the infernal Indians. The dark-skinned people of the subcontinent die much too easily anyway, and in droves: 'thousands' have been killed in riots, industrial 'accidents', and earthquakes. One is accustomed to thinking of life in India as cheap, worth little more than a farthing, and famines and earthquakes do the prophylactic work to which thick-skinned Indians will not give their easy assent. Perhaps, by a perverse twist of logic, Indians even ought to be grateful to the English for having relieved some of them of the onerous burden of their miserable lives. Famines aside, Indians have also been unsuccessful in obtaining an apology from the English for the atrocity perpetrated at Amritsar's Jallianwala Bagh in 1919, when a regiment of troops under the command of General Reginald Dyer fired for ten continuous minutes at a large unarmed crowd and massacred not less than 400 people.

Considering the trends of the last few years, nonetheless, one can reasonably hazard the speculation that the day may not be too far away when imperialist nations, and some of their hallowed institutions (such as the Red Cross, or missionary organizations), will daily be issuing apologies for one or more episodes drawn from the 500-year-old saga of rapacious colonialism. But to suppose that the West has now somehow become more civilized, or genuinely repentant, may well be a mistake, as the American perspective on issuing apologies suggests. Nearly forty-five years after the conclusion of the Second World War, at a time when the Japanese almost appeared to have a stranglehold over the world economy, and there was much talk in the United States of 'Japan as Number One', it must have seemed even prudent to apologize to Japanese-Americans. The Japanese have long been recognized as Asians who understand imperialism and the business of governance; the yen, moreover, was then poised to become almost as widely accepted as the dollar. An apology to Japanese-Americans, not to be confused with an apology to Japan, seemed in order: it could even be summoned as an instance of the narrative of Western exceptionalism, which states that what is distinct and unique about America and the West as a whole is the fact that the Western powers alone have had the courage to atone for their misdeeds. Germany's openness about its Nazi past is routinely contrasted to Japan's grave reluctance to admitting to wartime atrocities.

No people in the United States, barring perhaps the native Americans, have endured the relentless regime of oppression and genocide that African-Americans have had to face since the first slaves were brought to this country over 300 years ago. The office of Tony Hall, a Democratic senator from Ohio who a few years ago sponsored the bill that calls for the US Congress to issue a formal apology to African-Americans for the institution of slavery, has reported that two out of every three letters received expressed disagreement with Senator Hall's proposal. One man from the American 'heartland', describing Hall as a 'stupid' man, wrote: 'I should like to see our nation return to slavery.' Another letter expressed the opinion that members of the 'Negro race' should be thankful to 'us', white Americans, 'for having brought them here'; and speaking of four well-dressed African-American professional women he had seen on television making such a demand, he added: 'If we had not brought their ancestors here, they would still be running around over there in loin-cloths with their breasts hanging out.' But perhaps none of this is very surprising, considering that the American Constitution, supposedly humankind's cradle of freedom, construed the Negro as equivalent to three-fifths of a white person. We ought to recall as well the 1858 pronouncement of the 'Great Emancipator', Abraham Lincoln: 'I am not, or ever have been, in favor of bringing about in any way the social or political equality of the white and black races.'

It has often been suggested that any apology to African-Americans would be merely 'emotional symbolism', as though the country does not otherwise thrive on it; and the African-American spokesman and political leader Jesse Jackson has described himself as not reconciled to the idea of an apology, as it would be without 'substantial value'. The descendants of the Japanese-Americans were given something of 'substance' beyond a mere apology: in America nothing but money has ever been 'substance', but such a possibility cannot be contemplated in the case of African-Americans. For one thing, any reparations on so substantive a scale would leave the country bankrupt, and so its financial condition would echo its moral state. Many white Americans also believe, though they do not always have the gumption to state so in public, that money is wasted on an African-American.

But perhaps the meaninglessness of an official state apology to African-Americans can be reaffirmed for reasons other than those stated by the phobic opponents of such a gesture. To utter an apology is not only to say sorry, to beg forgiveness and to express contrition at one's actions or words but to express a willingness to forbear from such action or words in the future. An apology carries with it the declared intention to repudiate such action, language or behaviour as has been offensive or caused hurt, injury or death. It is very doubtful that Americans, or for that matter all those who have been so busy issuing apologies, are truly penitent. The brutal truth remains that a very sizeable number of the American 'people', in whose name undertakings are commenced, legitimized and sanctified, are far from being reconciled to the 'free' condition of African-Americans today, and certainly are not inclined to express remorse for the wretched deeds perpetrated by their ancestors. Were not the moral opprobrium of the world to descend upon those who may desire to perpetrate slavery today, it is possible that some Americans might actually welcome the re-enslavement of African-Americans, if on no other grounds than the frequently proffered one that equality between the white and black races is inconceivable, not to mention undesirable. Moreover, as Americans are aware, capital can flourish in circumstances other than those of slavery; indeed, whatever the American South's interest in preserving this (in historian Kenneth Stampp's phrase) 'peculiar institution', slavery was proving to be a rather expensive proposition. If Coca-Cola, Nike, Nestlé and Benetton can almost effortlessly penetrate the remotest markets worldwide, what is the need for a system of slavery?

An apology remains, with respect to spiritual and material considerations alike, a cheap and inexpensive way to gain the high moral ground. In the political circumstances of the present moment, it necessitates little or no introspection, and certainly does not require one to confront those parts of one's own self that, being incapable of conciliation, one expels outward or projects on to the other. It is instructive that five years ago, when the controversy surrounding the planned exhibition of the *Enola Gay*, the plane that carried the atom bomb used over Hiroshima, was at its height, President Clinton did not merely decline to issue an apology to Japan but stated with astonishing arrogance that an apology to Japan was unthinkable. That old and utterly indefensible canard which describes the atom bomb as having averted millions of American and Japanese deaths was again revived; nor was there any recognition that the atom bomb was not merely an intensification of conventional bombing but an entirely new nihilistic order of human self-debasement, a transgression of the ecological underpinning of our universe. Clinton was unable to apologize because the United States is unwilling to renounce the use of nuclear weapons, and a genuine apology is none other than a statement of intent that one repudiates one's conduct and promises never to engage in a similar undertaking again. A genocidal mentality is indubitably at the very heart of the American psyche.

Owning up to one's past will require far more than an apology. The present epidemic of apologies, and the sister discourses of multiculturalism and Western exceptionalism, should alike be scrutinized aggressively, treated with extreme caution and be placed at arm's length. We are yet to discover that the venomous benefaction of the West may kill us all. Such cynicism may well be undeserved, and yet one has no recourse but to say, 'Sorry.'

Architecture

R.L. Kumar

All the pillars of the Parthenon are identical, while no two
facets of the Indian temple are the same; every convolution of
every scroll is different. No two canopies in the whole building
are alike and every part exhibits a joyous exuberance of fancy,
scorning every mechanical restraint. All that is wild in human
faith and warm in human feeling is found portrayed on these
walls, but of pure intellect, there is little.

—J. Fergusson
A History of Indian and Eastern Architecture, 1897

Architecture, medicine and agriculture provide us with a ringside
view of the politics of knowledge in our times. Unable to
shake off the long shadow of the past and unable to deliver the
promise of modern universality, they endlessly reproduce the
classical differences between theory and practice, science and
technology, mind and body—and ultimately between profession
and practice. In most of the world outside the modern West, the
idea of an architect as a service professional is confined to a
handful of cities and particularly in the government and commercial
sectors. Most Indians, even in our times, consult a thatchan,
kothanar, maistry, achari or stapathi (colloquial names for
architectural craftspersons) when building a home, office, workplace,
cattle shed or temple. The other tradition of modern scientific
architecture, produced at the university, legislated by governments

and pressed into the service of various public engineering departments or the service of urban middle classes is not complementary but antagonistic to the older vernacular tradition. This antagonism can be understood in the context of three ideas.

The Idea of Scale

It was Lewis Mumford who coined the phrase 'human scale'. He was referring to the fact that measurement is fundamentally a human act, anchored to the human experience of body and space. The arms which measure a yard of stone, the fist which determines the space between rows of rice and the spanning palm which measures the width of the foundation of a building are excellent examples. The urban industrial world which transformed land into 'real estate' also transformed space into a function of scarcity. It redefined land. Land was no longer where agriculture was practised: it became a resource for agribusiness. A forest was no longer a dwelling for entire communities: it became a site of 'scientific forestry' to produce measurable timber. Land was no longer defined by its location in nature but by its location in the economy. It is a commodity connected to electrical power grids, sewage and water pipelines, road networks and address registries. It represented a model of life removed from the basic life-sustaining activities of agriculture and craft. Modern architecture is preoccupied with the management, distribution, utilization and surveillance of this space.

To appreciate the implication this has for the 'scale' of buildings, compare the Rashtrapati Bhavan, the official residence of a 'developing' republic's president, with the one-time official residence of the Viceroy of the British Empire who, before Indian independence, presided over the greater part of the Indian subcontinent. The Viceroy's former residence, abandoned after Rashtrapati Bhavan was constructed, is today the modest office of the vice chancellor of the University of Delhi!

Mumford's 'human scale' was indeed a modest one. It is only scale, coupled with the 'prestige' of a national state, that can produce monumental residences, symbols of power and authority that surpass all such previous symbolism. No wonder, then, that the symbol of the doctrine of national security must express itself with the dubious distinction of being the world's largest building— the Pentagon. With 30 kilometres of corridor space alone and a workforce of 30,000 people, the Pentagon building is the symbol of the American endeavour for national security and 'global peace'.

This practice of monumentality, of buildings as symbols of power and authority, is a secular one. It is vastly different from the drive to build the great pyramids of Egypt or a Taj Mahal. To understand this difference one must remember Adam Smith's well-known formulation of human desire. It was Smith who first articulated the connection between individual human desire and national wealth in post-Enlightenment societies. It is only the modified human desire to be gratified by another's envy, wrote Smith, that can be an engine to economic expansion and growth. Vale Laurence suggests that monumental buildings like the Lincoln Memorial, national parliaments and residences of presidents and other heads of states are symbols of a notion of power and authority that is distinctly modern and derived, I would add, from a theory of secular democratic republicanism. The English prime minister's house, the seat of real power (leaving aside the power of capital and industry for now), is an understated No. 10 Downing Street, lest it smack of the 'feudal past' denying the 'democratic revolution', while the Queen's residence is a Buckingham Palace, in London. In the true home of democratic republicanism, the US, which has done away with the distinction between formal and real heads of state, the American 'Chief Executive's' residence in Washington DC is an ambiguous 'White House' at 1600 Pennsylvania Avenue. It is another matter that today elite commandos and bulletproof technologies protect these democratic representatives of the 'people' from the people themselves.

In this sense national/public buildings are not only secular ones but also carry specific meanings. They are designed not to please the gods or to honour the dead; they are designed to create and govern the new subjecthood of citizenship in nation-states. They are supposed to inspire awe and remind the state's subjects of the canons of democratic revolutions.

If 'keeping up with the Joneses' was the way to creating a nation's wealth, such development wasn't always a matter of access to better technology. The spectacles designed to inspire awe were also technological marvels, but this is only half the story. Technology did not create the mimetic desire to display wealth— it only made it possible, perhaps even justified it. Hitler's plan for a presidential palace of the Reich where visiting dignitaries would walk a distance longer than the French king's court at Versailles is a good case in point. It is also here that scale loses its human reference point and its location in the natural world and becomes purely a function of technology and mimetic desire. There is also another crucial dimension to scale: that of surveillance. Prisons, schools and hospitals, which employ what Michel Foucault has called technologies of surveillance, owe their architectural inspiration to Jeremy Bentham's Panopticon. This project of total visibility and total surveillance is also a consequence of the loss of a human scale.

The Idea of Craft

The work of Laurie Baker, an English architect who has made India his home, and Hassan Fathy, an Egyptian architect credited with reviving the art of building Nubian vaults, an ancient technique dating back to pharaonic times, illuminates the idea of architecture as a craft. They emphasize the use of locally available building materials and following time-tested building designs, which are climatically and culturally attuned. Baker also insists that the practice of an architect not be divorced from that of a builder. Architecture as a craft means that its theory and its practice are indivisible.

The difference between industrial labour and craft activity is of crucial importance here. The enclosure of the commons, the depopulation of the countryside, the factory police of Germany and many other forms of dislocation and social engineering went into the making of what we know today as the industrial working class in Europe. But one precondition for the creation of working classes anywhere in the world was what Ivan Illich has called the 'war against subsistence'. Craft was a victim of this war, which we also know today as 'development' or 'modernization'. Most people outside the metropolises in India rely on the knowledge of the local building craftsmen, who rely on practices which are informed by traditional geometry, astronomy, weather science, soil science, arithmetic and accounting. Theoretical modern science might find these knowledges wanting, but they serve the purpose of their customers and practitioners admirably. Like other crafts, this knowledge is taught through practice; there is plenty of innovation, experimentation and professional communication. In the modern sector, however, this craft nature of architecture is lost because of the industrialization of the raw materials of architecture.

The Idea of Regeneration

Regeneration presupposes a kind of post-industrial need to connect with processes of nature. It is misleading to talk of regeneration with regard to societies that are not dislocated from nature as fundamentally as industrial societies are. However, I use the word to talk about what can be perceived as imperatives which go into the making of something we broadly understand as human. Humans, despite computers and cars, power grids and roads, Kevlar and Teflon, still eat bread, drink water, grow grain, build homes and wear silk and cotton. But here is the rub: these products of nature (grain, milk, water, mud, thatch, silk and cotton, for instance), in the post-industrial sectors of all societies, are less accessible or affordable to those who are its primary producers. Cotton growers and weavers dressed in cheap synthetic clothes, potters storing water in vessels made of recycled plastic, masons living in concrete boxes, farmers unable to afford the price of grain and suffering reduced access to milk and meat, are the symbols and symptoms of a dislocation which Marxist categories of alienation do not adequately capture. At stake here is not just the hostile relationship between producer and product, but a deeper redundancy of basic life-giving activities.

In India, as in many other parts of the world, the New Year would mean a time to clean and limewash one's home, marriages would mean a time to extend and alter, and changing seasons would determine the order of repairing and changing the worn elements of a building. *Regeneration* here is nothing but the endless cycle of life in nature's environment. But when all environments become 'built' environment, regeneration appears as a newly discovered lifestyle. Technophiles, who sing arias about the smart homes of tomorrow connected to WAP technologies, with their auto-managed lighting, temperature and security systems, automated 'work-performing' cybernetic systems and maintenance-proof architecture, forget that *re*generation is re-entering post-industrial culture in a new way while vernacular homes have *re*generation 'built' into them.

The basic elements of a modern building, such as cement, steel, glass, ceramic, plastic and synthetic fibre, are not connected to nature in the same way as mud, brick, lime, thatch, timber and grass. The industrial elements are what we know as waste, insofar as they are not, to use a trendy word, biodegradable. They also produce undisposable waste in their very production. In this search to be permanent and 'maintenance-free', architecture has lost its capacity to be *re*generative and, therefore, ecologically sensitive.

Fergusson must, perhaps, be allowed the last word on this tradition of architecture. The 'pure intellect' of which he found so little in the architecture of Belur and Halebid, the famous eleventh-century temples of South India, is, I suspect, a recognition of what a dominant culture of rationality can do to human faith and feeling. The search for perfection, permanence and immortality in architecture must look to him like a Faustian contract with technology threatening to rob architecture of its very soul.

Bollywood

M.K. Raghavendra

'Bollywood' is the name given to the phenomenally popular, extravagant genre of Indian cinema created in Bombay (now Mumbai). These films are usually in the Hindi language. The term is recent but it is applied retrospectively to traditional Indian cinema from the 1920s onwards. It has been evidently coined presuming an affinity between this cinema and the kind associated with Hollywood, but a comparison of the codes informing the two cinemas shows otherwise. The tenets of classical Hollywood film-making are tantamount to dogma, but Bollywood brazenly flouts the paradigms, and its heresies are lapped up with evident relish not only by local votaries but also by audiences widely distributed over Asia and Africa. There are rumours, perhaps exaggerated, that people of the ilk of Joseph Stalin and Mao Zedong were, in their respective times, also ardent Bollywood fans. Chairman Mao reportedly watched the Raj Kapoor blockbuster *Awaara* forty times.

Bollywood is distinguished by its refusal to recognize causality as an operating principle in narrative construction. The spectator seeking excitement must contend with stories in which characters exhibit natures that remain static for the normal three hours of viewing time. A dowager who dies in the film is, at every moment, a feeble woman due to depart and create a foreseeable emotional crisis. The boy who takes action twenty years later to revenge himself upon his father's murderer finds the villain unchanged, except for a notional graying at the temples. Where Hollywood insists on change and development as the raison d'être of storytelling, Bollywood finds its truths in the immutable. There are other symptoms that point to this core perceptions. Saints are born into sainthood rather than first being sinners, widows are perpetually in mourning, and courtesans never qualify to advance to the rank of family women.

The rasa theory of classical Indian aesthetics, which posits fictionalized emotions—such as grief, rage, wonder and fear—experienced through poetry and art, can be described as an 'essentialist' doctrine. Bollywood inadvertently owes something to it. Since the 'essence' of an object is 'eternal', by this logic the truths sought by Bollywood are therefore also undying and permanent. The love between two people does not begin and grow but is, rather, present in equal measure at all moments. A film, for example, will not attract notice if the hero and the heroine sing a duet before their initial meeting! This feat of the imagination is facilitated by references to mythological models and the only concession made to plausibility is that the lovers-to-be are in distinct spaces. Since the notion of universal time is founded in the inevitability of change, Bollywood rejects absolute time as an essential consideration and disregards also the possibility of simultaneity. Other notable casualties are historicity and topicality, both of which are founded on the notion of universal time. Bollywood's 'historical' films are love stories played out against period backdrops and when topical elements are introduced into the narrative, these elements are divested of their immediacy and of virtually all their contemporary significance.

The frames in Bollywood movies are, by and large, also flatly composed to resemble our experience of proscenium theatre. The spectator is not presented with the illusion of being included within the space of the narrative. The logic perhaps is that there is nothing corresponding to an 'elsewhere' in theatrical space and the implicit denial of universal time and simultaneity by Bollywood makes an 'elsewhere' redundant.

Another basic component of Bollywood formulae is their

unapologetic rejection of psychology and the goal-oriented character. Jorge Luis Borges remarks in one of his stories that, given an infinite amount of time, all things will happen to all people. The traditional Indian belief in the transmigration of souls and doctrine of karma draws emphasis away from 'free will', and the universe of Bollywood is therefore strictly 'determined'; the characters are at the mercy of destiny's dispensations and subject to a relentless proliferation of melodramatic coincidences. Regarding agency, the emphasis is not on 'choice'. Events 'befall' the characters swiftly and furiously. Action sequences in Indian popular cinema usually arrange fortuitous ends for hate figures and narrative construction is virtually in the 'passive voice'. If we are to illustrate the methods of Bollywood through a hypothetical scenario, we can say that, rather than participate in the excitement of a mountainous ascent, Bollywood would, more likely, simply show the crest as ascended. Films are therefore grievously handicapped in their exploration of character.

Bollywood's dependence on songs and dances is legendary. The kinds of songs and dances have changed considerably, and two consecutive verses may be sung in different landscapes in many modern productions. Unlike the Hollywood musical, Bollywood employs the song and the dance to actually disrupt narrative continuity and loosen the causality. This, along with the insertion of premonitions, abrupt coincidences and similar devices, makes the structure so porous and accommodating that generic inconsistency unacceptable in any other cinema can thrive openly. Films are therefore often 'conglomerations' with autonomous, interpolated subplots that have their own independent climaxes and resolutions.

Another recognizable feature of Bollywood is the manner in which it brings the family into the narrative. The presence of the father or the mother serves to provide Bollywood with a 'context', since historical markers are rarely incorporated, nor serve as a pivot for the action, or for sociological expression. The narrative is also an 'ideal construct' (as the world of classical Indian literature has been described) that is not a mimetic representation of the real world. The narrative must therefore be brought to a decisive closure in order to keep its world clearly separate from the historical universe. This is efficiently achieved through a family reunion or through the successful conclusion of a romance.

Although there is a relatively new 'art' cinema (that is closer in spirit to the European mode) after the advent of the Bengali director Satyajit Ray, Bollywood hit upon its mechanisms very early in its history. P.R. Tipnis's *Pundalik* (1912) is often credited to be the first Indian film, although D.G. Phalke's *Raja Harishchandra* (1913) was perhaps the first genuine feature film. Although Phalke's films apparently anticipate the direction taken by Indian cinema, the silent era, which ends around 1931, saw films being made that were considerably more 'realistic', and perhaps more in conformity with a Western model.

Much of India's silent cinema has been lost. There are available segments of some strikingly realist work in the 1920s that is a far cry from any of the Indian cinema that followed, with the exception of Satyajit Ray. Dadasaheb Phalke, it is believed, brought the mythological influence into Indian cinema and in his films the use of magic makes the sway of the film-maker and magician Georges Meliés evident. It is normally presumed that the realist aesthetic and mythology cannot go together, but some recently discovered and restored footage discovered shows differently. Baburao Painter's *Muraliwala* (1927), like Phalke's *Kaliya Mardan* (1919), is also about the god Krishna's childhood but it is notable for the realist aesthetic it brings to mythology. The forty minutes of the film now available show Krishna and his friends playing pranks upon the local people while Yashodha is a harassed mother who cannot control her foster-child's exuberance. For Krishna's friends the director uses local children dressed in the dusty, worn country clothes seen in Maharashtra's rural areas even today, and Yashodha's own house is cramped and soot-stained, with smoke billowing perpetually from the kitchen. The frames are also not flatly composed and there are several sequences in which people enter the space perpendicularly, from the camera's axis of vision. Krishna wears his traditional peacock feather but he is not the static being posing for the shot, as in *Kaliya Mardan* and most other films on this theme. In Painter's film Krishna's pranks genuinely harass the helpless villagers, and the child wriggles so violently in Yashodha's ineffectual grasp that he is able to free himself and remains generally at large. The vision of childhood contained in *Muraliwala* is so lyrical and so humanly vibrant that it is possible to see the film, quite justifiably, as a possible precursor to *Pather Panchali*.

Bollywood willingly misplaced this realist aesthetic after the sound era. Baburao Painter's own later films conform to the familiar mode and are a far cry from the vision informing *Muraliwala*. Even more strangely, a German film-maker named Franz Osten was in India in this period, and in 1925 made the 'orientalist' *The Light of Asia* (about the Buddha) according to the model made familiar by the German film company UFA in the 1920s. The image of a starving beggar on a narrow Indian street (in *The Light of Asia*) has an inherent exotic appeal, perhaps comparable to the attraction a field of tulips in Holland has for one of today's Bollywood blockbusters! But, by the late 1930s, Osten had renounced this aesthetic, and was making Hindi films indistinguishable from the product locally developed.

After Independence in 1947, Bollywood committed itself to a new mission, which was to give voice to 'national aspirations'. Being the only medium able to influence the entire subcontinent, films like Mehboob Khan's rural-themed *Mother India* (1957) responded to the spirit of secular optimism pervading the space of the nation. Other films of the 1950s are set in the city (usually Bombay) and engage with the issue of modernity. The city was one of the designated sites of progress in the India of its times, and these films are therefore historically relevant, although no historical question pertinent to the times is actually addressed by them.

Not being able to engage with the contemporary in historical terms, these films have a strange way of dealing with issues in the language of myth. Hardly any films deal with the freedom struggle and with independence as issues, but films after 1947 begin to privilege the institutions of the state (chiefly the judiciary), and the courtroom becomes the 'moral site' where the truth eventually prevails. It is only after 1947 that surrendering to the police (a consistent theme in the plot) also becomes an admission of moral guilt.

Ironically, India's excursion along the path of socialism made Bollywood believe in the social purpose of cinema, although this belief is sometimes only manifested in complicated love between characters from different classes, castes and religions. After the fall of the Soviet Union and the initiation of the economic liberalization process in India, a move has been seen to banish the poor from the realm of film narrative. This has spawned a new kind of kitsch—notably in examples like *Hum Aapke Hain Kaun* (1995) in which unbelievably wealthy people live happily, although the source of the wealth is left ambiguously undefined.

No systematic attempt has ever been made to justify Bollywood's film aesthetic, but the genre itself continues to flourish. That its narrative codes depart to extremes from the dominant 'global' model—much more excessively than Japanese cinema, for example—makes it an incredibly difficult phenomenon to grasp. Bollywood nevertheless demonstrates conclusively that there are other ways of perceiving modernity than in the dominant way and that these perceptions will continue to insist on their own complex idiosyncratic paths towards the 'real'.

Further Reading

Das Gupta, Chidananda. 1992. *The Painted Face*. New Delhi: Roli Books.

Pfleider, Beatrix, and Lothar Lutze, eds. 1985. *The Hindi Film: Agent and Re-agent of Cultural Change*. New Delhi: Manohar Publications.

Calcutta

John Hutnyk

You will think you will know Calcutta one day. But it cannot be known. It is all things, always, already. Rumours of Calcutta will continue to circulate around the world, as they have done for more than 300 years. Conjured with for all manner of ends—city of crowding, city of slums, city of joy, city of Ray, city built not on silt, but gold. The wealth of the Raj passed through its ports, the image of the world flashed on its screens—Ghatak, Sen, premieres and festivals—literary, musical, militant. Calcutta cannot but be the future we hope for because its avatars exceed all possible demarcation. In the future Calcutta will still be very much Calcutta (Tagore). It always has been a place of excess. It exceeds even now, its geography, its times, its spirit; be thankful for this excess, a city alive. Thus it cannot be known. Cannot be an object of scholarship, no subject for journalism. How could anyone profess to write up this city? A street is difficult enough, a suburb a speciality. Claims to knowledge are like false treasure maps. X mistakes the spot.

Once upon a long ago, Job Charnock and the English came and built a factory on the site of three villages. The British traders had entered India in 1612 and purchased land from local rulers with silver coin earned through the brutal slave-trade markets of the West Indies. These tainted coins began a city built on the backs of a population which has become a commodity. Marx called this twisted social relation 'fetishism'. No surprise that one of the big starts of the fetish is traced to Calcutta. No surprise that it continues there as well.

On the coin—which is perhaps to be passed to a hand in need in an imaginary Calcutta—the image of a woman's face, one eye crying, one eye alight with a knowing gleaming smile, is engraved. Mrinal Sen and, before him, Radharaman Mitra evoke this allegorical doubled face in their craft. The sound assessment of Calcutta is to take stock of pain and pleasure, lotus and mud, brilliance and joy. But others would have images of the photogenic poor, child begging like sadhu by the pavement, or wandering bovine beasts, sleepers on the streets. I'd call this fetishism. Representations of crowds, teeming, overflowing, congested on the Howrah Bridge—these replicate and circulate rumours of Calcutta that evince death and decay, the dark side of the coin. This dark convention of those who do not live in town. Rajiv Gandhi declared it dead prematurely; Winston Churchill was glad to have seen it so as not to have to see it again; Gunther Grass scratched insults and epithets in mire. The imagery serves an agenda that should be disaggregated in its many modes.

Calcutta suffered from a bad press in the twentieth century. Maligned and maltreated, its face was muddied by slur and scar. The British moved the capital to Delhi in 1910 to avoid Bengali militancy, and through the enforced famines of the 1940s and the fratricidal Left struggles of the 1960s and 1970s, the reputation of Calcutta has always been loaded with an interpretative charge from afar. Still mistaken for somewhere else in the horror psyche of the West by the likes of Lapierre and Joffe (of *City of Joy* fame), and marked by commercial billboard hoardings and speculative capital, more and more today as the advent of structural adjustment and NGO aid continues the hype.

Much sham scandal is still made, and will be made, here in this one-sided telling. Perhaps in future tellings we can disrupt the exaggerated sympathy of Mother Teresa and her ilk, whatever their good intentions, which have the same consequence as the old story of the Black Hole. This was a justificatory fiction that became the alibi for invaders and occupiers. Marx himself described the 'Black Hole' incident, and, since the story must be told again here, it may as well be in a critical version: It was Marx (1947) who called it a 'sham scandal'. In an extensive collection of notes made on Indian history, he comments that on the evening of 21 June 1756, after the Governor of Calcutta had ignored the order of Subedar Siraj-ud-daula to 'raze all British fortifications' in the city:

> Suraj came down on Calcutta in force ... fort stormed, garrison taken prisoners, Suraj gave orders that all the captives should be kept in safety till the morning; but the 146 men (accidentally, it seems) were crushed into a room 20 feet square and with but one small window; next morning (as Holwell himself tells the story), only 23 were still alive; they were allowed to sail down the Hooghly. It was 'the Black Hole of Calcutta', over which *the English hypocrites have been making so much sham scandal to this day.* Suraj-ud-duala returned to Murshidabad; Bengal now completely and effectually cleared of the English intruders.

Marx also reports on the subsequent retaliation against and defeat of Siraj-ud-daula by Lord Clive ('that Great Robber' as he calls him elsewhere), and Clive's 1774 suicide after his 'cruel persecution' by the directors of the East India Company. There seem to be very good reasons to conclude that the Black Hole incident is counterfeit (false coin, fetishized). The single report from a 'survivor' some months after Clive's savage response to Siraj-ud-daula's occupation of Calcutta—the notorious 1757 Battle of Plassey—reads very much like a justification forged to deflect criticisms of brutality on the part of the British forces. The Black Hole is a kind of souvenired past of imperial history faked to stand in for the theft of a city.

Enough of listening to Mayo Memorial Sanitation Committee sentiments on India, always seeking out stench and dung, blind to what ferments and fertilizes here.[1] What new versions of this

---

[1]The reference is to Catherine Mayo's *Mother India* (1927). M.K. Gandhi called this text a 'drain inspector's report'.

fiction will be deployed to ensure Calcutta does not manage itself, as it so patently can? Or, rather, what chance for knowing Calcutta otherwise than through the rumours that misrepresent it so?

No doubt future Calcuttas will proliferate as always in the bipolar pattern. It is and will be at once a fantasy site conjured with by global interests of all stripes, and also an actually existing and always dynamic specificity, a lived-in city, complicated and complicating. Certainly the city looks much lived-in at times; no one could doubt this, whatever the future may bring. However, it is just as certain that the many phantasmagoric and fantastic Calcuttas which circulate through media, literature, ideological representation and satellite TV are also worn and frayed, but in different ways.

Calcutta is and will at once be the sounding board of liberal indignation from the charity-NGO types through to the World Bank/International Monetary Fund and be host and home to raging debates about commerce, cinema, representation and power that would only be credited in places of much more refined reputation. Fuelled by the Coffee House culture, it is inadequate even to promote the place as the Princeton of the East, the Oxford of the swamps or the forum of a dhoti-clad Socrates—is it the Sirens of Odysseus that will lure us to stop at the silting port?

One thing is certain: in the future Calcutta will still be very much Calcutta—it will keep its Tagores, and I hope its Marx, but let it add many others, accumulating, proliferating. It is the promise of continuity that this place of excess offers us all, a continuity that recalls that the centre is not always the self-declared centre, but perhaps shifts and twists in the wind. Calcutta was the first city of Empire, not London. It was not built on silt, but gold, as Mr Kipling said. Through this same port flowed a seemingly unending stream of riches. Who are we to think this was only a consequence of a particular and past imperial period. What do we know? With China to the east, with the rest of India to the west, the city remains the node of possibility as long as the self-deluding myths of commercial monoculture don't obscure the plausible and the possible. There will, must and needs be other centres and nodes, and all the better for all of us that the city preserve a plural identity. What appears as the smog, smoke and the fog of *adda* may just be our future's best next hope. City of the twenty-first century, character, maverick, beautiful, many-rumoured Calcutta. More than the New York or the Paris of the East, it is Wonderland, only better.

By the way, did you forget that London was also built on pain? On silt? There is good reason to recall the stories of rippers and curiosity shops—that need not delay modernity. In the Calcutta to come, the mosquitoes, the famine of '42, the Naxalites, even the Black Hole, can be remembered and commemorated. There is much to learn from Subhas Chandra Bose as well as from Siraj-ud-daula—allegiance to centres can be tactical, compromised and shifting for good ends. Let us remember this as much as recall myths as true. Fictions build a city as much as stones crumble.

The Number 10 still wends its way to Jadavpur, and like all Calcutta buses, it may not arrive in the same shape as it leaves, but it keeps its promise of forward mission. Word needs to get round. Coin. Fetish. Rumour.

Further Reading

Marx, Karl. 1947. *Notes on Indian History*. Moscow: Foreign Languages Publishing House. (See the reference on p.81.)

———. 1978. *On Colonialism*. Moscow: Progress Press. (See the reference on p.86.)

Cancer

Manu Kothari and Lopa Mehta

August Bier, a German surgeon, declared in the earlier part of the twentieth century that all that the experts knew about cancer could be put down on a visiting card: We know nothing. Charaka, the Indian Ayurvedic legend, predating Christ by half a millennium, classified tumours into benign and malignant. Charaka warned the physician against meddling with the malignant lesion, for it often rendered the patient worse than before. Ernest J. Borges, an outstanding surgeon at Mumbai's Tata Memorial Centre, comprising the Cancer Research Institute and the Tata Memorial (Cancer) Hospital, declared at a public meeting in 1966, a few months before his death from cancer, that many of his patients had complained to him about the treatment being worse than the disease. Macfarlane Burnett, the Australian immunologist of wide renown, summed up in the 1970s the outcome of all cancer research in just two words: precisely nil.

James Watson, of *The Double Helix* fame, characterized cancer research as scientifically bankrupt, therapeutically ineffective and wasteful. Despite the continuing global animal slaughter on an astronomical scale and the fiscal Niagara down the laboratory drain, there is no reason to change mankind's *krebsanschauung*, or cancer-view. The eminent chemist Linus Pauling, who espoused the virtues of mega doses of vitamin C as a preventive against common cold and cancer, and who succumbed to cancer himself, had openly stated that the war on cancer is largely a fraud, and that the National Cancer Institute and the American Cancer Society have been derelict in their duties towards the unsuspecting public.

One of us had a chance to spend over two hours with the then director of the New-York-based Sloan-Kettering Institute, Lewis Thomas, in October 1977. Thomas confessed that oncologists were politically so committed to the cure of cancer that they didn't have the courage to be candid. Joseph Hixson's 1976 *The Patchwork Mouse* is the biography of the greatest scientific scandal of the century, perpetrated at the Sloan-Kettering Institute, and provides a brilliant diagnosis of the ills that plague the cancer establishment.

Cancer—far more benign than malignant mankind—*is what it is, and does what it does*, because of unalterable, unabrogable biorealities that attend this fascinating phenomenon. Alexander Solzhenitsyn, author of *Cancer Ward* and, through that, an authority on cancer more trustworthy than most oncologists lumped together, indicated in his Nobel address that a grain of truth can outweigh the whole world. Cancerrealism, comprising truths about cancer, provides to the open-minded lay and the close-minded learned a perspective that allows one to live with cancer, and die with it. Let the paranoia of humans be assuaged by a declaration at the very outset: the last thing a cancer in your body wants to do, or does, is to kill you. Rather, it chooses to go down the grave with you. Towards such a *krebsanschauung*, it is useful to fall back on the six teachers listed by Rudyard Kipling: what, why, who, where, when and how.

What

Life was, expectedly, preceded by 'pre-life' which originated in the ancient seas or primeval broth. Clyde J. Dawe has suggested that a cancerous—'neoplastic'—equivalent may have been the first form of pre-life endowed with infinite capacity to proliferate. Life evolved from cancer. Talking in the language of Charles Darwin and the German biologist August Friedrich Weismann, every life form bears the indelible stamp of its lowly origin from cancerous pre-life. Not surprisingly, then, canceration is a universal prerogative of normal diploid dividing cells. 'In a disconcerting way, the development of neoplastic cell populations in contemporary metazoans resembles not only a reversal of evolutionary processes but also a recapitulation of them' (Dawe 1969). From cancer thou art, to cancer mayst thou return.

Chemotherapy and radiotherapy, both sworn enemies of cells 'normal' and 'abnormal', have been deployed against cancer through the professionally propagated paranoia that the 'savage' cancer cells are multiplying too rapidly and, therefore, fall a prey to the therapy too readily. Alas, this idée fixe has no support whatsoever from the world of cytology: cancer cells multiply so tardily that before chemo- or radiotherapy may kill one cancer cell, it will surely destroy thousands of normal cells in the bowel and bone marrow. The other obsession, that therapy targets the abnormality inherent in a cancer cell, is nailed by the fact that a cancer cell is considered but a variant of normal cell, or to deploy the vocabulary of Norman MacLean, author of *The Differentiation of Cells* (1977), the cancer cell is the most stable, most committed, differentiated cell. The ugliness of a cancer cell truly lies in the eyes of the beholding cancerologist.

Why

Cancer is causeless, 'whyless'. Way back in 1918, Bertrand Russell exiled causalism from science on scientific grounds. It persists in modern medicine, for it is but an art wearing the garb of science. If the much-maligned Lady Nicotine is blamed for causing cancer, then statistics, read between the lines, reveal that those who smoke have a lower incidence of bowel cancer, brain cancer, Alzheimer's and Parkinsonism. Alex Comfort, the guru of gerontology-et-sexology, has caricatured medicos as 'the anxiety makers' in a book by the same name, where he ends up admiring the astounding resilience with which the common man bites the very apple that his doctor has denied, no matter what cancer the apple threatens to cause.

That one's cancer is preprogrammed prior to one's birth and

stays noumenally programmed after one's death is inferrable from the unfailing uniqueness that every cancer exhibits. No two cancers have ever been alike, for when present in anybody, a cancer must converse with all the cancers of the past, the present and the entire future so as to obey the TITE principle—Total Inclusion allows Total Exclusion—and thus to fashion its own uniqueness. The uniqueness of my fingerprint or DNA-print is a phenomenal outcome of its noumenal oneness with the entire cosmos, past, present and future. So it is for cancer. The very uniqueness of every cancer rules out the possibility of a specific drug or a vaccine.

Who

All are called, but a few (one out of five) are chosen. The benevolence of cancer is evident from the fact that cancer occurs everywhere on the earth, but in excess nowhere. Oncogenes, now granted a normal, universal status by the researchers, are present in all, but by a herd order, cross the cancerogenic threshold in a predictably fixed number to spawn the phenomenon. The saving grace is that the one who bears the cancerous cross is no more likely to die than the one who has been spared. Hardin Jones (1956), of the National Cancer Institute, from a global survey of cancer treated and untreated, concluded that cancer per se is *not* the cause of death, and that on an average the untreated outlives the treated.

Where

Cancer is universal—among all species in the plant and animal kingdoms, in all human races, and, in the body, from the scalp to sole. C.P. Leblond of Canada classified the body cells into perennial or immortal, expanding and renewing groups. The perennial cells are the sensory receptors, nerve cells and muscle cells. They can't divide normally, and hence can't divide cancerously. They are free from cancer. The expanding cells divide only on demand, and hence the occurrence of cancer therein is low. The renewing cell populations divide ceaselessly, and are the seat of the majority of cancers.

When

Cancer occurs throughout the human lifespan. It can occur in the newborn, and at all ages, but, in both animals and man, it closely parallels the mortality curve natural to the species.

The nature of the whenness of cancer exposes the greatest lie that cancerologists have been mouthing to date, namely the idea of early diagnosis and treatment. Following its inception, even the most rapidly growing cancer takes a quinquennium before it reaches a scannable stage, and yet more time before it diseases the owner. By the time a cancer is diagnosed, no matter how and by whom, it has had enough time and opportunity to settle itself as a cellular reality pervading the entire body. The few cancers—notably, primary tumours of the brain—that do not spread to other sites, nevertheless, observe their 'discreet silence' and undiagnosability for quite a while. On the medical claims about the early diagnosis and treatment of cancer, one could invoke Churchillian rhetoric: Never in the history of science has so much untruth been told by so few to so many for so long.

How

From the last of the Kipling's teachers, we shall learn how to deal with one's own cancerophobia, and with one's own cancer when it is a fait accompli. All the available data on cancer allow a robust approach to the problem, no matter what age, and what the cancer, as follows:

1. Cancer cannot be caused, cannot be prevented. Therefore, adopt a *que sera sera* attitude about its affecting you.
2. Remember that cancer has been with mankind for ages and its occurrence is neither a freak of nor a punishment from nature. Every cancer is a part of your own being. If you must not love it, you need not hate it either.

3. Each cancer, before it bothers you or your doctor, has been with you for a long time. Early diagnosis/treatment for a cancer is a myth to be buried.

4. For the reasons cited above, it is not at all necessary for you to get yourself screened for cancer. Bother yourself about cancer when, and only when, it really bothers you.

5. Cancer does not always kill, nor does it always connote a short post-diagnosis or post-treatment life. Decide to *live* with your cancer until it chooses to die with you.

6. Appreciate the fact that cancer need not necessarily disrupt either your profession or your joie de vivre.

7. Since there is nothing like a cure for cancer, insist on being treated symptom-far and no further. Any form of therapeutic radicalism is despicable overkill by medicine.

8. If you must be treated, seek surgery; should you be irradiated or given chemotherapy, insist on the minimal and be prepared for the cellular levy that your body must pay from head to foot as a consequence.

9. You owe a duty to your body and soul in the form of a dignified death. Do not deny yourself the experience of dying with dignity.

10. Cancer is a species, class or ordinal character. You can neither inherit it nor pass it on to your progeny.

Further Reading

Burnett, MacFarlane. 1970. *Immunological Surveillance*. Oxford: Pergamon. [See chapter on cancer cells]

Dawe, Clyde P. 1969. Phylogeny and oncogeny. *National Cancer Institute Monograph* 31:1.

Hixson, Joseph. 1976. *The Patchwork Mouse: Politics and Intrigue in the Campaign to Conquer Cancer*. Anchor Press.

Jones, Hardin B. 1956. Demographic considerations of the cancer problem. *Trans. N.Y. Acad. Sc.* 18:298.

Kothari, M.L., and Lopa A. Mehta. 1979. *Cancer: Myths and Realities of Cause and Cure*. London: Marion Boyers.

Cloning

Manu Kothari and Lopa Mehta

The Mythology

Genetics, with all the hype and hoopla over Dolly-and-after, has of late been at a low ebb. The sixty-sixth Ciba Foundation Symposium titled 'Human Genetics: Possibilities and Realities', held in 1979, concluded with the frank comment of its chairman, Sydney Brenner: 'Scientists should not promise society too much . . . Our promises have been made too easily . . . we are nearly always wrong . . . our symposium will be a landmark even if it only records our confused perception of the future of genetics and human biology.' Benjamin Levin's huge tome *Genes IV* (Oxford University Press, 1990) concludes on Nobelist Salvador E. Luria's 1986 'attitude of romantic pessimism', a note unchanged in the epilogue to the sixth edition of *Genes* (Oxford, 1997). Dolly-making arrived in 1997 without, alas, providing any reasons for changing the pessimistic note into an optimistic one, notwithstanding the media blitz on the Human Genome Project and its sequel, the Human Proteome Project.

Aldous Huxley set his *Brave New World* in the seventh century AF (After Ford). The Dolly-device seems to have achieved a time-contraction, raising the *BNW* spectre barely fifty years AF. Yet, there are saving graces. Soon after Dolly, *Time* (10 March 1997), scarcely the most enlightened expression of opinion, commented: 'But on the more profound question of what, exactly, a human clone would be, doubters and believers are unanimous. A human clone might resemble, superficially, the individual from whom it was made. But it would differ dramatically in the traits that define an individual—personality and character, intelligence and talents. "Here's the rule," says psychologist Jerome Kagan of Harvard. "You will never get 100 percent identity—never—because of chance factors and because environments are never exactly the same."' As if to underscore the aforementioned came rapid disclaimers from the Roslin Institute that spawned Dolly. The *Times of India* of 6 January 2000 ran a headline imported from the UK: 'Human cloning hits a natural barrier'. The report read: 'The cloning technology that produced Dolly the sheep will never be able to produce identical humans, research has shown.' Professor Keith Campbell, who directed the creation of a clone of four rams at the Roslin Institute, declared that 'physically and mentally the rams were progressively diverging from each other'. Campbell's concluding remarks are oxymoronic: 'The only real clones are identical twins and anyone who really knows twins understands that even they have different features and personalities.'

Nature Negatived Cloning Long Ago

The nine-banded armadillo, as a rule, delivers a litter of eight offspring, all of which develop from a single zygote, and yet each differs from the other. As if to match the armadillo, Oliva Dionne, a Canadian woman, had her ovum most naturally impregnated in 1933 by Elzire Dionne, the single zygote splitting into six, one getting aborted at three months and the other five being prematurely delivered but growing up fully, 'every one of them developing into a consummate woman by 1950' (see Murchie 1978). Regarding the Dionne quintuplets, the *Encyclopaedia Britannica* poses a question and then answers it as well: 'How alike and how different can five adults become, who began genetically as one person . . . the question is a reasonable one, since differences commonly occur even between the right and left side of a person's face or body.' Geneticists nurse many a dogma, which has been dubbed *geneticism* by Peter Medawar, this being 'a scheme of thought which extravagantly overestimates the power of genetical ideas ... which has the ill effect of bringing GENETICS into undeserved discredit.'

Identicality of Monozygous Twins Does Not Exist

Despite the averred identicality of the human twin pairs derived from a single ovum and single sperm, one-third of such pairs exhibit tissue incompatibility to reject grafts from each other as vigorously as 'non-identical' animals or humans. On the other hand, all dizygous, manifestly non-identical, cattle twins exhibit tissue compatibility, despite differing genetic constitutions. The secret of compatibility (or incompatibility) resides in the twins having had shared a common placenta. Two-thirds of 'identical' human twins and all cattle non-identical twins share a placenta and hence are able to swap tissues and organs, along the theoretical and experimental lines established by the acclaimed work of Medawar and MacFarlane Burnett.

Conception versus Cloning: The 2n Game

Circa 1894, August Weismann intuited that the germ cells—ovum, sperm—ought to have n number of chromosomes, just half of the 2n number characteristic of body cells. He proved to be right, allowing biologists to classify gametes as haploid (single) and somatic cells as diploid (double). At fertilization, leading to conception, the n-nucleus of the sperm fuses with the n-nucleus of the ovum to beget a cell called a zygote that has the 2n number of chromosomes, a characteristic of all body cells. Embryological development starts with the formation of the zygote, which could be seen as the first body cell that will clone itself to form the 100,000 billion cells that comprise a human being. The fertilization of an ovum by a sperm is usually achieved coitally, in the genital passages of the female. When such an act is achieved outside the body, in a petri dish, it is called in vitro (in glass) fertilization or IVF.

Cloning is conception by devious means. J.B. Gurdon in 1969

excised the haploid nucleus of a frog ovum and replaced it by a 2n nucleus of a body cell, and a frog was eventually formed. It should be clear to the reader that Gurdon created a zygotic cell—the first body cell—without the intervention of the sperm. This little experiment proves that the sperm is utilized by Nature primarily to diploidize the haploid nucleus of the ovum. Paternality rides piggyback on the sperm's haploidy. So does maternality. The cytoplasm of the ovum does not seem to bother whether its diploidy comes from the sperm or the ovum, or a body cell. All it wants is a 2n nucleus. Occasionally, an animal ovum that by itself has remained 2n or diploid, begets an offspring, a process called parthenogenesis (from the Greek *parthenos*, virgin, implying a virgin birth). Dolly-making, or Wakayama's cloning of mice, by 'impregnating' the cytoplasm of mice-ova by the nuclei of body cells, is merely mimicking the diploidy that the zygote had had to start with. The clonologists forget that any somatic cell is nothing but the clonal progeny of the zygotic cell and hence genetically no different from it.

The sine qua non in this genetic manipulation is the cytoplasm of the ovum or the female gamete, which carries within it the entire blueprint of embryo-making. All that it needs is nuclear diploidy that replaces the unipolarity (n) of an ovum by the 2n bipolarity. No two ova, even from the same ovary, are ever alike. The total possible number of chromosome arrangements due to reassortment in meiosis (gamete formation) alone is 2^{23}, which is more than 8×10^6. Further rearrangement takes place because of crossing over, so it is not surprising that the individual zygotes from the same parents are never alike genetically. Hence, no matter what nucleus and from where, it is the irrepressible individuality of the ovum-cytoplasm that begets an invariably variable progeny. As Robert Ardrey puts it, despite all the knowledge we have on gravity, the apple refuses to fall upwards. Despite all the experimental ingenuity, the individuality of the ovum and the uniqueness of the offspring it begets have the last laugh, rendering the past, the present and the future of cloning into a farce. An article in *Science*, 6 July 2001, has inspired media headlines: 'Healthy clones can carry genetic abnormalities'. Reading between the lines, one gleans the double folly of claiming cloning when it just does not exist and willy-nilly admitting that Nature's forethought inherent in ovum/sperm-making had better *not* be dispensed with.

Cloning Smacks of Male Chauvinism

The synonymy of sperm with a seed, and of diploidization with fertilization betrays the age-old obsession that the female and her egg merely provide soil through which the sperm spawns a progeny. 'Your wives are a tilth unto you. So come into your tilth when and how you will' (Quran: 2.223). In fact, the theory of preformation, popular long before the microscopy of cells came into its own, assumed that the fully formed human lies coiled up in the head of the sperm, and that landing into the ovum it merely grows to a large size during pregnancy. David Rorvik's infamous book had to have the title *In His Image*, betraying an obsession that the sperm rules the roost. Here too, male chauvinism was beaten to the post by the pioneering of Dolly in her image, as it were.

Cloning Is Mythology

The whole fallacy of cloning may seem to reside in the idea that in a cell, the nucleus is the boss, and cytoplasm the obedient servant. Hence, if a series of ova can be impregnated with the nuclei of the body cells of a person, all the resulting progeny should be identical. The idea has bitten the dust on the clear realization that the cytoplasm of the ovum calls the developmental shots, and all that the sperm, or body nuclei, do is to provide a nuclear bipolarity characteristic of all body cells. The cloning idea could well be called the greatest misconception of the second millennium, deserving a decent abortion at the very start of the third millennium. In any case, since the so-called cloning is a deadend exercise, so that a Dolly can't re-Dolly itself, the mythopoetic term *cloning* can be dropped forever from biological and medical lexicons. This despite *Time*'s cover story (26 February 2001) declaring that 'Human cloning is closer than you think'.

Cloning is conception by asexual, non-spermal means, a third-millennial version of the immaculate conception. Clonology is out to square a circle. When no two atoms, leaves, fingerprints or homozygous twins have ever been identical, clonologists promise to create identical copies of sheep, mice, pigs and, quite soon, human beings. Their 'proton pseudo' or the basic mistake is their calculated ignorance of the self-evident fact that it is not the nucleus of the zygote but the maternal ovular cytoplasm that has the entire mechanism of embryogenesis encoded into it. No two ova have ever been, are, or would be, alike. Likewise, no two 'cloned' individuals will ever be clonal to each other. Thank God, Huxley's *Brave New World* will never come to pass. Cloning shall, forever, remain a dream—not because of inadequate money, technology, intellect or will or ingenuity but because of the boon of *uniqueness* or *individuation* that St Thomas Aquinas clearly enunciated in the thirteenth century. It is a universal principle that no clonologist dare deny.

Further Reading

Murchien, Guy. 1978. *The Seven Mysteries of Life*. London: Rider/Hutchinson.

Coca-Cola

Ashis Nandy

The first principle of the philosophy of Coca-Cola is that Coca-Cola is substitutable only by another cola. The substitute may be Diet Coke at some point of time (indicating a concern with health) or Pepsi-Cola at another (indicating a subtler sensitivity to taste), but it has to be a cola. For, once exposed to the world of cola, life in a community cannot be any more defined without some version of a cola. The spectrum of human needs in the community expands permanently and can never again contract to what it was before the cola drinks entered it. Everything else about Coca-Cola is negotiable, but not the issue of non-substitutability. A cola can never be replaced by tea, coffee, beer, wine, fruit juice or water. That is why, in the global scene, Coca-Cola's archetypal Other, its chief competitor, is Pepsi-Cola.

Many of my cleverer friends—especially South Asians, North and South Americans—tell me how autonomous they are of what they contemptuously call the Coca-Cola culture. They do not drink Coca-Cola; they do not even like its taste. In some cases, they also force their children to be abstemious. Proud of their dissent from the global mass culture, they flaunt their 'deviance' by talking about Coca-Cola the same way others talk of McDonald's and Woolworth, or red meat, hard liquor and tobacco. Their attitude to the cola drinks is a mix of contempt (towards what they see as an important aspect of low culture) and fear (towards a caffeine-based drink which, according to health freaks, is bad for health).

This deviance is not as deviant as it looks. The very fact that one has to flaunt such dissent, that the dissent is dissent only with reference to the cola drinks and does not extend to other items of useless consumption, tells us that Coca-Cola has managed to become a world view, a philosophy of life, within which there is ample scope for variation and even some scope for dissent. This was forgotten during the brief tenure of the Janata party at the helm of the Indian polity during 1977–79. The then minister of industries, George Fernandes, threw the Coca-Cola corporation out of India. Fernandes thought he was being true to both his socialism and Gandhism, apart from contributing handsomely to India's drive for self-reliance. Actually, he was operating faithfully within the given framework of the philosophy of Coca-Cola. For Coca-Cola was duly substituted by Campa Cola, product of an Indian corporation, and by Thums Up, produced by another multinational. Now, more than a decade afterwards, to spite the likes of Fernandes, Coca-Cola has re-entered the Indian market triumphantly. It is also triumphantly competing with Pepsi-Cola to provide the ultimate prototype of market competition that is supposed to be the salvation of Mother India in the near future.

The secret of Coca-Cola, closely guarded by the company, and an object of greedy curiosity for every other producer of cola drinks, also constitutes a paradigmatic puzzle for our times. Many other companies in the world have come close to Coca-Cola's unknown formula, to judge by the tastes of their products. Others have often deliberately come close to, but not duplicated, the formula. They have sought a distinct or unique place for themselves in the cola market, a place not occupied by Coca-Cola itself. The success of these competitors has occasionally been spectacular. But that does not—in fact, cannot—detract from the mystery of the formula, the code still waiting to be cracked or the standard waiting to be approximated. No argument about local, regional or national variations in taste can ultimately work in such cases. Any such argument must fail as decisively as the touch of cinnamon and cardamom in some Indian cola drinks have failed to attract the Indian customers in the long run. The philosophy of Coca-

Cola has no place for—and does not have to bother about—popular cultures of different societies or regions. It bases itself on the global mass culture of consumption, apparently unaffected by local cultures, levels of economic activity and political preferences. Local cultures may be hostile to the strangeness of Coca-Cola, the economy may not be able to sustain its production or import and the politicians may for symbolic reasons seek to 'clean' a society of its colaphiles. But remove the external compulsions, and the attachment to or love for Coca-Cola comes back in its pristine purity.

Everyone knows this, though only a few acknowledge it. Thus, when India threw out Coca-Cola, Air-India, which had to woo Indians in competition with other international airlines, understood the logic of the situation perfectly well. It was neither impressed by slogans of self-reliance and basic needs nor by the industrial policy of its owner, the Government of India. Air-India never served its passengers any of the Indian versions of cola, and even Fernandes did not object.

Coca-Cola touches something deep in human existence. Like many other elements of the presently dominant global mass culture—such as pop music, blue jeans and hamburgers—it reminds its consumers of the simple, innocent joys of living which might have been mostly lost in the modern world but which survive in symbolic form in selected artefacts of modernity. But even more than most other elements of the global mass culture, Coca-Cola has come to symbolize something that is totally useless and hence useful to consume—to aggressively affirm one's conformity to a lifestyle. Hence the difficulty of giving up Coca-Cola, and the fanaticism of the lapsed colaphile. Like a heavy smoker who gives up smoking and becomes an anti-smoking activist, those rejecting Coca-Cola on ideological grounds or fulminating against the cola culture have to fight against a part of their own selves.

Coca-Cola, of course, is the ultimate symbol of the market. You cannot have a cola without a market. You can have orange juice or tea or beer without going to a market. Theoretically you can grow oranges and squeeze their juice manually at your home.

Theoretically you can grow your own tea and drink it, if you happen to be at the right altitude and in the right kind of territory, or brew your own ale, if you have the patience. None of these are possible in the case of a cola. There is no territory or altitude in the world where you can grow your own cola and consume it. You have to have your cola in some ready-made form, you do need a franchise for it and you have to be part of the global market to have access to the world of Coca-Cola.

I need hardly add that the philosophy of Coca-Cola is not confined to Coca-Cola alone or the colas in general. It informs many areas of life and the votaries of the philosophy would like it to ultimately inform all areas of life. They do not have to work hard for that, because the philosophy is blatantly phagocytic; it eats up all other adjacent philosophies or, alternatively, seeks to turn them into ornamental dissenting philosophies within its universe.

A neat example is the changing culture of liberal-democratic politics the world over. The most remarkable aspect of the democracies today is the way they are abstracting all politics out of elections. The elections are now primarily media ploys and secondarily politics. They are fought the way giant corporations fight media wars—through advertisement spots, with droves of media experts and public relations consultants remote-controlling the battle from the sidelines. The voters are given a choice between images, sold as alternatives to one another, while being only each other's flip side. The candidates think that the 'political' needs of the electorate can be engineered through experts. The experts think all candidates are edited versions of each other; only their public images differ. For both, the ultimate model of political contests is not the boxer's ring, but the advertisement battles between popular brands of consumables, none of which could be called essential except in terms of needs artificially created in the consumers. The strategy is borrowed straight from the titanic battle between Coca-Cola and Pepsi-Cola for higher market shares.

The consumers—also called the electorate—are never given a chance to stop and think or confront the possibility that they might be deciding their own fate. The philosophy of Coca-Cola insists you never acknowledge that the game might have ended or changed for you. It insists that you go on playing the game, for worse than losing is to opt out or own up that your needs could be or have become so different that the game is not relevant to you.

The philosophy of Coca-Cola is the paradigmatic social philosophy of our time. Those who talk glibly of the Coca-Cola culture subverting other 'superior' cultures know nothing of its appeal. Coca-Cola happily grants such superiority when the market or advertisement policies require it, for its appeal is nothing less than an invitation to worsen it at its own game. Following the model faithfully, that is the challenge the United States has thrown to the rest of the world. Japan, which can be called the Pepsi-Cola of the world economy, and China, which has the ambition of being so in the future, have shown that Coca-Cola can be 'defeated' if one joins the game sincerely and recognizes that the real battle is on TV, in our drawing rooms and in our hearts. It has also shown—as the five little East Asian economic dragons were doing before their economies collapsed—that one can win only if one retools oneself to withstand the rigours of fighting Coca-Cola on its own terrain.

In the 1980s, Yevgeny Primakov, Russian social-scientist-turned-politician, seemed surprised that in Düsseldorf, McDonald's employed more people than the steel industry and Coca-Cola paid more tax than Krupps. An old-style Marxist scholar, he failed to appreciate that mass culture was not only sane politics but also rational economics, that defiance of mass culture was already defiance of sanity and rationality. To have the luxury of that defiance, you have to take on not only the world of mega consumption but also the worlds of normality and rational knowledge.

Many years ago, when as a new scientific and cultural innovation Coca-Cola began its journey through the corridors of time, it allegedly included cocaine as an ingredient. If true, some may like to read this history as a standard example of corporate greed and immorality, a proof of how little the Coca-Cola corporation cared for the consumers. I read it differently—as a proof of how little the corporation itself understood the product it was unleashing in the global culture. The corporation, following the tenets of nineteenth-century capitalism, was selling something addictive, to hold on to its clientele and to make the demand for its product artificially inelastic. It had no idea that it was a pioneer selling a world view and a lifestyle. It did not know that even without using a physically addictive ingredient, it had produced a culturally addictive brew that could ensure as inelastic a demand as any bootlegger or drug pedlar might want.

In the mass culture which has begun to engulf the urban, media-exposed, modernizing South, Coca-Cola is an epistemological, not an ontological, statement. It is a way of thinking rather than a thought, perhaps even a way of dreaming that subverts other kinds of dreams.

Consumerism

Ashis Nandy

Consumerism is not the first choice of human beings. Nor is it a basic need. There is not an iota of evidence in contemporary psychology, anthropology or ethnology to confirm that consumerism is a part of human nature, that we cannot survive without unending consumption. Not even the great champions of free market have dared to claim that human happiness is inescapably hitched to the kind of consumption that the prosperous are encouraged to practice in the name of development today. Even much of the West, identified the world over with infinite consumption, had no genuine tradition of heavy consumption before the beginning of this century, probably not till the 1940s.

Consumption was discovered as a value and a lifestyle only about five decades ago. Previously, it had been a character trait of profligate rulers and the spoilt children of a few super-rich; now it was made a marker of social achievement and, thus, a part of everyday life. People now consumed stories of super-consumption through newspapers, journals and television—the way they earlier read of, fantasized about and vicariously entered the harems of Oriental potentates. Earlier, the aristocracy, when it consumed mindlessly, did not dare to advertise the fact, for it was incongruent with class status. Only the newly rich were expected to flaunt their wealth. High consumption now became a marker of social status and success and a patented remedy for feelings of social inadequacy and personal inferiority.

Perhaps no other country has become so deeply identified with consumption in our times as the United States, though some of the most powerful critiques of consumption, too, have come from that country. The reason for both these facts may be that in no other country has consumption been so systematically institutionalized as a need in itself. A few city states like Hong Kong and Singapore, and a few small kingdoms acting as city states, such as Dubai, have also jumped on the bandwagon of 'consuming societies'. These are societies where not only is consumption an end in itself but the entire country often looks to a casual observer like a huge supermarket, and the country's political economy, if not life itself, is organized around consumption. However, the global cultural impact of such city states is not a fraction of that of the United States.

In America the successful institutionalization of consumption might have come about perhaps because it is mainly a society of immigrants that has tried to build a public culture hitched to the psychological and social needs of the exiled and decultured. The institutionalization of consumption is an incidental byproduct of this larger cultural process that has been going on for the last 200 years thanks to the changing colour of industrial capitalism, erosion of communities and the emergence of 'lonely crowds' in the large parts of the world. As I have already said, consumption has anxiety-binding properties, particularly in the lives of the uprooted, the lonely and the massified.

This culture of exile also provides a clue to the unique status that the United States has began to enjoy as everyone's second country. In pre-war Europe Paris claimed the status, I am told, of being every European's second city. For many subjects of British and French colonies as well, London and Paris had a similar status. Today, it seems that only the United States can claim this prerogative. The size of the American market (including the market for conformity and deviance and for new faiths, ideologies and creeds) has a role to play in this. The United States is the consumer's paradise. Even dissent has a better market there than elsewhere; it is consumed more avidly and widely there than almost anywhere else. This critique of consumption can also be consumed.

In the 1940s, the psychoanalyst Erich Fromm coined the term 'marketing orientation' to describe a personality type that included people who sold their selves, rather than things in the modern marketplace. He did not foresee that one day we shall have another personality type that would consider it 'normal' to consume for the sake of consuming. The consuming orientation is now a hallmark of style and high fashion; there are persons and groups in the world famous only for their flamboyant consumption. These hyper-consumers would have put to shame the greediest rich before the Second World War.

Usually when justifying consumption, the marketeers claim that it will lead to greater consumption of the physical essentials of life by the poor. Alternatively, they extol the technological growth or economic modernization that follows a consumption explosion, allegedly serving as an engine of development. It has, however, already become obvious that the kind of consumption they have in mind—or are comfortable with—has nothing to do with any such grand social vision. For, once built, a culture of consumption becomes a self-perpetuating affair. As has been the case with the super-consuming rich, it becomes an end in itself. This is not unknown to the development experts; they expect consumption to lead to a consumption-oriented development and technology. I am not saying that their economic logic is faulty. I am arguing that their justifications of consumption only capture a small part of the phenomenon and spirit of consumption.

To understand that spirit, one must first face the fact that to make consumption a value, human beings have to be re-engineered. The first step in this process is to isolate or uproot a person from his or her community, traditions and family. In their place, he or she has to be given a large, anonymous quasi-community called the nation, a more manageable set of cultural artefacts called traditions (artefacts that can be consumed in a theatre, gallery, classroom or a tourist resort) and a nuclearized unit called family where the elderly and the underaged both become either intrusions or liabilities that have to be sometimes borne but never treated on the same footing as the conjugal pair, bonded together by a commodified concept of sex.

Simultaneously, an ideological basis has to be laid for consumption. The possessive individual who, according to many European scholars, provides the very basis of modern liberal capitalism, has to be redefined as the consuming individual. Simultaneously, the right to property has to be redefined as the right to consumption. The sovereignty of this consuming individual has to be declared so that the apparent sacredness that attaches to the individual in many theories of the state, freedom and rights begins to attach to the act of and the right to consumption. Some social and political activists claim that standardized production systems are now producing standardized consumption patterns, for only such patterns now make economic sense. Many popular ideas of democracy in the global mass culture seem, on closer scrutiny, to be an attempt to protect this pattern and the particular form of individualism that goes with it. Speaking of the Kyoto protocol on world environment, which the United States refused to sign, President George Bush, Sr, once said, 'Gentlemen, the American way of life is not negotiable.' As some others put it, 'dollarized poverty' is now matched by dollarized wealth and dollarized individuals.

To such an individual—lonely, narcissistic and decoupled from community ties—consumption becomes the ultimate value, a guarantor of social belonging and status. He or she compensates for an empty social life by consuming. One is, because one consumes.

This lonely individual is the basic constituent of all projects of global marketing. Marketing is all about creating needs. Basic needs do not have to be advertised; people automatically try to meet them and are willing to work or pay for them. Advertisements become necessary to create artificial needs. Marketing is the art and science of creating such needs by linking them to basic human needs. This linkage is often not noticed. Many talk of consumerism as a form of a conspiracy to cheat the ordinary innocent citizen with the help of smart, high-pitched advertisements. Ordinary citizens are not that easily cheated. They are influenced by advertisements, but first a void has to be created in their lives so that the seductive properties of advertisement can work on them.

It is crucial to create this void. Only when his or her life is emptied of a deep sense of belonging to a community, family or tradition does the atomized individual begin to seek meaning in various pseudo-solidarities. One of the most important of these today is the solidarity of the consumers. Presidents and prime ministers in the First World are now made or unmade on the basis of the threat they pose to—or the promises they offer of—mega consumption. Consumption, or the hope of it, now gives meaning to the lives of many, however odd that may sound to a large proportion of the world. This has even produced a new internationalism which, paradoxically, relieves one from any responsibility to learn about other countries or communities. You do not have to, for others also consume, and therefore they are. They also can be known through their consumption patterns.

Yet, consumerism is not anti-cultural. Being a world view, it has a place for culture. The place is not for culture as we have known it—vibrant, unmanageable, fuzzy and often subversive of the projects called modernity and development—but for a consumable culture. Once such a culture becomes triumphant, many known entities in our world acquire new meanings. For instance, I notice remarkable and rapid changes taking place in ancient civilizations such as China and India. There are already signs that, under a consumerist dispensation, the Indianness of India may become a liability and yet, at the same time, a capital. Much effort, we may presume, will be made in the coming years to encash that Indianness as a form of commodified classicism or ethnic chic, 'viewable' on the weekends and saleable in the tourist market.

Do cultures resist consumerism? I do not really know. But I like to believe that they can hit back when threatened with extinction, whether the threat is real or imaginary. Human biology can be even more aggressively resistant. A large majority of the fatal diseases in the First World have to do with over-consumption. Worse is the fate of those ethnic groups in the First World which have not developed any scepticism towards consumption. The incidence of cardiac diseases among expatriate South Asians in some of the Western societies today is three times that among the native whites. This is probably the way nature and culture seek to restore balance and ensure their survival.

Coronary Care

Manu Kothari, Lopa Mehta and Vatsal Kothari

The nearly fifty-year-old saga of invasive treatment of coronary artery disease by bypass (CABG) and/or angioplasty (PTCA) owes itself to the pioneering work of three Nobelists: Alexis Carrel, who introduced suturing of blood vessels, and Andre Cournand and Werner Forssmann, who evolved catheterization of blood vessels to pave the way for coronary angiography. A visualization of 'coronary blocks' inspired bypass. The ingenuity of covering a catheter's tip with an inflatable balloon led to the equally widespread procedure of angioplasty. The widening of an artery by angioplasty was made to 'stay' by yet another refinement introducing at the site a plastic/metallic stent that would prevent the blood vessel from collapsing and let the blood flow through. To the lay person, and also the medically learned, the abovementioned procedures seem perfect straight-line plumbing solutions.

However, the gains for the patient seem to be nil. The *Current Medical Diagnosis and Treatment* (2001) is blunt: 'Controlled trials have not shown any advantage in increased survival or lower infarction rates with CABG or PTCA compared to medical therapy.' So much is done; nothing seems to be gained. In fact, the patient is the loser. According to Dean Ornish, 25 per cent of bypass subjects manifest a lowering of their IQ. The collateral damage to the brain during—and consequent to—bypass surgery is perhaps as high as 53 per cent, if the reasonably authoritative *New*

England Journal of Medicine (344:395) is any guide. No wonder *Current Diagnosis* shies away with a guarded statement: 'Avoiding bypass may lessen the risk of cerebral complication.' Bottom line: the heart fails to gain; the brain fails to lose. Angioplasty is akin to harpooning an already diseased coronary artery with the harpoon-head carrying an explosive charge. The *Concise Oxford Textbook of Medicine 2000* describes angioplasty as 'inflation of a balloon to compress an atheromatous lesion, creating one or more tears within the plaque or the normal vessel wall opposite.' Coronary tear/s as part of coronary care!

Coronaries Are Blocked: Circumvent Them; Deblock Them

On 4 April 1999, the *Times of India* devoted a full page in small print to the medical miracles that are there for the asking for anyone with a coronary problem. The menu card's prized item is CABG: 'You can describe cardiac surgery as a dignified plumbing job: creating a detour around a blocked pipe. In medical terrain, it involves creating a new passage for blood to reach the heart when the arteries in the human "pump" get blocked. This is the essence of that sophisticated procedure called Coronary Artery Bypass Grafting (CABG).'

Well said. The authors have followed the magnificent American tome *Harrison's Principles of Internal Medicine* from 1983 through 2001, tenth edition through the fifteenth. Despite twenty years and countless bypasses and immeasurable research, the learned textbook clings to an apologetic refrain. While musing over how bypass works, it offers three explanations: (i) placebo effect—a theory that justifies bypass being christened the costliest aspirin; (ii) sensory neurectomy—the heart remains status quo ante, but the patient, no longer feeling any pain, does not work up into a coronary frenzy; and (iii) the reader should hold his breath for, as the learned tome states, bypass probably works by killing the complaining segment of the heart. A composite verbatim quote from the latest edition is appropriate: 'Angina is abolished or greatly reduced in approximately 90 per cent of patients following coronary revascularization. Although this is usually associated with graft patency and restoration of blood flow, the pain may also have been alleviated as a result of infarction of the ischemic segment or placebo effect . . . CABG does not appear to reduce the incidence of myocardial infarction in patients with chronic IHD; perioperative (i.e. in the immediate post-operative period) infarction occurs in 5 to 10 per cent of cases but in most instances these infarcts are small.' If bypass cures pain by killing the heart, angioplasty can behave no differently.

Is modern medicine barking up the wrong tree? *The Annals of Internal Medicine* (72:181) hinted that coronary blockage could be the consequence and not the cause of cardiac dysfunction. This was clearly buttressed when JAMA published a Centennial Series of '51 Landmark Articles in Medicine'. Among these is the 1912 benchmark article by James Bryan Herrick on coronary occlusion, and a 1983 postscript on it by the redoubtable J. Willis Hurst, editor-in-chief of the voluminous *The Heart* (McGraw-Hill, 7 editions, 1966–90), that reads rather tellingly: 'A debate still exists as to whether coronary thrombosis is the cause or the result of infarction, and whether it is always present in myocardial infarction. The debate as to the frequency of thrombosis identified at angiography and the frequency of thrombosis found at autopsy in patients with myocardial infarction is an important one and is not settled.' The fact that a phenomenon called reperfusion injury— significant damage to the heart because of medically restored blood flow—is clearly accepted to exist—in the carotid field as well—puts paid to the idée fixe of restoration of the coronary lumen as the summum bonum of invasive cardiology. Coronary or carotid occlusion or narrowing is the result of altered demand from the heart or the brain and not the other way around. Hence all attempts at revascularization, no matter what the sophistry, end in a no-gain, no-win situation, for one can gain nothing out of treating an effect. In the whole Coronary Arteries Disease game, the coronaries are treated as the driver and the heart as the driven. Coronaries could as well be the chauffeur driving under backseat orders from the human heart.

Give Me a Prejudice and / I Will Move the World

'Give me a prejudice and / I will move the world.' This profound observation by the investigating magistrate in Gabriel García Marquéz's *Chronicle of a Death Foretold* is perversely applicable to the issue we are discussing. The prime prejudice that moves the cardiological (and medical world) was defined by William Osler, the modern Hippocrates, way back in 1894: 'But know also, man has an inborn craving for medicine . . . the desire to take medicine is one feature which distinguishes man the animal from his fellow creatures. It is really one of the most serious difficulties with which we have to contend . . . the doctor's visit is not thought to be complete without a prescription.' The universal creed that 'something can and hence must always be done' views the coronaries and the blood flowing therein as the root of all the troubles, that have to be set right, given the power of modern medicine.

An unwitting portrayal of such strong prejudice can be gleaned from the state-of-the-art *Management of Complex Cardiovascular Problems—The Consultant's Approach* (Futura: New York, 2000). It has five editors, thirty-nine contributors from six countries, and a preface by Eugene Braunwald, the guru of all cardiological gurus. The thirteen chapters have cited 439 references from impeccable sources, 413 of which are from the 1990s, most of these from 1999. What comes through the circumlocution of the 240 pages is an apology for the failure of all the non-invasive or invasive approaches to coronary care. And yet, each chapter ends on the classical note: The show must go on. The enormity of cardiologic conundrums makes a patient, in poor and rich countries alike, feel that all this cannot be wrong, spawning thereby the Everest complex of seeking a remedy just because it is there to be sought—the costlier the better. An affluent male in his late fifties or more can now trumpet a bypass as one of his achievements; it is a mark of some success. A bypass now takes its place alongside private-club memberships, a taste for golf and fine culinary experiences as something which announces to the world the status of its recipient.

An extensive study in the 23 December 1999 issue of the *New England Journal of Medicine* concludes that there is no evidence that stents reduce the most important complications of a heart attack, namely, death, stroke or a repeat heart attack. In the controlled trial of stents vs no-stents, the mortality was 4.2 per cent with stents and 2.7 per cent with no-stents. The editorial annotation to the foregoing confesses that, despite 500,000 stentings a year in the US, 'It has yet to be shown that they can save lives.' It should be little wonder that the *Consultant's* book referred to above has described in-stent (stent-begotten) restenosis as the commonest iatrogenic malignant disorder. Stenting has turned the art of coronary-care into a malignancy.

Our advice to the lay and the learned is to stay away from the well-conceived but useless and harmful procedures comprising invasive coronary care. The cardiologists and coronary surgeons are riding a tiger they fear to dismount, lest the dollar Niagara come to a sudden end. Angiography, by itself untrustworthy, inevitably spawns—plasty and/or bypass, the trio comprising costly iatrogeny on a global scale. A wise person avoids any assault on the coronary tree, no matter how sophisticated the laser, reamer, rotor or what have you.

Further Reading

Current Medical Diagnosis and Treatment. 2001. 40th ed. New York: Lange and McGraw Hill.

Corruption

Sudhir Chella Rajan

Ask a postcolonial what she is least proud to reveal about her country to a 'Westerner', and the answer most often will concern the national level of corruption. Corruption is one of those words that more easily generates malaise than a desire for comprehension, and it is often intriguingly linked to the self-worth of the society to which one belongs. In fact, the shame of corruption appears to spread completely across the postcolonial nation; almost no individual other than its strongest perpetrators seem to be free of it, which is perhaps why it is so common to hear calls to 'purge' the evil of corruption from the land.

But surely, discomfiture concerning corruption is not just a colonial hangover? It seems not, for the bodily metaphor of certain internal processes causing damage to or, indeed, *corrupting* the social fabric has been used widely enough and in contexts as different as ancient Egypt, Kautilya's India and present-day Italy, Japan, Nigeria and the US. This suggests that there should be some value to dehistoricizing the word, in the first instance, to appraise it generically, as it were, before examining the multiple cultural significations and skin tones it has imbued, particularly since the twentieth century. A good place to begin is to ask why the readily identifiable and largely domestic practices of corruption would cause such gloom to the national imaginary as a whole.

One answer seems to be that corruption represents a social injustice that, once accepted within the body politic, is supremely capable of reproducing itself 'like a cancer'. The scourge can cause stable institutions to become off-centred by rewarding ill-gotten gains and can turn into a race to the moral bottom, but a race in which the least competent and wiliest individuals secure all the handicaps. The shame of corruption, then, is largely the despair about being powerless to play the game fairly, but it is also the humiliation of having to concede to the new rules just to be able to acquire the scraps. Compounding the direct psychological impact, of course, is corruption's economic toll: large amounts of wealth meant for productive activities are diverted, if not squandered entirely, to private hands for extravagant consumption that generates little or no trickle-down.

However, corruption doesn't always destabilize the nation's larger sense of dignity and honour. Consider, for example, the frequent cases of corruption in various police forces in the United States during much of the twentieth century. The most notorious occurred during the period of nationwide alcohol prohibition in the 1920s, which created vast opportunities for both bootleggers and enforcement officials to make money, by working within the new system of rules that had been created. The impact of corruption on the credibility of public officials as well as on the national exchequer was evidently large, but at no point did it translate itself into general despair or gloom. (Instead, prohibition was simply removed thirteen years after it was instituted.) In terms of financial impact, the US government's bailout of failing savings and loans institutions in the late 1980s to the tune of $500 billion, reportedly under pressure from lobbyists, was perhaps far greater, but even more remarkable was the lack of popular outrage it caused.

A possible reason for the relative apathy of the American public towards even these hefty cases of corruption is that they were seen as exceptional instances that could rock, but not seriously damage, established institutions. In other words, there was little indication of a severe breakdown in American public culture occurring as a result of corruption, no matter how scandalous. In fact, the more scandalous, often the more titillating, to the extent that the level and type of corruption that surfaced could exist only as spectacle but not really become part and parcel of one's daily life.

It is useful at this point to map out different expressions of corruption. A common feature of nearly all forms is that a public office is used to conduct private and sometimes illegal transactions that always result in unfair outcomes. In other words, someone who is entrusted with the task of allocating a public good in some just and reasonable manner betrays this trust for private gain, whether it is the ration shop distributor, the examiner in a standardized test or a minister charged with sanctioning investment projects. Of course, one could also call private agents corrupt if they act as touts or illegally require payment for entry into places or for carrying out routine tasks, but such behaviour would typically call into question the role of public authorities who ought to prevent it. In all instances, a bribe, or incentive payment, is either demanded by the person controlling the good or one is gratuitously offered to him.

Within this landscape, one can distinguish three broad types. First, bribes may be needed where there is inadequate supply of, or excessive demand for, a valued good, like public housing, college admissions, government jobs, etc. Sometimes, supply may be artificially restricted, as in the case of government officials controlling driving licences or passports and visas. In other instances, bribes may help 'lubricate' the process of getting something legitimate done expeditiously, like a telephone line or a ration card. Second, there are opportunities for corruption when public officials are in a position to assist persons who want to engage in an illicit activity, like driving without a licence, smuggling, producing excessive emissions and avoiding paying taxes or customs duty. In these instances, criminal behaviour (in addition to the act of bribery itself) is authorized, if not actively encouraged. Arguably, this causes more significant economic and social damage than the first type of corruption, which by and large only makes available short-cut routes to legitimate goods for certain players at the expense of others.

Third, there is a whole class of so-called 'back-room deals', where favours are exchanged among elite members of a political establishment, or between contractors and politicians or civil servants, to the disadvantage of other, sometimes more deserving contenders. Typically, there are conflicts of interest in these types of deals, where parties authorized to dispense rulings or award legitimate grants could personally benefit directly or indirectly from their actions. In some cases, this type of corruption can be quite subtle. For instance, those in power may assume that their mere status as benefactor requires that they be given special privileges from those who may even legitimately be given awards; for instance, a civil servant who sanctions a contract after an otherwise fair bidding process may feel it is her right to demand personal travel or meals from the contractor.

What appears to be distinctive about corruption in the postcolonial nation-state is the proliferation of all these forms across sectors. But in advanced capitalist countries, while the third type is not uncommon, the first two have largely been squeezed out of everyday experience. There are simply too few opportunities available within prevailing institutions—rules, regulations, laws— to permit individual public officials to do much outside the framework of what is allowable by the state apparatus. Indeed, one might say that a super-panopticon is at work to guard against individual infractions: while there is no Big Brother to monitor daily operations, the very act of conducting government business implies the creation of a set of databases in the form of accounts and procedures whose internal checks and balances considerably reduce the potential for individual 'gaming'.

Clearly, bureaucracy per se is neither a necessary nor sufficient condition for this outcome. That would create a paradox for the postcolonial world, where bureaucracy is often the perfect setting for obfuscating corrupt practices and for avoiding penalty upon detection. Rather, Western bureaucracies seem to survive relatively smoothly because of the particular structure of their intricate web of regulations, which have locked-in transparent bidding processes and opportunities for redressal from third parties like administrative tribunals and courts. For the most part, these processes have evolved in response to modern capitalism's demand from the state that it ensure minimum congestion for routine transactions. In other words, it has become evident that capitalist enterprise cannot function efficiently if there is a 'gatekeeper' every step of the way. Precisely for that reason, government procedures and processes have been transmogrified from what might have been a Kafkaesque nightmare into a 'necessary evil' that keeps internal check on its own excesses. And the additional reward is a populace that resembles contented drivers on an efficient road system: they don't mind having to play by the myriad rules of licensing and traffic control, so long as they are provided the autonomy to move relatively fast and independently to achieve their individual purposes.

This perhaps throws more light on why the third type of corruption—the back-room deal—where it does proliferate, seems to produce little or no popular anxiety in the West. Indeed, if the parties' corrupt transactions do not cause individual pain to the vast majority of the population, only an active civil society that concerns itself with public affairs would have cause to care. On the other hand, when corruption is rife in its first two forms, it resembles a road full of potholes and checkposts, and simply forces every member to take extra precautions to adjust his or her routine activities.

The latter is clearly a stressful situation, but could it also be shameful? Conceivably, yes, if the postcolonial nation was created under an original cloud of suspicion concerning its ability to create mature institutions without the guiding hand of its former masters. Indeed, the disgrace of corruption is tracked through indices that tell the world that Nigeria, Kenya and India are still, a half-century after birth, just as corrupt, if not worse, year after year. And insofar as that the dishonour is locked in as a cultural legacy, the postcolonial will want to avert his or her eyes when faced with the question from his or her highly ranked interlocutor from the West.

Further Reading

Bardhan, Pranab. 1997. 'Corruption and development: A review of issues.' *Journal of Economic Literature* 35:1320–46.

Rose-Ackerman, Susan. 1999. *Corruption and Government: Causes Consequences and Reform.* Cambridge: Cambridge University Press.

Transparency International. 2000. Corruption Perceptions Index, http://www.transparency.org/

World Bank Group. 2001. Anti-Corruption and Fraud Resources. http://wbln0018.worldbank.org/acfiu/acfiuweb.nsf/

Dammed H₂O

Dipak Gyawali and Ajaya Dixit

Water flows. It rises in evaporation from the oceans to the atmosphere, where it swirls to various continents and falls as rain or snow. It then cascades down mountains and valleys, evaporating a little, seeping underground a bit, being picked up by living things here and there, until the H_2O molecules cycle back to the seas and their deep ocean currents, only to begin evaporating and flowing anew. Even in living things, water flows as blood or sap and defines in the process life itself. Indeed, when the flow stops with cardiac pump arrest in animals or capillary dystrophy in plants, vital pranic force is said to ebb away, leaving behind the cold shroud of death.

Human beings have devised much of their settlements and social institutions by arresting the natural flow of water and diverting it elsewhere to serve anthropocentrically ordained functions. The powerful tantric imagery of *sarva stambhanakari*, the power of universal stoppage that throttles the free flow of natural energy, also conveys the idea behind dam building. When a rushing current of water is stopped, whirls and eddies gather greater momentum and overwhelm the obstruction or bypass it to flow into new channels. The tantric vira (hero) arrests the flow of breath through yogic practices to force otherwise dissipated pranic energy to course through and rejuvenate all the nerve channels of the body. Similar to the tantric, the modern civil engineer too heroically stops a river through the yantra of a high dam and channels the waters through canals and pipes to power plants and irrigated fields as well as urban or rural drinking water systems. Like the tantric, the *dakshya* engineer is also looked upon in awe by the laity for his seemingly supernatural powers.

Water engineering has a long history: indeed the rise of civilizations is attributed to irrigated agriculture and the permanent settlements it necessitated. From the great Egyptian pyramid builder Imhotep in about 2550 BC to Roman aqueduct engineer Vitruvius in the first century AD, down to today's US Army Corps of Engineers, arresting the natural flow of water to serve societal needs has been a prime function of powerful states. So it has been in South Asia also, with its rice-based civilization that requires streams to flow through paddy fields before draining back to the river and flowing out to the sea. Kautilya (circa 320 BC), the Machiavelli of South Asia, describes the state's role in water management in his *Arthashastra*. The link between state power and the will to modify river regimes has meant that water engineers were mostly part of a military engineering culture who knew how to use a river to deluge an enemy or, with moats and aqueducts, to defend one's fortress. Fountains with gargoyles and artificial ponds in urban capitals were merely cultural artefacts, symbols of power created by military engineers for their governors and generals.

Their exclusive clientele changed in the seventeenth and eighteenth centuries with the rise of mercantile capitalism. Trading houses and artisan guilds and also the labouring class, to some extent, became customers of water engineering expertise. Indeed, the term 'civil engineers' emerged in mid eighteenth century to distinguish them from military engineers. The notion also gave legitimacy to the fact that skills in hydraulic manipulation could be used in normal civilian life to promote trade and business.

It is said that the function of a scientist is to know, but that of an engineer is to do. The fact of the matter is that the moment voluntary intellectual curiosity goes beyond aesthetic pleasure and acquires a commercial value, we are blessed with technological prowess. Solving mathematical puzzles is rational logic and science;

the moment the solution helps a software company to make money, it becomes technology. This innate link with moneymaking means that engineers do not solve problems of inborn interest to them: rather, they apply their skills, for a reward, to untangle some investor's difficulties. Because the boundaries within which solutions must be optimized are set by society, engineers must work within the norms of cost, safety, equity and fairness that are socially acceptable. However, when society finds itself in turmoil over these values, that is, when values themselves are being contested, the engineering profession can suffer ailments ranging from conflicts to paralysis.

One such technology to suffer from value turmoil is that of high dams. Dam engineers are finding out that, while governments and businesses generally support their plans to build a barrier across a river to store and divert the flow, other segments of society vehemently object to their plans. Engineers are often surprised and resentful of these attacks, but the reasons are fairly straightforward. From a technical point of view, an ideal dam site is one where at least two rivers converge in a wide valley and then flow downstream through a narrow gorge. Akin to a wide flask with a narrow neck that can be corked, the narrow gorge allows a narrower (and hence less expensive) dam to be built, while the wide valley behind it would provide space for storing the water. The narrower the dam and the larger the storage space, the better (cheaper and more efficient) the dam and its output, whether electricity or regulated water for irrigation, flood control, navigation and fisheries.

Unfortunately, ideal dam and reservoir sites are also ideal for farms, settlements and (especially in Hinduism) traditional sites of pilgrimage. People in any case object to having their habitations inundated and themselves thrown upon the mercy of an uncertain future. Even if no humans lived in these valleys, there would still be significant impact on the environment upstream and downstream of the dam. Engineering schools often do not sensitize their graduates to these social concerns, and when they do, it is often grudgingly. Modern dam builders are acolytes of cement technology, and they exhibit an almost Pavlovian response to pour concrete whenever they see a river. From their perspective, anything or anyone standing as an obstacle to this mission would need to be bulldozed with techniques reminiscent of the profession's non-civilian past.

Modern dam building is a multi-generational enterprise. For some of the larger and more complicated high dams, the estimated time gap between the first bulldozer's move and the first hum of a turbine generating electricity is about fifteen years, if nothing goes wrong. When one adds to this the time for planning, design, financing, contract bidding and negotiations (if resettlement or contesting of water rights occurs, as is often inevitable), the enterprise can take two decades or so. The controversial Tehri high dam in India's western Himalaya, decided upon in 1969 and begun in earnest in 1972, was nowhere near completion three decades later.

Projects with long gestation periods such as high dams are difficult to initiate and more difficult to sustain without a wide-ranging social consensus. In poor societies, the struggle for subsistence takes place on a daily basis, and being ousted by modern dams and reservoirs means losing one's subsistence base. The time horizon of a dam builder is aeons longer than that of the poor farmer, and a consensus between these constituencies requires the mediation of socio-political institutions that just do not exist in much of the South, where dams are being planned today. It is not that the poor do not harness the waters of the rivers: they do, and mostly with the use of temporary brushwood dams that are washed away every year during the floods and are built anew. However, most modern civil engineers as well as those that patronize their expertise, such as government bureaucracies, foreign aid agencies and multinational private companies, ignore these traditional activities. These coping skills are either consigned to the limbo of non-existence or (if existence is grudgingly acknowledged) are deemed inefficient from a modern development perspective. This makes the engineers' expertise in effect unavailable to South Asia's toiling farmers, and their efforts to redefine land and water use through industrial cement techniques result in anti-dam conflicts that have fuelled several well-known protest movements around the world.

The impasse has led some to declare that the age of dam building is over. This view has gained added support as shifting social values begin to ordain that water for salmon or rafting is more beneficial than irrigation for alfalfa. Old dams are being 'decommissioned' in the US, the biggest dam builder ever, to allow rivers to revert to their wild and scenic stage. This obituary, however, may be somewhat premature, especially in many countries of the non-industrialized South where there is genuine unmet demand for water in its varied functions. Indeed, so intense are these demands that a former UN secretary general even feared that the next major war would be over water. Since dams provide the means to meet some of these demands in these impoverished societies, they will continue to be built. The debate in the South therefore will not be about dams or no dams but rather about good or bad dams.

Between 1997 and 2000, an attempt was made through a World Commission on Dams to bring together representatives of pro- and anti-dam lobbies with the intention of finding mutually acceptable ways forward. Contrary to what is often projected, the commission's report did not say, 'Don't build dams!' Rather, it acknowledged past mistakes in dam building and suggested guidelines that would improve decision making and eventual outcomes from this enterprise in the future. While many environmentalists have taken them as the bare minimum that needs to be done, many water bureaucracies, especially of China and India, which are heavily involved in dam building, have rejected the report outright.

Such a response is unfortunate because it will ensure that future engagements between the protagonists and opponents of this particular technology will continue to be confrontational and destructive. The angry response of the hierarchy, however, is understandable: accustomed as they were to operating within an uncontested terrain, the challenge to their judgement by social and environmental activists, from an ostensible moral high ground of equity and justice, erodes the very legitimacy of their authority. In this arena, globalization has not been the sole monopoly of governments and construction enterprises. Environmental groups have transcended national boundaries to confound grandiose plans of bankers and bureaucrats, and will in all probability continue to do so as effectively in the future.

To revert to the tantric imagery, the dammed-up energies of resentment against the inequities of one large development project will course through many channels to enmesh in debates on good and bad dams at the local level. Local entrepreneurs will engage local critics while the village and town councils strive to adjudicate between them. All social solidarities—profit-seeking businesses, egalitarian 'social auditors' as well as busybody managers—will get not everything each wants but something less, which is more than the nothing that would be their lot if the terrain was uncontested. Dams do have a future, but only if technological choices occur in a pluralized democratic terrain.

Further Reading

Ahmed, I., A. Dixit, and A. Nandy. 1999. Water, power and people: A South Asian manifesto on the politics and knowledge of water. *Water Nepal* 7:1.

Gyawali, D. 2001. *Water in Nepal*. Kathmandu: Himal Books and Panos South Asia.

Harden, Blaine. 1996. *A River Lost: The Life and Death of the Columbia*. New York: W.W. Norton & Co.

Illich, Ivan. 1985. *H₂O and the Waters of Forgetfulness: Reflections on the Historicity of the 'Stuff'*. Dallas: The Pegasus Foundation and The Dallas Institute of Humanities and Culture.

Democracy

C. Douglas Lummis

In the case of a word like democracy, not only is there no agreed definition but the attempt to make one is resisted from all sides. It is almost universally felt that when we call a country democratic we are praising it: consequently the defenders of every kind of regime claim that it is a democracy, and fear that they might have to stop using the word if it were tied down to any one meaning.

George Orwell stated this at the very beginning of the cold war. Today, after the cold war has ended, his words remain true. His remarkable insight is that democracy inspires fear not only in its enemies, which is obvious, but also in people who claim to be its friends. A clear definition might reveal that the practices of many of those who call themselves democrats are not democratic at all, and they would be forced either to give up the title or change their ways. The practice of most democratic theorists today is to conceal democracy by burying it under a huge pile of words, none of which mentions it.

Democracy is the most avoided topic in political theory. This may come as a surprise, as there are whole libraries of books alleging to discuss the subject. But consider this fact: in the entire canon of classic works in political theory, there is not a single work that is directly devoted to the subject. Plato held it up to ridicule, Aristotle ranked it low in his taxonomy of constitutions and from then until the nineteenth century the subject is hardly mentioned. Democracy is always there, but only in a negative sense: in the various proposals for systems of government, democracy is always silently present as the system *not* chosen. To discover it we need to borrow a method used in astronomy. Imagine democracy as a planet radiating negative gravity; we will be able to locate it by tracing the paths of all the other great planets as they swerve to avoid it.

In fact it is not at all difficult to 'tie down' the word to a clear definition; it is, however, difficult to grasp what that definition could mean. Democracy comes from the Greek words *demos*, 'the people', and *kratia*, 'power'. It means a situation in which the people hold the power. Considered carefully this may seem a bit like saying 'hot ice'. That is, you can say it, and the words are clear and not at all obscure, but you can't see how the thing could happen. Put the heat together with the ice, and the one will melt while the other cools.

The problem is that since we generally conceive of power as power over something, and of political power as power over people, it is difficult to see how the people could hold the power without either the power melting or the people cooling. As John Cotton famously asked, 'If the people be governors, who shall be governed?' Of course this was no problem for the ancient Greek democrats—they ruled over women, slaves and whoever they could conquer in war.

But this is no longer an option for contemporary democrats—'at least', as they say, 'in theory'. It is no longer considered democratic to set up a category of non-people for the people to rule over. What, then, is to be done? Mainstream contemporary democratic theory solves the problem by saying it can't be solved. The standard democratic theory text typically begins, generally in the first pages of the first chapter, by saying that 'direct democracy' is not feasible (the modern state is too big, life is too complex, knowledge is too specialized, the people are too apathetic, etc.), so what we have instead is government by elected representatives who govern by consent. Thus is the door slammed in the face of the people's power before the book even begins.

This is the classic bait-and-switch of democratic politics: you are told of a system called 'The People's Power', only to discover that it doesn't mean you get any power, just that you get to help those who do, by voting for them. This is comparable to the classic bait-and-switch of capitalist economics, where you are told of an economic system that makes people rich, only to discover that it is not going to make you rich, but that you will have the opportunity to help select those who do get rich, by buying their products.

Thus the 'whole libraries of books' on democratic theory, mentioned above, turn out mainly to be on the theory and operation of a system of representative government. If the model for this form of government is the US Constitution, it is important to remember that the framers of that Constitution never called it democratic, or themselves democrats. The democrats of that time were to be found among the Anti-Federalists, the party that opposed the Constitution (the state it formed would be too big, society within it would be too complex, knowledge would become too specialized, people would become apathetic, etc.; in short, democracy within its framework would not be feasible). It was only later, in the nineteenth century, that the representative republic came to be called 'democracy'. Of course, representative government has many virtues to recommend it, as we all know. But the fact remains that to call it 'democracy' is to commit a category mistake. It was this that severed democracy from its original meaning, and began the process towards vagary that Orwell described: if democracy didn't have to mean the people's power, why not apply it to whatever kind of regime you want to defend?

So here is the paradox: every sort of thing is labelled democratic, while democracy = the people's power is dismissed as a chimera: impossible-by-definition. But surely much of the puzzlement comes from our inability to get away from our standard notion of power: power over others. Of course, within the framework of this notion all sorts of 'solutions' have appeared: power might be exercised over the minority (tyranny of the majority), or over foreigners (democratic empire is, as I mentioned above, ruled out in theory today, but is still practised), or over the owning class (dictatorship of the proletariat); alternatively, different sections of the people might take turns ruling each other.

All of these things can happen, and some do, but none is very attractive (well, dictatorship of the proletariat might be, depending on how it is carried out). But is there no notion of power that does not require someone to assume the role of the powerless, that is, the victim? Fortunately, while very little has been said about it in the writings of political theory, for it is very hard to write about, in the world of experience the appearance of this kind of power is not at all uncommon. When people join together in sustained political activity (it is true that under contemporary circumstances they are likely to do this for the purpose of generating conventional power to direct at an external 'enemy', typically, but not always, the state), they often find that they have simultaneously generated a different kind of power, one which gives order to their community without this order being dependent on domination. This experience is often only fleeting, and the people may quickly revert to their former ways. But the fact that this is experienced as a 'reversion' is itself evidence that in the intervening period something different has happened.

What has happened is that a community has shifted over to the mode of spontaneous self-governance, a mode in which the ordered activity of the community, or at least a big part of it, is not enforced 'from above' by an authority, but is the direct result of a collective choice. This process is never easy; it always involves lots of discussion and argument (and 'politics'), but it does occur. People who have experienced this shift of mode, as in the 1954 bus boycott in Montgomery, Alabama, or Japan's 1960 anti-Security-Treaty struggle, or the Philippines' People's Power, or Poland's Solidarity, or Thailand's Parliament of the Streets, or (on a larger scale still) India's Satyagraha, often find it difficult to find the words to describe it, since the phenomenon cannot be fitted into the jargon with which we ordinarily talk about politics. Nevertheless, this very rare but real experience has a precise name. It is what is called democratic freedom.

Further Reading

Finley, M.I. 1973. *Democracy Ancient and Modern*. Reprint 1985. New Brunswick: Rutgers University Press.

Lummis, C. Douglas. 1996. *Radical Democracy*. Ithaca and London: Cornell University Press.

Trend, David, ed. 1996. *Radical Democracy: Identity, Citizenship, and the State*. New York and London: Routledge.

Development

Majid Rahnema

In the last sixty years, few words have been as intensely discussed, glorified or attacked as 'development'. At the end of the Second World War, the word came to symbolize the hopes of almost every human being dreaming of a future liberated from colonialism, hunger, destitution, exploitation and all other forms of injustice and suffering. Today, for the billions who shared these hopes, the dream has become a nightmare. The increase in the world's productive capacity has made it possible, indeed, to provide enough food for nine billion people, that is one and a half times the entire population of the earth; yet more than one billion are today suffering from hunger and malnutrition.

Many questions therefore arise. Is development what its votaries say it is? Does it still represent the hopes of 'change' and liberation that the word carried with it in its infancy? Or is it now only a mask and a modern Trojan horse, one that paradoxically serves the same old colonial or hegemonistic interests that the development discourse was meant to combat? Finally, if that discourse is no longer trusted by the populations concerned, what other prospects are open to the millions of people whose lives and livelihoods are more than ever threatened by so-called economic development?

The Story of a Corrupted Word

To deal seriously with these questions is not an easy task, for development has become an 'amoeba' word. It means everything and nothing. It has different meanings in different places and contexts. For many people in the North, it still refers sometimes to a child's mental or physical development, sometimes to the development of a game, a plot or a strategy, sometimes to a housing project. For Webster's dictionary, to *develop* has also meant 'to unfold gradually like a flower from a bud'.

Trying to convey similar messages of an 'unfolding' effect, modern promoters of the word have tried to use it as a substitute for such concepts as *âbâdi* (in Persian, a clement place to live), or *'imrân* (the word, often used by Ibn Khadûn, that comes from the Arabic root *'imr*, meaning to fulfil a life, to dwell in a place, to cultivate land, to make it prosperous), or *fidnaa* (an Ethiopian Borana concept signifying the flow of life as it moves ahead through times and generations; a fertile environment coupled with the absence of conflict, dissatisfaction, hunger and disease). In short, it was introduced in the languages of the older civilizations with a view to co-opting all forms of endogenous processes of improvement in the ways communities were historically coping with necessity.

As such, in the new language of modern economics and of national or international institutions, the word is generally used instead of 'growth and change', particularly in projects aimed at modernizing life and dealing with such 'problems' as 'poverty eradication', fighting 'underdevelopment', malnutrition, homelessness, disease, ignorance and socio-economic inequalities.

Thus, modernized elites in 'underdeveloped countries' take pride in presenting themselves as champions of national development. Their enthusiasm is, however, no longer shared by their 'target populations', even if they had initially welcomed the concept as an answer to colonialism or foreign domination. As it stands, the concept either means nothing to them or it is perceived as a legitimizing cover for a host of totally different phenomena, namely, policies associated with new and more sophisticated forms of domination, of the compromise and destruction of the people's own power and economy, and of the selling out of their countries to the new masters of the world market.

The main reason for this disenchantment is that the banner of development has had, particularly in the last six decades, a substantial role in uprooting entire populations in the South and in forcing them to participate in the destruction of their own livelihood. Huge masses of people have thus been led to migrating into shantytowns and transformed into modernized poor, whose tiny incomes never allow them to meet their socially generated needs. Almost everywhere, development is now identified with governments that mainly serve the interests of the 'developed world'. Paradoxically, the word has now come to legitimize oppression at the national level, the law of the jungle, the destruction of people's immune system, the selling out of their resources and talents to the best buyer; in short, it means the opposite of everything that once represented the liberating promises of the development discourse.

Had Webster's dictionary to be re-edited to take into account these trends, the updated definition of the word could be something of the sort: 'To develop is to unfold a modern process of mutation, similar to that used by corporations specialized in genetic engineering, where the latest devices of modern management, technology and economy are used to genetically modify the buds of different botanical species with a view to making them produce the one and only flowers or fruits that are more profitable on the world market.'

Why Is Development Still a Seductive Word?

The question is often asked: How is it possible that only a few years ago, on the occasion of the fiftieth anniversary of the United Nations, the representatives of all its member states still unanimously confirmed their unconditional support of the concept, pleading for a universal commitment to the development objectives?

The answers to this question may be found in at least two sets of reasons. The first can be related to the highly manipulative uses of the word 'underdevelopment'. In less than a century, the promoters of modern economy have succeeded in introducing, in almost all the world's languages, this totally new construct as a substitute for all forms of human deprivations and of shameful and degrading conditions born out of pre-economic times. Thus, in a global environment dominated by the modern binary mode of thinking, 'development' is proposed as the undisputed and only answer to the miseries of the past. In other words, the overpowering message to all the wretched of the earth is that they are now given, for the first time in their history, the unique chance to choose 'freely' between their status quo and the promises of an ideal life embodied in the concept of development.

The other set of reasons is related to modern forms of knowledge and power. Development supporters are thus composed of two main categories of persons. The first group often includes even well-intentioned persons who sincerely believe in linear 'progress', whose model is biological. This group is convinced that, regardless of their cultural specificities, societies, too, evolve like species or children. They go through stages of development that tend to move them forward, towards an achieved state, embodied by modern industrialized countries. With a few exceptions, the belief in such a linear progress, embodied in the ideas of the Enlightenment and the French Revolution, has dominated the thinking of the world's 'educated elites' for nearly two centuries.

The second category of development votaries is composed of individuals and institutions for whom development has become a major instrument of livelihood and power. Autocratic and repressive nation-states in need of legitimation; economic institutions and modernization projects whose objectives require the destruction of convivial and human-centred economies; 'developing' economies and their growing need for foreign capital and technologies are among this second category of development supporters.

For both groups, it is neither desirable nor possible to perpetuate 'outmoded' modes of living and producing that could retard or prevent the rapid transformation of all human societies into 'fully developed' ones. They both feel that it is imperative and high time that all the 'underdeveloped' populations of the world, considered to be the dropouts of history, be given their rightful chance to join the winners. Hence, the duty of all the developed and the rich, everywhere and at all national and international levels, to join the universal crusade for development.

The Truths behind the Development Discourse

The combined attempts of all these groups and the powerful media at their disposal cannot, however, conceal the following facts:

For the underdog exposed to the growing needs created by economy, be they in its so-called underdeveloped or developed parts, development has *not* represented a change for the better, or a sustainable alternative. It is true that modern systems of production have allowed the emergence of a 'middle class' of people with enough income to take advantage of a host of new goods and services to meet their growing needs. Yet the 'trickling down' processes that have enriched these few have, at the same time, propelled a much greater number of people into structural destitution. The most tragic and irreversible impact of the new modes of production has been the systematic destruction of the people's own regenerative capacity to adapt themselves to externally produced threats. In the name of assistance to the developing economies of the South, the loan policies of major credit institutions of the North have imposed, on the recipient countries, huge debts that have acted as a death blow to local modes of production.

A constant strategy of development has been to show the populations in distress that their only choice is between the frying pan and the fire. A disastrous effect of this binary logic has been to dispossess them of their own cultural wisdom and insights for finding imaginative alternatives to their own problems. As a result, development policies have actually hindered rather than helped the blossoming of the endogenous 'human resources' of their 'target populations'. The destruction of traditional and culturally defined modes of production, together with the combined effects of the rural exodus and the brain drain phenomena, have been particularly detrimental to the promotion of self-reliant and people-oriented economies.

The more the 'target populations' have shown indifference and hostility to the development practices, the greater has been the temptation, by the nation-states committed to the development discourse, to use it as a major instrument of power, control and repression against all possibilities of dissent. The banner of development has thus been systematically utilized for the strengthening of the various apparatuses of subjugation, for obtaining more funds for repressive and military expenditures, and for adapting national economies to the needs of the world market rather than to those of their own people.

At the international level, the unholy alliance of corrupted 'developmentalist' regimes with those of the so-called developed countries has become a basic threat to all the peoples of the world, preventing them from seeking genuine alternatives to current mechanisms of social change. The alliance, even when it is made under the aegis of a formally democratic institution like the United Nations, serves primarily the interests of all those opposed to such alternatives.

Can There Be 'Good' Development?

To put it in the language of the United Nations, can development be given a 'human face'?

It is clear that the first failures of the development discourse and its practices did lead a whole generation of well-intentioned persons to seek new ways of delivering 'good' development to populations in need of modernization. These attempts brought in new concepts such as 'endogenous', 'human-centred', 'bottom-up', 'participatory' and finally 'sustainable' development.

A thorough analysis of such efforts aimed at giving development a 'human face' suggests however that the search for alternatives within the dominant development paradigm has continued to be a lost cause. The paradigm is based on the assumption that development programmes should all aim at integrating every human activity into a system of modern economic production. Such alternatives tend, at best, to make it easier for this system to pursue the destruction of people's own and autonomous modes of living and producing. Thus, 'good' participatory development programmes have often served only as analgesic palliatives while the overall economic project of which they are a part has destroyed the whole body's regenerating capacity.

Inspired by hundreds of imaginative grass-roots movements that have been initiated by the very victims of development, new currents of thought have emerged, in the last few decades, that question the paradigm itself. Most of these movements advocate the creation of new ways of interaction to help communities find their own alternatives to the development paradigm, rather than helping the market-oriented development projects achieve greater efficiency within the paradigm.

An interesting trend of thought foregrounds the role that can be played by all social actors in breaking the binary logic of economic development. Individuals and groups, acting as endogenous agents of change within their various fields of social and economic production, thus continue to search for radically new alternatives in their own specific areas of competence, rather than focusing solely on abstract social and institutional changes. These new actors realize that modern systems of power based on the market economy lead all social actors to participate, directly or indirectly, and in one way or another, in the creation of scarcity and various social injustices. As long as the causes of people's sufferings and of societal dysfunctions are reduced to abstract ideas alone, and as long as the expected desirable changes are perceived as exogenous factors coming from 'above'—or from indefinable categories or institutions—processes of social transformation remain at a superficial level. True and deeper changes occur only when the social actors constituting civil society are ready, first, to change themselves and, second, to use all their creative potential to finding new alternatives for a better life—alternatives destined both to changing their own personal ways of being, living, producing and relating to their community, and to changing the societies to which they belong.

Further Reading

Esteva, Gustavo, and Madhu S. Prakash. 1998. *Grassroots Postmodernism: Remaking the Soil of Culture*. London: Zed Books.

Rahnema, Majid, with Victoria Bawtree, eds. 1997. *The Postdevelopment Reader*. London: Zed Books.

Sachs, Wolfgang, ed. 1993. *The Development Dictionary*. London: Zed Books.

Economics

Roby Rajan

A number of years ago, peasants from the Bocage region of France were asked whether they still believed in witchcraft. Almost all of them began their answer 'Some people believe . . .' Anthropologists doing fieldwork among 'primitives' on the subject of their superstitions are frustrated that hardly any will say 'I believe . . .' It is always 'Some people believe . . .' In today's networked global economy driven by consumer and investor confidence, when one actually sets out to track down the confident consumer or investor, he proves to be as elusive as the superstitious primitive. We quickly find ourselves in a hall of mirrors in which the belief of each consumer and investor turns out to be the belief that there are others who believe . . . that inflation will continue to be low, that labour markets will be tight, that the trade deficit will fall, etc. Beliefs about the economy cannot be found to reside in any concrete subject, only in the opinion poll—the place towards which each particular consumer or investor, lacking direct belief, may orient himself and find a guarantor of others' beliefs. As a web of consumption and investment decisions, the economy turns out to rest on this quasi-subject of others' beliefs—a non-existent subject supposed to believe—through which each may believe without himself believing. The economy can in this way produce its reality for each in the name of the indefinitely deferred beliefs of others, without having to furnish either believing subject or believable object. Economics is best understood as the set of beliefs about this (non)belief about others' beliefs about economic reality.

Although an overall harmony of beliefs was taken as more or less self-evident by Adam Smith (1723–90), it was explicitly spelt out for the first time by James Mill (1773–1836) and christened as Say's Law after J.B. Say (1767–1832). The essence of this law is that while there may well be situations of partial overproduction in which particular firms or industries are unable to dispose of all their output, at the level of the economy as a whole such disturbances could not escalate into a general glut. Assuming no significant obstacles to the mobility of capital and labour, partial overproduction would in course of time correct itself through withdrawal of resources from glut sectors and their redeployment in sectors enjoying buoyant demand. Income not spent on consumption would be channelled into investment without significant leakages. It was the Reverend T.R. Malthus (1766–1834) who first cast doubt on the beneficence of this invisible hand: a glut, he feared, could be both general and chronic. In the line of distinguished sceptics toward Say's Law were to follow J.S. Mill (1806–73), Karl Marx (1818–83) and J.M. Keynes (1883–1946).

To Say's problem of reconciling investment and consumption, we may now add a third consideration: money. Unlike the Middle Ages when a gold coin could guarantee its value by being directly equivalent to the value of the gold it embodied, paper money is intrinsically worthless. To proclaim one's own individual belief in money would plainly be meaningless—the value of paper or electronic money can only be guaranteed through a *subject supposed to believe*. Once money enters into a monetary relation with itself, so to speak, it becomes as subject to fluctuations in value as any other commodity. Keynes's innovations take root precisely in the gap that opens up between the Middle-Ages notion of money as a pure medium of exchange for other commodities, and money as susceptible to changing valuations itself. If part of the income stream were to leak away from consumption and investment into hoarding, speculation or as a hedge against future losses, an economy might find itself stuck at a high level of unemployment with scarcely any prospect of improvement if left to its own devices. In *The General Theory of Employment, Interest and Money* (1936), Keynes argued that the desire to save does not always lead to benign consequences; by reducing aggregate demand, an excess of saving could lead to lower output and investment. Keynes's remedy for this oversaving problem was for the government to inject more demand into the economy by raising government spending—borrowing, if necessary—to spend the excess savings.

With this gesture, Keynes becomes the first economist to suspend the link to the 'natural ground' of economics that had implicitly consisted of such grandmotherly maxims as one should not spend more than one rightfully earns, one should not borrow from the future, one should settle all of one's accounts, etc. These were elevated to the level of guiding principles for an entire nation's consumption and investment decisions. Keynes is the first to notice the emperor's (non)clothing: that the entire edifice of economics is built not on 'real believing subjects' but on a subject supposed to believe, and that there was no reason why this subject could not be made to believe (against the claims of the economic puritans) that borrowing and spending by the state would result in higher 'real growth', after which all accounts could 'eventually' be settled at this higher level of economic prosperity. However, this moment of final settlement was for Keynes—like economic belief itself—subject to indefinite deferral, not an eventuality that was to materialize at some concrete historical date. Hence his most famous aphorism: In the long run, we are all dead.

The stagflation of the 1970s, characterized by high unemployment and high inflation, furnished the occasion for the revenge of the puritans. Look, they said, this is what comes of profligacy, of incurring debts, of welfare without work, of governmental meddling with the market; in short, stagflation was just punishment for moving away from the economy's natural ground. All the economics since Keynes has been a massive rearguard attempt to reinstall the proper believing subject of economics who knows just what his limits are, who will consume but not overborrow, who will at the end of the day settle all his accounts both at the level of the individual and at the level of the nation. The dream of post-Keynesian economics is to regulate the excess and restore the balance. But this Minerva's Owl of the well-balanced believing subject of economics has (always) already flown, no matter how well the economist gilds his cage to trap it.

The gilded cage of contemporary economics has arrived in the form of iron rules to enforce low levels of inflation, government borrowing and public spending. This has translated into defanging the fiscal power of governments to tax and spend in pursuit of social objectives, and a reliance on the mechanical lever of monetary policy to keep the economy on course. Economics holds out the promise that if only its iron rules are adhered to, the social organism could once again restore itself to stable homeostasis and regain mastery over the excessive element that was threatening to displace it. In this respect it harks back to the memory of the secure closure of pre-modernity, while amnesiacally forgetting that within the pre-modern the economic was only a secondary moment of the social totality, not an end in itself. Having thoroughly reordered the social formation by subordinating all other moments (cultural and political, among others) to the status of residual, it wants to put this Humpty Dumpty back together again, this time under its own sign.

Even Keynes, despite his seeing through to economy's *subject supposed to believe*, was an accomplice here in believing that all that had to be negated was Say's Law and in assuming that the only leakage in the system was away from consumption into non-investment forms of saving. The reality of it was that the enthronement of the economic as the paramount principle of social structuration had introduced a permanently destabilizing force into its very core. It was beyond the power of aggregate demand management to tame this. Leaks had begun to spring all over: the more the economy produced to satisfy needs, the more the unsatisfied needs it produced; the more the number of prisons it built, the greater the number of criminals; the more the number of highways built to ease congestion, the more congested the highways became; the more the pharmacological cures discovered for mental disorders, the more rapid the multiplication of newer pathologies . . . Unlike pre-modern authority, economics could no longer rely on the performative power of symbolic ritual to regulate the excess; its only recourse was a manipulative one—to forcibly embed its authority into the procedural rules of public policy and thereby to produce economic reality as its own effect. This is why when an economic prediction such as 'a rise in social expenditures will result in a fiscal crisis' comes true, all this means is that economy's *subject supposed to believe* believes a fiscal crisis will occur; it in no way proves that fiscal discipline is therefore an 'objective requirement' for the avoidance of crises because the rules that economics has itself put into place have ensured in advance that a crisis will indeed ensue.

Through fiscal and monetary policy, economics gains a back-door entry into the traditional preserve of political theory to discredit one of the latter's key premises: that interest groups in a liberal polity mediate the relationship between a universal electorate and state policy through a bargaining process with built-in checks-and-balances, the aggregated outcome of which reveals society's preferences with regard to public goods, distributional issues and the appropriate macroeconomic trade-offs. In the economic understanding of politics, it is this very process that fatally contaminates allocative efficiency in the economy. Hence the conclusion that political choices be severely curtailed so that economically efficient outcomes may emerge overall.

Into this economic usurpation of politics, the authentically political must now insert itself: between a global order in which each part has been assigned its proper place and the subordinated particular within this order. For this to occur, politics—which economics would circumscribe as one among other social sub-systems in which different interest groups compete for control of resources—would need to fall out of its confinement as a sub-system, and generalize itself across the entire space of economy. This political task of reclaiming economics's *subject supposed to believe* on behalf of the subordinated may not be as insurmountable as it first appears. I recently performed an informal experiment on some economist colleagues of mine by individually asking them if they *really believed* in the hallowed principle of methodological individualism that undergirds all economic research. Without exception they all began their reply, 'Some economists believe...'

Education

Gustavo Esteva and Madhu S. Prakash

The beginning of the end of the era of education has already started.

For the experts, the state of education cannot be worse. The educational systems teach badly and the limited and poor learning you get there is useless: they do not prepare people for life or work. The experts thus claim urgent reforms to cure education of its plagues.

Educational reformers can be grouped in three categories. Some look to improve the classroom: its methods, equipment or personnel. Others attempt to liberate it from any bureaucratic imposition, and argue that parents and communities should decide by themselves the content and methods of education. Still others attempt to transform the whole of society into a classroom: the new cyber technologies should substitute for the closed space of the classroom, paving the way for open markets and distance learning. A reformed, free and worldwide classroom: three stages in the escalation of interventions to increase social control and thus prevent the bankruptcy of the main modern tool to subjugate people.

The educators have educated the world in the fallacy that education is as old as the hills. But it is exclusively modern: it was born with capitalism, and for the same purpose. We colonize the past if we consider education as an equivalent to other past or present practices and institutions to learn or study.

Children's education is mentioned for the first time in a French document of 1498. It was still a novelty in the seventeenth century, when a new conviction arose in Europe: man is born stupid and lacks vital competence unless he is educated. Education was thus established as a new original sin, defining the inverse of vital competence.

Everywhere education is promoted in the name of equality and justice. It is presented as the best remedy for the oppressive inequalities of modern society. It produces exactly the opposite. No matter how much every society invests in education, most people fail to reach the end of the process and are disqualified as unfit for a manmade world. Education creates the most oppressive of the class divisions now existing. It separates people in two groups: the educated and the uneducated or undereducated, the knowledge capitalists and the destitute. In the new class structure, more value is attributed to those consuming more knowledge; since society invests in them, for the creation of 'human capital', the means of production are reserved for them. Some get all kinds of privileges; the rest suffer all kinds of discriminations and disqualifications.

Beyond any consideration about the quality of the disabling services provided by educational institutions, the fact remains that everywhere their outcome is the same: to disqualify the majority of the population. According to UNESCO, 60 per cent of the children now entering first grade will never be able to reach the level that in their countries is considered obligatory in terms of being educated. They will live forever with the handicap of all dropouts. Meanwhile, a small minority will get twenty or thirty years of schooling.

The compulsion to reform the educational systems, which is reaching epidemic proportions, derives from two well-established facts: most people in the world are uneducated or undereducated, and an increasing number of the educated can no longer find a job in whatever stream they were educated or oriented towards.

The reformers continually dispute the content or method of the reform, but share the same purpose: to reaffirm the social prejudice that education is the only legitimate way to prepare people to live.

As education becomes equivalent to the consumption of knowledge, the new generations are thus educated to participate in that addiction, under the assumption that their success will depend on the quantity and quality of their consumption of that commodity, and that learning about the world is better than to learn from the world.

The most dangerous reformers today are those who substitute for the classroom the massive distribution of knowledge packages, and establish their consumption as a basic need for survival. While traditional reformers are still promising more and better schools, their current enemies are winning the race. They present themselves as the only ones who will be able to reach the accepted goal of everyone: equality of access.

Those reformers may contribute to disestablish the school, if only to extend its function. They attempt to transform the global village into an environmental womb, in which pedagogic therapists will control, under the appearance of a free market, the complex placenta that nourishes every human being. The regulation of intellectual rights, now being negotiated in international institutions, will protect the activity of the corporations producing and distributing the knowledge packages that from now on will define education.

Education, like capital, achieved primitive accumulation through force once it came under the jurisdiction of the state. The police and the army are still being used to extend and deepen educational control. In the process, however, education became established as a personal and collective need. Much like other needs, is was soon transformed into a right. It operates today as a bureaucratic imposition and as a legitimate and universally accepted social addiction: it stimulates knowledge consumers to freely, passionately and compulsively acquire their chains and thus contribute to the construction of the global Big Brother.

Marx's rhetorical question 'Who educates the educators?' is still valid. Tolstoy observed that education is a conscious effort to transform someone into something. More and more, that 'something' is a sub-system, a creature of an oppressive system.

Education is already the main tool to reproduce it. Modern technologies, particularly those linking TV and Internet, will lead the oppression further than ever before.

Marx also observed that the blind compulsion to produce too many useful things will end up producing useless people. The current global escalation accentuates the process. Perhaps capital has more appetite than ever, but it has not enough stomach to digest everyone. It cannot offer employment for most people and is closing the globalized markets to them. An increasing number of people thus become disposable human beings; there is no way for capital to exploit them. By giving them, through public funds, access to knowledge packages, capital educates them as consumers and prepares them for the moment in which it can subsume them again in the system of exploitation.

Such 'disposable' people, however, have started to react everywhere. There is a proliferation of initiatives escaping from the logic of capital: they transform the drama of exclusion into the opportunity to follow their own path and to produce by themselves their own life. One of their first steps is to escape education.

In 1953, when education was included in the promotion of development launched by Harry Truman in 1949, UNESCO experts concluded that the main obstacle to education in Latin America was the indifference or resistance of most parents. Eleven years later, the same experts warned that no Latin American society would be able to meet the demand of education. The campaign had been successful. Parents educated in the idea of education began to agitate for more teachers and schools, always insufficient for the majority. The same process was reproduced everywhere, in different periods.

During the last twenty years, however, the impulses to resist-and/or-claim began to be transformed into a struggle for liberation. The illusion that education delivers employment, prestige and social mobility leads many people to accept its high price: severe cultural destruction and the dismembering of family and community life. Step by step, the majority of the population understood that diplomas did not certify competence or skills: they certify a number of hours and years during which the student sat in a school chair. Far from guaranteeing employment, diplomas doom many to permanent frustration. The humiliation of engineers or lawyers, forced to work as taxi drivers or hotel porters, becomes an opportunity for liberation for those without diplomas or possessing one of minimum value: they are thus able to revalue their own wisdom, their skills, their competence to live.

While the Internet accelerates the disestablishment of school, suggested by Ivan Illich thirty years ago, the social majorities are bypassing it, as they do, whenever they can, just as they overcome all bureaucratic impositions and the allurements of the wealthy. They may send their children to school, for them to obtain diplomas which operate as a passport to circulate in modern society. But they are no longer surrendering themselves to the illusions of education.

People are saying: Enough! They recover little by little their old art of learning, in which every baby is an expert. Given the fact that education is the economization of learning, which transforms learning into the consumption of a commodity called knowledge, people recover their own notion of learning to live. Since the noun 'education' imposes a radical dependence, of any educator, upon the public or private system of education, they substitute for it the verb 'to learn', which re-establishes the autonomous capacity to keep a creative relationship with the others and with nature. People acknowledge again that to know is a personal experience, and that the only way to know, to widen the competence to live, is to learn from the world, not about the world.

Everywhere, dissident groups enjoy the sufficiency of their initiatives, which are opening new spaces for freedom. Here and there some people close the schools or put them under community control. In Oaxaca and Chiapas, for example, in the south of Mexico, many communities closed the school and reclaimed the control of the learning process of their children. In the area occupied by the Zapatistas, in Chiapas, hundreds of 'schools' have been built by the communities themselves and operate under their control, without any intervention of participation of the state or professional teachers. They initiate public campaigns to impose heavy taxes on schooling, such as those on alcohol and tobacco, instead of allocating public funds to schools. Other campaigns struggle to abrogate all laws making education obligatory. But the main impulse follows another direction. While the educated persist in their competitive struggle to consume more knowledge, the uneducated or undereducated acknowledge again that to know is a personal experience and relationship, controlled by the person learning. Towards the propaganda of 'education', they adopt the attitude they take towards junk food: they know that the latter does not nourish, although it sometimes may satisfy hunger. The propaganda of 'education' is junk knowledge, unable to generate wisdom.

While Bill Gates and his colleagues prolong the agony of education, some people are anticipating its death with creative, convivial initiatives, which widen their capacity to learn, to study and to do (instead of the capacity to buy and to consume) and redefine their responsibilities in their old or new commons. So, undermining the dominant institutions, they prepare for their inversion. They hope, for example, that the extinction of the educational rituals, which has already appeared on the horizon, will signal the beginning of an era ending privilege and licence.

Further Reading

Berry, Wendell. 2000. *Life Is a Miracle*. Washington: Counterpoint.

Gandhi, M.K. 1995. *Towards New Education*. Ahmedabad: Navajivan Press.

Illich, Ivan. 1971. *Deschooling Society*. New York: Harper.

Illich, Ivan, and Barry Sanders. 1988. *The Alphabetization of the Popular Mind*. San Francisco: North Point Press.

Prakash, Madhu S., and Gustavo Esteva. 1998. *Escaping Education*. New York: Lang.

Ethnic Cuisine

Ashis Nandy

Ethnic cuisines have always existed, though called by other names. The cuisines of other groups were always a part of one's life—as markers of cultivation and class, as indicators of social status or as esoteric rituals, meant for adventurers, travellers and, beginning in the nineteenth century, anthropologists. French cuisine did traditionally perform an important function for the European elite. For a long time it had a particular cultural role to play, for instance, in the English cultural scene, despite widespread stereotypes of English insularity. English cuisine, in turn, had a place in colonized societies like India where, to spite the detractors of English food, many Indians accepted it as a marker of cultivation and others developed its more labour-intensive, spicier, tropical versions. However, in the 'civilized' world, ethnic styles of cooking were mostly organized within a stable, hierarchical frame. Even in bland Scandinavia and in the gloomy, self-sure ambience of Victorian and Edwardian London, on formal occasions the cognoscenti, the learned and the beautiful people served French food or some domesticated version of it. It is true that some members of the gentry seemed committed to good old healthy English food, but that was often a self-conscious gesture rather than a matter of preference. British Islanders in general, and not merely the English, have for centuries lived with feelings of inferiority as far as food and wines are concerned, and even their love for their own food is tinged with a certain ambivalence. This is best reflected in Somerset Maugham's well-known saying that one could eat very well in Britain if one decides to have breakfast morning, afternoon and night.

In the United States too, despite occasional paeans to the beauties of home-grown American food, there has been a similar reverence towards French and, to a lesser extent, Italian and Viennese cuisines for a long time. On formal occasions, presidents, members of the cabinet, generals and university professors have tended to serve French food or some Frenchified version of domestic fare. Sometimes, as an elegant variation, it has been Italian food. Everyone sings the glories of the dedicated American mom and her wholesome exploits in the kitchen, but formal public banquets are another matter. There you choose cuisines that are recognized as valid for exactly such occasions.

Many societies have similar ideas of occasion when it comes to food. In my native Calcutta, Bengalis have always sung the glories of Bengali food but, when it comes to eating outside the home in a restaurant, they tend to choose some version of Mughal, North Indian or, less frequently, 'continental' food (by which they mean Indianized British food, given fancy French or Italian names). The famous clubs of Calcutta, true to their colonial heritage, also serve English food that, unfortunately, often tastes like English food. The city's first recognized Bengali restaurant was founded in the 1960s, and it was a particularly modest affair, run by a women's cooperative. The city's first upmarket Bengali restaurant opened in the 1990s. Kasturi in Dhaka, the capital of Bangladesh, is arguably the best Bengali restaurant in the world. But it also is relatively new; it began functioning in the 1980s. Among Bengalis there still persists the belief that you do not eat Bengali food in a restaurant; you eat it at home, or on formal occasions like marriages and anniversaries, as long you do not organize them as events in restaurants. Bengali food is only now becoming restaurant food.

When it is not occasion, it is a combination of occasion and lifecycle. For a long time, Chinese food in the United States was meant for university students with meagre budgets, eating out on the weekends or playing host to their friends and teachers. It was different and it was cheap. For decades, Indian food has played a roughly similar role in London and other large cities of Britain. An entire generation of British women have been brought up, thanks to their boyfriends and classmates, with random but sustained exposure to an amalgam of Mughal and Punjabi curries, cooked mainly by Bengalis. Exactly as an entire generation of older Americans now lives with their memories of Chinese food consumed in their student days in the company of their dates.

Things have been changing gradually but radically during the last three decades or so. Ethnic food is now serious business. It has made deep inroads into global metropolitan culture all over the world. It has become a marker of the width of one's cosmopolitan experience. You can now talk for hours with erudition and sensitivity on ethnic food, and the listeners are unlikely to be bored. The ability to discriminate among the different shades of a specific ethnic cuisine and the ability to have an informed chat with the waiters before ordering food in a restaurant that serves lesser known fare, such as Ethiopian, Moroccan or West Asian food, have become signs of learning, elegance and sophistication. These abilities are now the contemporary analogues of the older status ritual that became popular during the Victorian period: the ability to address waiters by name in well-known restaurants. Exogenous cuisines are now acquiring the status of African safaris and are becoming the arena of a different kind of power play. No cuisine, however limited or flat, is considered inferior, except probably a few European ones, and certainly they cannot be called so in polite company. It is basically determined tourists and the brave at heart who are expected to frequent restaurants serving local fare in countries like Scandinavia, the Netherlands or Scotland. If you find Argentine, Filipino or sub-Saharan food uninteresting or not distinctive enough, you are supposed to keep your feelings to yourself.

Ethnic food has become the measure of one's tolerance of social and cultural diversity. Only philistines are supposed to grumble about any ethnic food served to them. You make a social and political statement if you dislike a particular ethnic cuisine, not if you like it.

Simultaneously, some of the old cast of suspects have acquired new stature and cultural meaning; they are basking in reinvented glory. Eating Chinese food in Chinatown is no longer a downmarket venture, nor is the act of eating Indian curry in an Indian restaurant in a university town like Oxford. However, you may convey something about the level of your cultivation and cosmopolitanism if, when your business partner or research collaborator asks what kind of food preferences you have, you blandly proclaim your love for Chinese or Indian food. You are expected to specify what version of Chinese or Indian food you like. Your host will have much more respect for you if you suggest a Hunanese or Szechwanese restaurant, or if you specifically demand that he take you to a Malayali joint for appam or even to a Gujarati fast-food stall for bhelpuri or khandvi. (Indeed, ethnic fast foods are never stigmatized, unless they get associated with multinational chains.)

Everyone is looking for newer, stranger and rarer kinds of ethnic restaurants, and so the variety of ethnic cuisine available in global metropolitan culture has proliferated enormously in the last twenty years. So have the skills demanded from those who patronize these restaurants. On the one hand, customers visiting a Sri Lankan or Thai restaurant are expected to order the more fiery versions of the curries and not the milder domesticated editions that may be kinder to one's palate and taste buds. On the other hand, such restaurants have to distinguish or distance themselves from their more familiar neighbouring cuisines so that their customers do not feel cheated. Nepali restaurants in Manhattan naturally try to avoid preparations that are close to or indistinguishable from some forms of Indian food, however central to Nepalese cuisines these preparations might be in real life. In a global metropolis, a Cambodian restaurant just cannot serve the same fare as the Laotian or Vietnamese restaurant next door. At the same time, the former must cleverly include a few familiar things from the neighbouring cuisines to give itself a wider range and a longer menu, perhaps even a touch of familiarity.

There are other subtle shades in the canvas that cannot be all enumerated here. However, a couple of examples should give the reader a flavour of how, in global cosmopolitan culture, the expanding tradition of ethnic dining has turned itself into an institution and a billion-dollar enterprise. All visitors to ethnic restaurants in North America and Europe must have noticed the growing tendency to serve or offer country-specific beers with ethnic food. You may choose your wines from all over the world, but you are supposed to drink Ethiopian beer with Ethiopian food and Japanese beer with Japanese food. The demand is relaxed only in the case of American food; no one insists that one must only have American beer with it. There may be some justification for this practice in the case of cuisines that use less spice and depend on flavours that are not overwhelming. But a good case can be made that in the case of cuisines that have 'overwhelming' tastes and flavours, the choice of beers becomes partly notional. Before you dip into a fiery Thai curry, you might legitimately claim to enjoy the subtleties of Singha beer, which is after all a light ale, as the British call it. But once you start eating, nearly all beers will taste more or less the same. Perhaps a Guinness with its strong taste will better survive the onslaught of chillies and spices. At least there is some chance that one's palate would be able to savour the stout's personality. But drinking a Guinness with a hot-and-sour soup would be considered blasphemous in the present dining culture of global metropolitanism.

Likewise, for years experts on food and gourmets have advised those eating Indian food to opt for beers, not wines, because the heavy spices drown the flavour of wines. But that is no longer considered acceptable in the new food culture. It is seen as an insult to Indian food—and to Indian civilization—to say that it is not compatible with sophisticated, expert choice of wines. A plethora of columnists on food and wine have begun to dole out a plethora of advisories on how to choose 'correct' wines for different kinds of Indian food—to the utter surprise of Indians, who are accustomed to drinking mainly plain water with their meals, and who have learnt, during the last 200 years, that gallons of Scotch whisky of dubious quality and, in its absence, home-brewed arrack—the poor man's tequila—is the ultimate in dining pleasure.

One suspects that the culture of ethnic cuisine and ethnic dining has become more and more sophisticated and complex because it has become a major symbolic substitute for the cultures it is supposed to represent. This culture of food is paradoxically becoming more autonomous of the cultures where the cuisines originate, and the civilizations or lifestyles they represent. Most people seem to believe that things should go this way. Ethnic cuisine is expected to survive the demands of culture and, as the contemporary world pushes more and more local cultures into extinction even while it produces and disseminates the rhetoric of multiculturalism and democratic tolerance, ethnic cuisine becomes more and more like a museum or a stage on which a culture ceremonially inscribes its details, or signs an attendance register for the sake of appeasing our moral conscience and declaring its existence and survival.

The Los Angeles Holocaust Museum displays some artefacts of Jewish culture thoughtfully collected by the Nazis for a projected museum on 'an extinct race' that was to be established after the Final Solution. Those were not the days of ethnic cuisines. Otherwise the Nazis would have surely added a wing to their museum where one could get, in a well-appointed restaurant, traditional Jewish fare from all over Europe.

Exile

Sudesh Mishra

Howlings attend on the exile, subject as well as concept. Banished to the delta of the Danube, the poet Ovid exclaims, *'Exilium mors est.'* His is the bitter jeremiad of the subject for whom banishment is indistinguishable from the terminality of death. Not metaphor but synonym. Here the exile stands in a relationship of morbid otherness to living entities, to those anchored in the familiarity of native soil. Corporeality, mass, weight and gravity are reserved for the non-exile. More apparition than body, haunted by the known, haunting the strange, the exile is nowhere grounded. Wrenched from routine, speech, gesture, cuisine, custom, turf and history—the stuff of belonging—he is pursued by signs of a past legitimacy, even as the present, with its estranging context, beings and practices, betrays the spectral thinness of such signs. In Ovid's vision, the exile never attains the condition of absolute otherness to his living, corporeal self. For this reason, he cannot enjoy the homely oblivion of the dead. Vexed by signs of his erstwhile plenitude, the exile empties the present context and being of all significance and potentiality. Since he exists through memory in another time, the exile is dead to the present. It follows that the present (illegible, illegitimate) temporality, from this same perspective, is brimming with symbols of death. Ovid proposes an aporia. The exile is torn between the today of non-being, the 'here' (nowhere) of death and otherness where he mournfully *is*, and the yesterday of being, the impossible 'there' of culture and corporeality where he longs to be.

Ovid's unhappy conception of exile is turned on its head by Victor Hugo's jubilant assessment of his time on Jersey island: 'Exilium vita est.' For Ovid, the memory of sameness at the location of difference is tantamount to death and an awareness of death, whereas for Hugo difference (and the memory of sameness in the time of difference) affords the raison d'être for existence. Hugo suggests that the stuff of belonging is the stuff of deathly sameness; the tremors of unheimlich engendered at the site of difference and remoteness is what fuels existential creativity. Ovid howls with grief while Hugo howls with joy.

From antiquity to the present, exilic utterances (and utterances on exile) hinge on these contrasting howls. Virgil, Shakespeare, Dante and Byron are partial to Ovid's melancholia, while Aeschylus, Cicero, Joyce and Rushdie, although markedly less sanguine than Hugo, generally cast a positive eye on the experience of deracination. Undoubtedly, perceptions of exile are bound up with the voluntary or involuntary nature of banishment. Driven out by the political state, Ovid, unlike the self-banished Joyce, is incapable of extolling the pleasures of displacement, of moving beyond what Cicero calls 'a circumscribed habitation'. Obviously there is a distinction to be had between banishment, a condition brought about by coercive factors (judicial decrees, imperial edicts, etc.) external to the victim, and conscious or self-willed expatriatism. The poet Robert Browning volunteered to live away from England while Wole Soyinka, the influential Nigerian playwright, is kept away from his country by a highly repressive nation-state. Even so, it needs to be acknowledged that subjective volition, to varying degrees, is socially determined and that the banished figure is not routinely innocent, as some would have us believe, in the politics of their banishment. In recent times, the figure of the literary exile has met with fashionable controversy. Usually identified with the itinerant postcolonial thinker, this modern exile, according to one account, exploits 'sexy' metaphors of banishment, ostensibly on behalf of minority groups settled in metropolitan centres, but with the undeclared aim of extracting the intellectual, moral and economic profits of victimhood. Exile as a trope for the privileged modern intellectual is, it is argued, at odds with the damaged, unhappy lives of the truly banished: political refugees and outcasts exposed to violence, hunger and loneliness (see Ian Buruma, 'The Cult of Exile', *Prospect*, March 2001, pp.23–27).

While admittedly there is no correlation between traumatized homeless refugees and salaried postcolonial thinkers, this account blinds itself to the genealogy of exile as *posture* and *imposture* (political, religious or literary) that, historically, has little to do with the unmediated suffering of outcasts or refugees. Exile does not refer to an actual, alienated body in pain, but to its *persona*. This fact separates the subaltern outcast, the one who suffers materially and physically, from the discursively aware, privileged wearer of exile as a sociocultural mask. Encumbered with the semantic aura of a genre, exile is not a meaningful term for the Vietnamese boat person, the Tibetan refugee, the Indo-Fijian runaway or the Kurdish outcast. It alludes to the aesthetics of banishment rather than to its ontology. When Ovid cries, 'Exile is death,' the fact of his utterance conveys the impossibility of the synonymous contract between banishment and death. In designating himself as that subject, the exile, Ovid alerts us to an attitude, to a trope and hyperbole (yes, conceit) that brings into being this new figure, this double. Possessing a value equivalent to death, the exile is patently *not* the speaking subject. Exile is posture, implying the figuration of an other. For this reason, every posture is a species of imposture—the generation of a contrived self—but emptied of values pertaining to sincerity or its obverse.

It is, then, *artifice* that announces itself in the figure of the exile. From Virgilian eclogues and Hindu epics to Baudelaire's verses and Bollywood ghazals, the exile is rarely free from the aura of simulation that betrays his presence as a generic creature, as an artifice. Virgil's exile is nothing less than a type identifying the rules and marks of the pastoral tradition; Valmiki's Rama is, likewise, hardly more than a figure of edification swaddled in the accoutrement of allegory; Baudelaire's flâneur is, as the term suggests, a bourgeois poseur whose meanderings bring into being the urban eclogue; while the banished lover or drinker of the popular ghazal is a facilitator of catastrophe (the classical 'turn') in a genre where conceit is emperor. No doubt I elide too many differences here. Since they are creatures of dissimilar epistemes, Homeric/Virgilian and Hindu epics present different types of exile. Odysseus and Rama. The structure of the tirtha yatra (pilgrimage, but in a specifically Hindu sense) dominates the Hindu epic tradition. The violation of dharma (Kaikeyi's in the Ramayana, Duryodhana's in the Mahabharata) impacts on cosmic law and has to be righted through the logic of banishment and return. In contrast, the Homeric/Virgilian tradition is mainly concerned with the geopolitical and the (profanely) secular. The seven-year digression by Odysseus on his journey homeward after the battle of Troy is really an exercise in narrative jouissance. Even historical exiles, such as Ayatollah Khomeini, Gandhi or Garibaldi, are *written into* exilic discourses and carry about them the same whiff of simulation. Of course we must be careful not to confound a methodology that draws on exilic discourses to describe a political subject with other forms of history writing. At the time of India's independence Gandhi was comforting the 'internally displaced' victims of Partition, not celebrating Mother India's return from an enforced British exile. Nonetheless, it pays to be wary of the tag of exile when applied to anonymous outcasts and scapegoats. Such tags suggest a taxonomy that is bound up with aesthetic effects, transforming the suffering person into a persona of suffering.

Large-scale demographic shifts, fostered by advanced capital, famine, ethnic conflict and war, have led—in less than six or seven decades—to the emergence of significant global diasporas. The migratory trend has largely been towards the hypercities of the 'developed' world and, without exception, to the detriment of economically hobbled nation-states. Writers, poets and critical thinkers have drawn on exilic metaphors to describe the symptoms of (dis)continuity experienced by members belonging to these communities. No longer the vassal of isolated decisions and arbitrary edicts, the modern exile is perceived as representative of a category of subjects pulled or pushed by historico-economic factors. The classical vision of exile is more or less psychological:

the persona is exposed to a strange milieu that induces in him feelings of nostalgia, fury, insomnia, resignation, death, rapture, reverie, self-pity and so on. By contrast, the view of the modern exile is largely sociological and speculative: the persona is not a hopelessly marooned individual reacting to his milieu but a historical actor whose experiences, for better or for worse, impinge on the world at large. In Salman Rushdie's novels or Homi K. Bhabha's essays, exilic symptoms tend to function as signs of a general assault on older forms of knowing, being and belonging. The exile 'straddles' unlikely localities, cities, memories, cultures, peoples and languages, endlessly changing and being changed by them. Subject and object begin to leak into each other. Whether this conception of exile affords us a form of historical truth is, at best, debatable. What seems certain is an alteration on the level of posture: the classical exile, whether howling in grief or with joy, is able to differentiate between the states of banishment and belonging, whereas the modern exile, oscillating at a vertiginous pace between discrepant times, memories, spaces and languages, is inevitably deprived of such certitudes.

Food

Philip McMichael

Food embodies world history like no other substance. European expansion to the Orient and the Americas in the fifteenth century followed the pepper trade, anticipating the 'Columbian exchange', whereby wheat came to the New World with Columbus, and American maize and tomatoes and the Andean potato travelled to Europe. From there the potato was introduced into Africa and India. Today, potato is a dietary staple for Indians as much as the tomato is for Italians, their respective cuisines featuring foods originally from the New World, such as chillies, potatoes and capsicums. Well before this, sugar travelled from Polynesia to Asia, to the Mediterranean, and back to the West Indies with Columbus. In the twentieth century, soya circulated from East Asia, supplying expanding global needs for cooking oil and protein for livestock and vegetarians alike. Many diets and cuisines across the world are at one and the same time 'local' and 'global'.

The notion of thinking globally and eating locally is, then, not as straightforward as it might seem. We can distinguish, however, between incorporating foods from afar into local diets ('creole foods') and local agricultures, and the imposition of monoculture as a process of the alienation of local resources for global markets. In the former case, the nurturing of a local 'foodshed' is vital to the process of cultural and ecological sustainability as well as dietary diversity. The latter case, of export monoculture, stems from the colonial project of expropriating non-European lands to provision consumer markets elsewhere. Export monoculture is increasingly dominant, but unsustainable in its assault on biodiversity and its consumption of chemicals and fossil fuels; therefore eating locally has become a matter of social and ecological necessity.

The globalization of monoculture is embodied in the rise of the beef culture. The introduction of European cattle to the New World anticipated an agribusiness complex that now links specialized soy producers, feed-corn farmers, and lot-fed cattle across the world. The global cattle complex embodies a series of commodity chains binding the world into an animal protein dependency that imposes monocultures on local ecologies and competes with the consumption of food staples like wheat, rice and beans. Beef followed the lead of sugar, a formerly aristocratic food whose modern availability to the emerging European proletariat depended on a global system of slave plantations. In the nineteenth century, beef moved down the social scale from the aristocracy to the swelling urban classes who dined 'up' the food chain, consuming North American beef financed by British investors. By the mid twentieth century, mass consumption subdivided the beef industry into lot-fed high-value beef cuts, and grass-fed cattle supplying the cheaper, lean meat for the global fast-food industry. In this sense, beef has come to symbolize modernity, and the representation of its social hierarchy in class-based diets.

Diets have a political history framed by class, cultural and imperial relations. Animal protein consumption signals rising affluence and the emulation of Western diets. Movement up the food-chain hierarchy (from starch to grain to animal protein and vegetables) is identified with modernity. This hierarchy is a political construct, and beef has typically been a vehicle of legitimacy for political and corporate regimes. This is exemplified in the World Bank's current sponsorship of the emerging domestic 'livestock revolution' in China, and previous export strategies encouraged by development agencies in Central America to develop an offshore source of hamburger meat for US consumers. The food-chain hierarchy is also socially constructed through markets that routinely privilege the supply of affluent, over staple, foods. As wealthy consumers 'dine up' on beef and shrimp, local peasants and fishermen, displaced by cattle pastures, shrimp farms and deteriorating coastal lands and mangroves, must depend on tenuous low-protein starchy diets.

Food systems around the world reveal the framework of 'globalization'. There is a brisk and growing trade in foodstuffs supplying affluent urban populations with exotic, high-value and all-seasonal foods supplied through global sourcing. Yet only about 20 per cent of the world's six billion people participate in the cash or consumer credit economy, and about 90 per cent of the world's food consumption occurs in the country in which it is produced. While urbanites depend on the market for almost all their food consumption, rural populations consume 60 per cent of the food they produce. In other words, there is a discrepancy between the image and affluent experience of globalization, and global reality. But it is this very discrepancy that drives the politics of globalization.

The food and biotechnology corporations view global hunger as their challenge, holding out the promise of transgenic crops and foodstuffs. The full implementation of the corporate project threatens to destabilize the world's remaining three billion farmers, intensify environmental jeopardy (with the growing threat of biological, on top of chemical, pollution) and reduce global biodiversity to agro-industrial monocultures, increasing the vulnerability of crops and livestock to disease. Meanwhile, growing numbers of small farmers, environmentalists and consumers contest this undemocratic and unsustainable globalization project.

The commodification of food underpins the rise and reproduction of capitalist culture and the ideology of 'development'. But this role is double-edged, since its singular logic undermines non-capitalist food cultures, and adulterates distinctive capitalist food cultures via 'McDonaldization' and genetic engineering, incubating serious epidemics of diet-related cancers, obesity and unforeseen health risks. It is now common to refer to a 'global epidemic of malnutrition', in which the 1.2 billion underfed are matched by the

1.2 billion overfed, expressing the intensification of global food inequity. In this context, food's staple, cultural and biophysical qualities position it as a central site of resistance to the project of capitalist globalization.

Agribusiness targets the World Trade Organization (WTO) to institutionalize transnational rights to source food and food inputs, to prospect for genetic patents and to gain access to local and national food markets. The trade-related intellectual property rights (TRIPS) protocol empowers corporations to patent genetic materials such as seed germplasm, potentially endangering the rights of farmers to plant their crops on the grounds of patent infringement. This expropriation of genetic resources developed by peasants, forest dwellers and local communities over centuries of cultural experimentation is termed 'biopiracy'—such as the patenting of Indian basmati rice by the US company Rice Tec, which sells 'Kasmati' rice and 'Texmati' rice as authentic basmati. Patenting intensifies an already monopolized global seed industry. The significance of the TRIPS is that intellectual property rights on gene patenting privilege governments and corporations as legal entities, and disempower communities and farmers whose rights over traditional knowledge go unrecognized. One powerful example of resistance to this patent regime is the mobilization of village youth in Pattuvam, Kerala, to document local plant species and crop cultivars, and register ownership of biodiversity in local names to pre-empt genetic prospecting.

Under a corporate-WTO regime, food security is reinterpreted as the reduction of barriers to agricultural trade, privileging agri-exporting regions as global 'breadbaskets', and global agribusinesses as instruments of regional 'comparative advantage'. In Mexico, two and a half million households engage in rainfed maize production, with a productivity differential of 2–3 tons per hectare compared with 7.5 tons per hectare in the American Midwest. The estimated 200 per cent rise in corn imports through the full implementation of the North American Free Trade Agreement (NAFTA) by 2008 is expected to undermine over two-thirds of Mexican maize production. The additional casualty here is the destruction of the local biodiversity that complements cash crops, but is invisibilized in the monocultural language of comparative advantage.

In addition to discounting regional (agri)cultures, this project embodies several tensions:

First, market liberalization intensifies the centralization and power of agri-food capital via global sourcing and global trading. Not only does this portend a future of nations and/or populations being held hostage to corporate food suppliers (and their states of origin), but we know that Japan's quid pro quo for supporting formation of the WTO regime was the guarantee of unrestricted access to food from export regions even in the grip of famine.

Second, while biotech/food corporation clusters claim to have the answer to world hunger, most of the food products (milk, soybeans, animal feed, canola, sugar beets, corn and potatoes) targeted for transgenic development enhance the profits of the chemical business first before addressing the supply of food to the world's hungry.

Third, the corporate embrace of transgenic technology seriously threatens human and environmental sustainability via the replacement of diversity by corporate monopoly of genetically altered seeds (that is, commercial bio-serfdom for small farmers). The introduction of transgenic crops could contaminate remaining centres of crop diversity through gene drift from transgenic plants to landraces (gene-complexes with multiple forms of resistance to disease).

Fourth, the corporate project of dismantling public farm and food subsidies amounts to a massive recommodification of one of life's basic staples. Global corporate sourcing and trading encourages a 'nutrition transition', involving a declining consumption of cereals and legumes and a rising consumption of meat and dairy fats, salt and sugars, including exposure to the diseases of affluence associated with processed foods.

Fifth, a global public health crisis induced substantively by dietary substitution, on the one hand, and formally by a market regime that discounts health (if not environmental) considerations.

The market regime aims to institute multilateral bodies such as the Northern/corporate-dominated Codex Alimentarius Commission, whose function will be to remove from national institutions the role of adjudicating questions of food contamination by pesticide and hormone residues, chemical additives and genetically engineered foods. We have already witnessed the subtle introduction of genetically modified (GM) food components into mass-produced foodstuffs.

Sixth, a swelling resistance to the attempt to institute market rule by environmentalist, consumer, farmer and fair trade movements providing an array of alternatives.

Food and environmental safety is driving an active countermovement, which emerged in the late 1990s. For example, food labelling is now on the political agenda in the North. French farmers attacked a storage facility owned by Novartis and destroyed 30 tons of transgenic corn seed, when the French government allowed planting of GM corn. In Bangalore, the Karnataka Farmers Union (claiming a membership of ten million) challenged Cargill's attempts to patent germplasm, and burned Monsanto's GM crops, giving life to other grass-roots organizations in this struggle. Sustainable agricultures crop up across the world. The Centre for Conservation of Traditional Farming Systems in Madhya Pradesh is now cultivating unirrigated wheat varieties by traditional methods. This is a bid to reverse the green revolution, to reverse the socially and environmentally unsustainable impact of high-input agriculture and to model small farming and subsistence agriculture as the alternative to big-dam-based irrigated agriculture. In the Andes, the PRATEC group consciously rejects Western methods in the context of the regional collapse of the formal economy, recovering traditional Andean peasant practices.

In these various ways, and more, food security/safety and environmental movements express the crisis of development. The central issue is that the corporate logic is culturally reductive and unsustainable, and food may be the strongest litmus test of this. Of course cuisines have evolved over time and across space, but we stand on a threshold beyond which the proverbial 'frankenfood' beckons to populations in what we may now call the Fast World. There is a dialectical relation between the greater abstraction associated with corporate foods and the intimacy of the Slow Food movement, and of fresh and organic food that expresses both locality and sustainability. For the majority of the world's population, food is not just an item of consumption, it is a way of life. It has deep material and symbolic power. It embodies the links between nature, human survival and health, culture and livelihood, and it will, and has already, become a focus of contention and resistance to a corporate takeover of life itself.

Further Reading

Hobhouse, Henry. 1987. *Seeds of Change: Six Plants That Transformed Mankind*. New York: Macmillan.

Lappé, Frances Moore, Joseph Collins, Peter Rosset, with Luis Esparza. 1998. *World Hunger: Twelve Myths*. New York: Grove Press.

Magdoff, Fred, John Bellamy Foster, and Frederick H. Buttel, eds. 2000. *Hungry for Profit: The Agribusiness Threat to Farmers, Food and the Environment*. New York: Monthly Review Press.

Mintz, Sidney. 1986. *Sweetness and Power: The Place of Sugar in Modern History*. Harmondsworth, UK: Penguin.

Rifkin, Jeremy. 1992. *Beyond Beef: The Rise and Fall of the Cattle Culture*: New York: Dutton.

Shiva, Vandana. 1997. *Biopiracy: The Plunder of Nature and Knowledge*. Cambridge, Massachusetts: South End Press.

Genocide

Michael Sells

In such countries, genocide is not too important.

—French President François Mitterand, 1994,
with reference to Rwanda

On 9 December 1948, the UN General Assembly adopted the Convention on the Prevention and Punishment of the Crime of Genocide. The convention was the culmination of efforts led by the Polish-Jewish jurist Raphael Lemkin to criminalize genocide (defined as acts 'committed with intent to destroy, in whole or in part, a national, ethnic, racial or religious group, as such') and to assert international obligations to prevent and punish it.

As the category of genocide gained moral and legal authority, problems of application arose. Armenians have pressed an intransigent Turkish government, for example, to admit that in 1919 genocide was committed against them. Organized mass killings in Guatemala, East Pakistan (Bangladesh), Tibet and areas of the Soviet Union went unpunished and remain politically unrecognized as genocides. Large-scale development in Latin America, Africa and Asia led to the destruction of numerous peoples whose existence, as a people, was tied to the habitat that was systematically or suddenly taken from them and then marketed or destroyed.

Disputes as to which categories to use (race, religion, ethnicity—

but what about political position, class or gender?) lead to a deeper paradox: before the genus can be destroyed, it must first be constructed as monotonic. People carry multiple, partially overlapping identities. Constructions of monotonic identity occurred with the Khmer Rouge division of Cambodians between 'new people' and 'old people', with one group marked for liquidation; colonial construction of rival and fixed Hutu and Tutsi groupings; and violent transformation of Muslim Slavs into a separate ethnicity from their Christian neighbours. The examples are numerous and by now familiar, thanks to media presence and commitment. Genocide is a real crime and real people are destroyed; and the forced construction of a monotonic genus is part of the genocidal process itself.

In 1993 the UN Security Council, responding to international outrage over the massive war crimes in Bosnia, established the International Criminal Tribunal for War Crimes Committed in the Former Yugoslavia (ICTY). In 1994 it authorized a similar tribunal for Rwanda (ICTR). Only then have indictments, convictions and acquittals of the crime of genocide begun to set international legal precedents on the scope and applicability of the charge.

Genocide was defined and criminalized in the wake of the Holocaust of the Second World War, which imbued the concept with much of its original gravitas. But movements against genocide have been caught in a dependency upon the Holocaust linkage. Threatened groups use the terms Holocaust and genocide (often interchangeably) to draw attention to their plight. In reaction, others define genocide as nothing less than another Holocaust. Bosnians appealing for international protection evoked the post-Holocaust slogan 'Never again'. Those who first saw through the euphemism 'ethnic cleansing' and the screen of moral equivalency ('all sides are to blame') included many Jews sensitized by the Holocaust. 'Death camp!' headlines accompanying photos of the notorious Omarska camp forced public recognition of the organized mass-killings in Bosnia, even though the reporters using the term acknowledged that the killings were carried out without gas chambers and crematoria. Although such appeals moved a resistant international public to the recognition of genocide in Bosnia and a final intervention that saved many, the same appeals also contributed to efforts to deny the genocide—a denial based, precisely, on the logic that crimes in Bosnia were 'not an Auschwitz'.

Neglect of the terms 'in whole or in part', and 'as such', has also limited anti-genocide efforts. With a widely dispersed 'people' of defined ethnicity, race or religion, eradication 'in whole' would require complete world domination—both in extent (across all boundaries) and in depth (to the village and communal level). Apologists for Hutu 'genocidaires' argued that they were not trying to destroy all Tutsis, only those in Rwanda. Deniers of genocide in Bosnia argued that the goal of 'ethnic cleansing' was expulsion, not annihilation. True, Bosnian Muslims may have survived as individuals, but after systematic annihilation of all witnesses and testimonies to the past (teachers, artists, writers, libraries, mosques, museums, shrines and secular architecture) they would have been stripped of the collective historical and cultural memory central to their existence as a people 'as such'.

The performative function of the word genocide, its evoking the responsibility to prevent and punish it, has in some cases encouraged genocide denial. UN and American officials avoided the term 'genocide' in discussing Bosnia and Rwanda, precisely to circumvent the obligation to prevent or stop it. Only shame over the 1995 UN betrayal of 7500 unarmed captives from the 'safe area' of Srebrenica, sheep led to slaughter, forced a UN-authorized NATO air campaign that helped bring a quick halt to slaughter. In Rwanda, only the military victory of Rwandan rebels stopped the killings.

There is no conceivable justice (in terms of retribution or restitution) remotely commensurate with the crime of genocide, and only a small percentage of perpetrators can be prosecuted. Yet, a publicly recognized acknowledgement of the crime (however inadequate) helps prevent demonization of the people in whose name the crimes were committed and possible future revenge against them as a whole. The importance of tribunal records has been confirmed, ironically, by many indicted criminals. Before arrest, they deny the atrocities took place. After arrest, confronting the victims and overwhelming evidence, they change their story, admitting they knew of the crimes but had not perpetrated them and had not been able to prevent them. Whether convicted or acquitted of their role in the crimes, their acknowledgement that the crimes occurred serves as a vital antidote to revisionism.

The convention is unequivocal on the obligation to prevent and punish, but vague on the legitimization of intervention. In 1999, NATO engaged in a bombing campaign to force the withdrawal of the Serb forces from Kosovo, citing imminent genocide. After Serb military withdrawal, the fact that fewer Kosovar Albanians had been killed than had been feared (though the number was still of a tragic enormity) generated strong criticism of the intervention. The lack of completed genocide, however, may not entail by itself the illegitimacy of an intervening force; it may mean that a planned genocide was successfully prevented. Serb nationalists had openly proclaimed their intentions in Kosovo. Failure to believe early proclamations led directly to Srebrenica.

Others argued that only the UN had the authority to intervene. If NATO may intervene on its own, other regional or national forces may evoke the genocide convention to justify military actions, with no recognized forum for determining the validity of the claim of imminent or ongoing genocide. The dilemma is stark. The UN, its credibility damaged after complicity at Srebrenica, was not in a position to act effectively. The NATO operation, though self-authorized, succeeded in enabling nearly a million people to return to their homes (a refugee return unparalleled in modern history) and saving the probable destruction of Kosovar Albanians as a people.

Even were it properly authorized by the UN, intervention would still favour the powerful. The permanent members of the Security Council are unlikely to approve intervention against Russian forces in Chechnya, French acts of complicity in Rwanda, Chinese policy in Tibet, or US-led embargo and betrayal of Iraqi dissidents that has led to the death of hundreds of thousands. Some of these powers oppose a permanent criminal tribunal that would make them subject to the same scrutiny as occurred in the Balkans and Rwanda.

Then there are the hapless Balkan and Rwandan genocidaires who have ended up in court. Their final appeal: the court is illegitimate, authorized by an institution dominated by great powers not subject to the same scrutiny. Yet no court is based on pure legitimacy or free of implication in a systemic bias. 'Others get away with it' is a valid condemnation of a system, but not exculpatory. In this sense, justice is never fair (at least outside utopia).

Debates over intervention and trial should need some principles of argumentation. Willingness to look at the full evidence is a first principle. Serb nationalists and a dismayingly large number of sympathizers worldwide denied the Srebrenica genocide, claiming that only a few bodies had been found (later several thousand bodies were discovered, and new DNA techniques have begun to make identification possible). Looking at the evidence means facing the victim. Denying the killings at Srebrenica should entail willingness to travel to Bosnia and speak to the tortured souls who think their loved ones are dead, and explain where they are. Opposing NATO intervention, and the International Tribunal, as illegitimate should entail willingness to make that case to the people endangered or their survivors and engage in an alternative practical action against the atrocity.

The moral stakes were raised when genocide was singled out as a particularly grave crime. The higher the moral capital, the more dangerous the uncontrolled market. In 1986, Serb clergy, politicians and intellectuals claimed that Albanians were committing genocide against Serbs in Kosovo. Dissident Serb journalists had exposed the charges as fabrications, but the historical memory of the Second World War and a resurgent ethnoreligious mythology rendered people blind to counter-evidence. By 1992, Serb radio broadcasts of fabricated genocide plans of Bosnian Muslims became a signal for Serb militias to begin liquidation of Bosnian Muslim civilians. Non-genocide had become genocide; victims of genocide were attacked as its perpetrators. It will not be possible, or wise, to establish a full international jurisdiction without safeguards against such Orwellian inversion.

Guilt must be distinguished from responsibility. Each person alive today is here today because some ancestor was part of a group that destroyed or expelled the people who occupied it previously. Recognition (and acceptance of responsibility for our living on the lands and economies of previously destroyed peoples) need not lead to rejection of efforts to prevent or punish new genocides, but rather enhance efforts to eliminate genocide. The Milosevic argument—'Who are you to judge: look what you did to the American Indians!'—should be accepted fully (without offering any exculpation to a Milosevic if convicted). The hapless genocidaire who is unlucky enough to be caught and punished will become a most effective advocate for recognition of other crimes which have remained invisible in various degrees.

Lemkin's category of 'genocide' has increased the sense of responsibility to prevent such mass atrocity and, in a limited way, helped promote increased efforts at prevention. There is so little recognition of injustice, however, that persecuted groups feel a need to compete for what little recognition exists. In the economy of zero-sum, many refuse to recognize one genocide out of fear that it will entail less attention given to another. I have here focused on the cases of Rwanda and Bosnia, leaving out many other cases. If prevention of genocide is to succeed, it will be through a logic of non-competition, where acknowledgement of one crime will increase—not compete with—the ability to acknowledge another.

Further Reading

Gourevitch, Philip. 1998. *We Wish to Inform You That Tomorrow We Will Be Killed with Our Families*. New York: Farrar, Straus and Giroux.

Bartov, Omer, and Phyllis Mack, eds. 2001. *In God's Name: Genocide and Religion in the Twentieth Century*. Oxford and New York: Berghahn Books.

Grass Roots

Gustavo Esteva

The new initiatives at the grass roots resist interpretation. People write their own scripts—if any—as they go along. Their own participatory self-transforming trial-and-error approach and their prodigious adaptability are a continual source of puzzlement and misunderstanding. These new initiatives do not fit well into the fashionable label of 'new social movements'. The epic now evolving at the grass roots is inspired by old and new traditions, but cannot be reduced to them. It is radically new.

The myth of progress is now ripe for the museum. It generated a view of the world in which unity would come in the future: history, always following an upward road, would integrate the world under the rule of reason and welfare. There are some attempts to resurrect such illusions: globalized capitalism would be the stage crowning history and ending it. But people at the grass roots have begun to acknowledge that the arrow of time is broken and the belief in progress has crumbled. They are recovering the present. They know that the coherence of the world cannot be achieved by pushing ahead along a common path towards some distant promised future, but only in the actual condition, in the present. Against the elitist obsession to unify the world through the homogenization of realities, aspirations, beliefs and dreams, they are celebrating the fiesta of diversity. Fully aware that ethnic or local fundamentalisms prompt mutual destruction and renovate dangerous forms of nationalism, they look for a dialogue among cultures to construct accords transcending the totalitarianism of the Western logos.

At the grass roots, people oppose localization to both globalization and merely localist resistance. They carve their own places with courage and imagination in the shapeless zones created by the market or the state. So entrenched, they resist the rhetoric of evangelization, capitalism, development, democracy or human rights. The uncertainty brought by globalization stimulated some groups to transform that tradition of resistance into a new form of dangerous fundamentalism. But more and more people become aware that in the era of globalization mere resistance is not enough: all localisms will be razed to the ground. Still affirmed in their places of belonging, convinced that David can beat Goliath if he fights him in David's territory, they open themselves to wide coalitions of discontents. They share a common rejection of the dominant mythologies and global forces. But instead of subsuming themselves into alternative global ideologies or organizations, they retain the multiplicity of their ideals and motives. Their politics of 'No'—the shared opposition to what they don't want—always expresses many 'Yeses': the differentiated affirmations of what they want. Without falling into relativism, they opt for radical pluralism, to create a world in which many worlds can fit.

The expression 'civil society' is often used to allude to grass-roots initiatives. It finds wide echo, but it is also a source of confusion: its long and convoluted history has deprived it of any precise denotation and it carries connotations that are the opposite of what one attempts to say. The expression has recently been used to allude to popular movements which did not use class or party organizations to dismantle authoritarian regimes in eastern Europe and South America; to organizations created by the citizens out of the state or the business sector (the 'third sector' or the 'non-profit sector'); to the cultural sphere, which generates meaning and social norms, different from the political and economic spheres; to men and women, groups and individuals, that come together to realize activities by themselves to change the society in which they live; to a rejection of the centrality of the state and its capacity to organize society and to promote the good life, a capacity attributed instead to civil society. The latter approach evolves into the notion of 'widened democracy', in which civil society does not substitute for the state, but operates as an independent force that controls it, as well as the political parties. Civil society is thus redefined as the sphere which organizes itself autonomously, in opposition to the logic of capital and to the sphere established and/or directly controlled by the state. It is not a substitute for expressions with the same antagonism and the same political orientation. It is not 'the vanguard party' operating as the agent of historical change. Civil society does not rise up and seize the power of the state; rather, in rising up, it empowers itself. Unlike mass society, civil society is not a herd but a multiplicity of diverse groups and organizations, of people acting together for a variety of purposes. Civil society does not create the 'tyranny of the majority' or a bureaucratic dictatorship in charge of the revolution.

In this context, democracy does not mean the transfer of power through the system of representation. It means people's power. It defines an attempt to maintain political power in the people's autonomous spaces, and to use political and juridical procedures to generate social consensus. This new incarnation of civil society is thus directly and immediately political, not only in its function of opposition or resistance but to get back in its hands, at the grass roots, the function of government. It gives new meaning and direction to the old notion of constituent power. At the grass roots, people until now overwhelmed by toil are celebrating the beginning of the human adventure. The expanding dignity of each person and each human relationship is challenging all existing systems.

The Zapatista movement in Mexico exemplifies these traits of the current grass-roots initiatives. On 1 January 1994, two hours after the North America Free Trade Agreement took effect, a small indigenous group, poorly armed, waved its dignity in the south of Mexico and said Basta! (Enough) to 500 years of oppression and forty years of 'development'. The rebels, calling themselves Ejército

Zapatista de Liberación Nacional (EZLN), expressed the hope that a new political regime would allow the country's Indians to reclaim their commons and to regenerate their own forms of governance and their art of living and dying. Since then, surrounded by 50,000 troops, the Zapatistas have been one of the main political actors in Mexico. For many people, all over the world, they are a source of inspiration and mobilization.

The Zapatistas are still a mystery and a paradox: a revolutionary group with no interest in seizing power, and explicitly rejecting any position in the national government, now or in the future; an army shooting civil resistance and non-violence; a locally and culturally rooted organization with a global scope; a group clearly and firmly affiliated to democracy, yet functioning as democracy's most radical critic. The Zapatistas are singular, unique and, at the same time, typical. They come from an ancient tradition but are also fully immersed in contemporary ideas, problems and technologies. They are ordinary men and women characterized by extraordinary behaviour, exemplifying the epic now unfolding at the grass roots.

The EZLN is not a guerrilla movement. It is not 'a fish that swims in the sea of the people', as Che Guevara would say. It is not a revolutionary group attempting to stimulate people's insurrection, in order to seize power to establish the regime it prefers. The Zapatista force was organized as a collective decision of hundreds of communities and has always been subordinated to a civil command: it is the sea, not a fish. Furthermore, the armed struggle lasted only twelve days. The EZLN complied immediately with the mandate of civil society to try the political approach. Since then, the weapons of the Zapatistas are words, organization, civil resistance, dignity.

The movement triggered and still nourished by the EZLN is not fundamentalist, nationalist or ethnic. It is ecumenical and very open in religious matters. It opposes the fragmentation of the country. Almost all members of the EZLN are indigenous people, but they are not an indigenous or ethnic movement and project their pluralism to both indigenous and non-indigenous people of civil society.

In their culturally differentiated communities, the Zapatistas affirm their commonality as their form of being in the world. Well committed to wide coalitions with others like themselves, their open and even cosmic world view is the opposite of fundamentalist localisms and of the parochialism and short-sightedness of national governments, transnational corporations or international institutions affiliated to the neo-liberal credo. The Zapatistas dismantle the illusions of equality and representation. They recognize that representative democracy has been used to good effect by the people. Fully aware that it has become a regime in which the citizens 'freely' elect their oppressors, they use it as a political 'umbrella' for the transition to radical democracy. Fully conscious that the nation-state is a regime of domination, a straitjacket that dissolves or prevents cultural diversity, they accept it as a provisional framework for the transition to a new political design. Through juridical and political procedures, they generate a social consensus to create a new social order, which can forge the communion of different ideologies through intercultural dialogue. The challenge, say the Zapatistas, is to live together with the differences, with whatever aspect in which the 'other' appears in a society, without renouncing one's own being.

The Zapatistas, in short, propose a radically democratic localization, not neo-liberal or social-democratic globalization; ruralization of the cities and regeneration of the countryside instead of conventional urbanization; local-regional self-reliance and marginalization of the economy instead of intervention by the market or the state; and the regeneration of the commons or the creation of new commons instead of modern and capitalist individualization.

The Zapatista uprising changed the balance of forces in Mexico. During the first months of 1994, the political opposition obtained more concessions from the regime than in the previous fifty years. The mutation of civil society, stimulated by the Zapatistas, further undermined the 'system' and paved the way for the outcome of the federal elections of 2000, which operated as the funeral of the authoritarian regime governing Mexico for the last seventy years.

The International of Hope, created during their Intercontinental Encounter, illustrates the new style of the coalitions at the grass roots. Their shared rejection of the system they hope to bring to an end avoids any centralized ideology, bureaucracy or organization. Radical hope, the very essence of popular movements, is not the conviction that something will go well, but (as Vaclav Havel has somewhere said) the conviction that something makes sense, no matter what happens. In that Encounter, the Zapatistas acknowledged that to change the world is very difficult, next to impossible. They suggested instead that humanity try to create a new world: this is not a futuristic fantasy, like all modern projects, but a pragmatic attempt to recover the present. As Gandhi once said, the idea is to yourself be the change you wish for the world.

Further Reading

Esteva, Gustavo, and Madhu Prakash. 1998. *Grassroots Postmodernism*. London: Zed Books.

Frank, Andre Gunder, and M. Fuentes. 1987. *Nine Theses on Social Movements*. Amsterdam: ISMOG.

Negri, Antonio. 1999. *Insurgencies: Constituent Power and the Modern State*. Minneapolis: University of Minnesota Press.

Shanin, Teodor. 1983. *Late Marx and the Russian Road*. New York: Monthly Review Press.

Human Rights

Vinay Lal

The notion of human rights is deeply embedded in modern legal and political thought and could well be considered one of the most significant achievements of contemporary civilization. Certain classes of people in all societies have from the beginning of time been endowed with 'rights' which others could not claim. Diplomatic emissaries, for instance, were conferred with 'rights' that even an alien state could not abrogate, and elites arrogated to themselves certain rights and privileges. *The Declaration of the Rights of Man and Citizen* (1789), Thomas Paine's *Rights of Man* (1791) and the 'Bill of Rights' attached to the US Constitution are conventionally seen as having extended rights to a much broader class of people, and the post-Second-World-War Universal Declaration of Human Rights is described as the rightful culmination of these democratic propensities. Some 'rights' were such which the citizen could claim against the state, others placed restraints on the state's agenda to produce conformity and contain dissent.

In this liberal vision of human rights, what is uniquely modern is that never before have individual rights been so squarely placed under the protection of the law. Moreover, it is only in recent times that the 'international community' seems prepared to enforce sanctions against a state for alleged violations of such rights. With the demise of communism, the principal foes of human rights appeared to have been crushed, and the very notion of 'human rights' seemed sovereign. Should we then unreservedly endorse the culture of 'human rights', as it has developed in the liberal-democratic framework of the modern West, as a signifier of the 'end of history' and the emergence of what V.S. Naipaul called 'our universal civilization'? Or, rather than acquiescing in the suggestion that the notion of human rights is the most promising avenue to a new era in human relations, is there warrant for considering the discourse of human rights as the most evolved form of Western imperialism? Is it the latest masquerade of the West, particularly the United States, the torch-bearer since the end of the Second World War of 'Western' values, which appears to the rest of the world as the epitome of civilization and as the only legitimate arbiter of human values?

The 'individual' and the 'rule of law' are the two central notions from which the modern discourse of human rights is derived. Since at least the Renaissance it has been a staple of Western thought that while the West recognizes the individual as the true unit of being and the organic building block of society, non-Western cultures have been built around collectivities, conceived as religious, linguistic, ethnic, tribal or racial groups. 'Whatever may be the political atom in India,' we find unabashedly stated in the 27 February 1909 issue of the *Economist*, 'it is certainly not the individual of Western democratic theory, but the community of some sort.' In the West the individual stands in singular and splendid isolation, the promise of the inherent perfectibility of man; in the non-West, the individual is nothing, always a part of a collectivity in relation to which his or her existence is defined, never an entity unto himself or herself. Where the 'individual' does not exist, one cannot speak of his or her rights; and where there are no rights, it is perfectly absurd to speak of their denial or abrogation.

Regarding the Western view, moreover, if the atomistic conception of the 'individual' is a prerequisite for a concern with human rights, so too is the 'rule of law' under which alone such rights can be respected. In a society which lives by the 'rule of law', such laws as the government might formulate are done so in accordance with certain normative criteria—for example, they shall be non-discriminatory, blind to considerations of race, gender, class, linguistic competence and so on. These laws are then made public, so that no person might plead ignorance of the law; and the judicial process under which the person charged for the infringement of such laws is tried must hold out the promise of being fair and equitable. As in the case of the 'individual', the 'rule of law' is held to be a uniquely Western contribution to civilization, on the two-fold assumption that democracy is an idea and institution of purely Western origins, and that, contrariwise, the only form of government known to non-Western societies was absolutism. In conditions of 'Oriental despotism', the only law was the law of the despot, and the life and limb of each of his subjects was hostage to the tyranny of his pleasures and whims. In the despotic state, there was perhaps only one 'individual', the absolute ruler; under him were the masses, particles of dust on the distant horizon. What rights were there to speak of then?

Having suggested how the notions of the 'individual' and the 'rule of law' came to intersect in the formulation of the discourse of human rights, we can proceed to unravel some of the more disturbing and insidious aspects of this discourse. Where once the language of liberation was religion, today the language of emancipation is law. Indeed, the very notion of 'human rights', as it is commonly understood in the international forum today, is legalistic. Customs and traditional usages have in most 'Third World' countries functioned for centuries in place of 'law'. Even without the 'rule of law' in a formalistic sense, there were conventions and traditions which bound one person to respect the rights of another. However, this is not something that proponents of the 'rule of law', convinced of the uniqueness of the West, are generally prepared to concede. By what right, with what authority, and with what consequences, do certain states brand other states as 'outlaw' or 'rogue' states, living outside the pale of the 'rule of law', allegedly oblivious to the rights of their subjects, and therefore subject to sanctions from the 'international community'?

There is, as has been argued, one 'rule of law' for the powerful, and an altogether different one for those states and non-state actors that do not speak the 'rational', 'diplomatic' and 'sane' language that the West has decreed as the universal form of linguistic exchange. It is not only the case that when Americans retaliate against their foes, they are engaged in 'just war' or purely 'defensive' measures in the interest of national security, but that when Libyans or Iraqis do so, they are transformed into 'terrorists' or ruthless and self-aggrandizing despots in the pursuit of international dominance. The problem is more acute: who is to police the police? Or, in the more complex variant of that query, how do certain particularisms acquire the legitimacy of universalisms, and why is it that Western universalisms have monopolized our notion of universalisms? In an astounding judgment rendered in the early 1990s, which was barely noticed in the American press, the United States Supreme Court upheld the constitutionality of a decision of a circuit court in Texas which allowed American law enforcement officers to kidnap nationals of a foreign state for alleged offences under American law, and bring them to the United States for trial. Such a decision arbitrarily proclaims the global jurisdiction of American law. Some centuries ago, such occurrences on the high seas were referred to as piracy.

There are still more significant problems with the legalistic conception of a world order where 'human rights' will be safeguarded. The present conception of 'human rights' largely rests on a distinction between state and civil society, a distinction here fraught with hazardous consequences. The rights which are claimed are rights held against the state or, to put it another way, with the blessing of the state: the right to freedom of speech and expression, the right to gather in public, the right to express one's grievances within the limits of the constitution, and so forth. The state becomes the guarantor of these rights, when in fact it is everywhere the state which is the most flagrant violator of human rights. Not only does the discourse of 'human rights' privilege the state, but the very conception of 'rights' must of necessity remain circumscribed. The right to a fair hearing upon arrest, or to take part in the government of one's country, is acknowledged as an unqualified political and civil right. However, the right to housing, food, clean air, an ecologically sound environment, free primary and secondary education, public transportation, a high standard of health, the preservation of one's ethnic identity and culture, and security in the event of unemployment or impairment due to disease and old age is not accorded parity. Such an ecumenical conception of human rights is admitted to by no state, and is infrequently encountered in the vast literature. Nor is it amiss to suggest that the 'individual' rather than the 'human person' predominates in human rights precisely because the individual is an abstraction, while the person is present in every gesture, action, word, relationship and transaction.

Certainly there are organizations, such as the Minority Rights Group (London), Cultural Survival (Boston) and Doctors without Borders, among others, which have adopted a broader conception of 'human rights' and whose discourse is as concerned with the numerous rights of 'collectivities', whether conceived in terms of race, gender, class, ethnic or linguistic background, as it is with the rights of 'individuals'. But this is not the discourse of 'human rights' in the main, and it is emphatically not the discourse of Western powers, which have seldom adhered to the standards that they expect others to abide by, and would use even food and medicine, as the long-lasting embargo against Iraq so vividly demonstrates, to retain their political and cultural hegemony even as they continue to deploy the rhetoric of 'human rights'. Never mind that state formation in the West was forged over the last few centuries by brutally coercive techniques—colonialism, genocide, eugenics, the machinery of 'law and order'—to create homogeneous groups. One could point randomly to the complete elimination of the Tasmanian Aboriginals, the extermination of many Native American tribes, the Highland Clearances in Scotland, even the very (seemingly 'natural') processes by which a largely Breton-speaking France became, in less than a hundred years, French-speaking. The West homogenized itself before it colonized various others; it is now homogenizing these others. Thus the Western discourse of human rights is entirely abstracted from the language of duty, with which the notion of rights is inextricably linked, partly because the West absolved itself of its duties to those whom it colonized.

We should be emphatically clear that what are called the 'Third World' countries should not be allowed the luxury, the right if you will, of pointing to the excesses of state formation in the West to argue (in a parody of the ludicrous evolutionary model where the non-Western world is destined to become progressively free and democratic) that they too must ruthlessly forge ahead with 'development' and 'progress' before their subjects can be allowed 'human rights'. One has, in some respects, heard too much of 'Asian values'; the idea of 'human rights' is noble and its denial an effrontery to humankind. Yet our fascination with this idea must not deflect us from the recognition that 'human rights' is the Maxim gun of the twenty-first century. Perhaps, before 'human rights' is flaunted by the United States as what most of the rest of the world must learn to respect, the movement for 'human rights' should first come home to roost. As Noam Chomsky (1991) has written, people in the Third World 'have never understood the deep totalitarian strain in Western culture, nor have they ever understood the savagery and cynicism of Western culture'. The further rejoinder to these critiques cannot lie in the recourse taken by some to endow their pets with rights while humans are shunned as incurables. Human rights will only flourish when there is a plurality of knowledges and each is furnished with its ecological niche—when, that is, different cultures put forth their own universalisms, and thereby set their own terms for a fruitful engagement with Western human rights discourse.

Further Reading

Chomsky, Noam. 1991. *Media Control: The Spectacular Achievements of Propaganda*. Westfield, New Jersey: Open Magazine Pamphlet Series.

Just World Trust. 1996. *Human Wrongs: Reflections on Western Global Dominance and Its Impact upon Human Rights*. Pune. The Other India Press.

Lauren, Paul Gordon. 1998. *The Evolution of International Human Rights*. Philadelphia: University of Pennsylvania Press.

Imperial Economics

Roby Rajan

With the end-of-millennium dogma of privatization, liberalization and deregulation having firmly established itself, a set of imperial economic formations has been entrusted with global governance. Of these, the best known are the World Bank (WB) and the International Monetary Fund (IMF), which were both created together in the aftermath of the Second World War at the 1944 Bretton Woods Conference in Bretton Woods, New Hampshire. The IMF's role was to provide short-term loans to countries facing a shortage of foreign exchange, whereas the WB was to finance long-term development and reconstruction by providing project-specific loans for infrastructural investment. The WB has since shifted its lending towards microeconomic 'structural adjustment' in specific sectors of the economy, and the IMF's role has expanded to include oversight of macroeconomic 'stabilization' in countries facing balance-of-payments difficulties. Both these institutions impose severe conditions on borrowing countries, with the common objective of facilitating rapid transition to a liberalized market regime.

At regular intervals the pinstriped representatives from these imperial formations land in Third World capitals, laptop in hand, dispensing the same formulaic advice to local supplicants: fiscal tightness by scrapping public programmes, monetary tightness through interest-rate discipline. Recently, however, these tried and tested rules collapsed in the face of large and abrupt movements of short-term capital that liberalization had itself made possible in the countries of East Asia. These countries were then left entirely at the mercy of global creditors; policy makers subsequently had no choice but to do whatever it took to 'restore confidence' in capital markets and attract capital back on terms favourable to global investors.

The crisis was precipitated by the practitioners of currency speculation, a spectral profession conjured into being by the floating of exchange rates and the enormous increase in international capital flows due to worldwide deregulation. The depredations visited by this profession on the Asian countries have lately thrust it into the global spotlight. In theory, as soon as speculators push a currency too far up or too far down, the country's central bank reacts by raising or lowering interest rates to attract or repel capital flows. The central bank also attempts to calm the waters by selling currencies that are in demand, or buying up weak currencies. But this kind of interest-rate jiggling and foreign exchange operations can at best cope with routine fluctuations. When a currency starts sliding beyond its routine limits, as was spectacularly the case in Asia, the central bank is powerless to stop it. This is when the IMF and WB step in, peddling their tonics of structural adjustment and stabilization. At this point, the country in question has little choice but to swallow their medicine in return for loans which then establish it in a relation of indefinite dependency. The weight of the standard IMF-WB ministrations— reducing the fiscal deficit by cutting spending and raising taxes, raising interest rates to attract foreign capital, devaluing the currency to make exports competitive in world markets—predictably falls most heavily on the worst off. These poorest of the poor are then under instructions to calculate their opportunity costs, invest in human capital, undergo austerity measures and do whatever else it takes so these imperial formations can then validate themselves.

A third leg of the quadruped of global governance is the World Trade Organization (WTO), which embodies the gospel of 'comparative advantage' and is charged with opening markets for goods and services worldwide, as well as being responsible for determining whether the rules of free trade have been violated. Before the formation of the WTO, 'free trade' meant the reduction of tariffs, and little else. The extension of free-trade principles to 'non-tariff barriers' marks a vastly expanded role for the WTO— regulations to protect the environment, health, safety, intellectual property, agriculture, worker rights, all now fall under this rubric, and the onus is on local governments to prove that their laws are the 'least trade-restrictive means' to achieve regulatory goals. Nations that fail to abide by the judgements handed down by the WTO face the threat of trade sanctions.

The WTO is the econocrat's dream of a rule-based economic constitution come true on a global scale. But there are some vital differences between this constitution and the constitutions of nation-states: there is no individual or community Bill of Rights here, its fundamental entities are corporations and the only right it concerns itself with is the unrestricted right of businesses to enter markets everywhere. Only one barrier now remains: removing all local, state and national restrictions on investment capital. If free trade could be coupled with free investment, the goal of total global governance would finally be realized: corporations would be free to move their plants around anywhere in the world, hire the lowest wage labour under conditions most favourable to profit-making, sell their products worldwide, all with no threat from those whose lives stand to be affected by these decisions.

A key element in the role that has been scripted for the Third World in the unfolding drama of comparative advantage is that these countries should exploit their low wages, access to natural resources and lower environmental standards to become globally competitive. In a memo notorious even by the lax standards of the World Bank, its then chief economist (and, subsequently, US Treasury Secretary) had offered the recommendation that the poorer and relatively less polluted areas of the world ought to accept a fairer redistribution of the industrial world's wastes so as to rectify the current toxic imbalance. Sniffing a golden opportunity for the countries of sub-Saharan Africa to be integrated into the global economy on the strength of their comparative advantage, the chief economist mused, 'I have always thought that underpopulated countries in Africa are vastly underpolluted; their air quality is probably vastly inefficiently low in pollutants compared to Los Angeles or Mexico City' (*The Economist*, London, February 1992).

Thus, in the chief economist's utopian vision, tropical timber, oil, coal and other natural resources would flow from the Third World to the First, while a reciprocal cargo of banned pesticides, leaded petrol, chlorofluorocarbons (CFCs), asbestos and other toxins would make its way from the First World to the Third through equal exchange. Overseeing these mutually beneficial transactions would be the WTO, invested with the authority to decide which national, state and local government laws conflict with its trade-maximizing goals. Among the national prerogatives now taken away in the name of such free trade are the right of a country to restrict bio-piracy of genetic material found in its rain forests, the right to produce and distribute low-cost medicines, and the right to prevent dependence on food imports.

The fourth and least known of the imperial economic formations is the Bank for International Settlements, a shadowy bankers' club that prefers to stay out of the limelight, letting the central banks of individual countries do most of its work. Although ostensibly not 'international organizations' in the strict sense, central banks play a significant role in integrating country policies with the overall logic of global governance. Endowed with the power to create money and to set the rate at which it is borrowed and lent, individual central banks proceed to unabashedly use it whenever needed to slow down economic growth before unemployment drops too far and wages start to rise. The role of economic knowledge here is at best an apologetic one. The hard-nosed world of economic policy-making has never let the finer points of theory stand in its way, and its practitioners show scant concern with keeping up appearances of fealty to the doctrine. The theory of 'rational expectations' that was in vogue until recently claimed that actions of the central bank have no effect on real output, but the bankers never took this seriously. Nor was much heed paid to the famous Austrian laissez-faire economist Friedrich Hayek's call to denationalize money altogether and leave its creation to the private market.

Central bankers today make up a high priesthood that has cut itself loose from parliaments and politics. Their terms of office are also of papal length for fear of 'unsettling the markets', and elevation from priesthood to sainthood usually comes with retirement and subsequent entry through the pearly gates into Wall Street and other financial Meccas. Unlike the theorists, these men in dark suits understand that it is important to be pragmatic in discharging their responsibility to keep profits growing while warding off serious threats of collapse, and the lodestar of inflation-targeting is what appears to be 'working' for now. With pursed lips and furrowed brow, these mandarins appear periodically before the media to make oracular pronouncements to an awestruck congregation: 'disturbing signs of incipient inflation', 'alarming warnings of mounting inflationary pressure'—thinly veiled econospeak for rising wages. This redistribution away from profits to wages is what the priesthood must oversee and control by raising interest rates at the proper time to 'cool down the economy'. Economic theorists have spilled much ink and defaced much paper constructing models to determine the precise level of 'the non-accelerating-inflation rate of unemployment (Nairu)' below which wages start rising, but the priesthood has never let such theoretical disputations distract it.

The central banks, the IMF, the World Bank and the WTO together make up a gargantuan machinery of global economic control freed from any democratic interference or public accountability. No set of institutions in recent memory has claimed such prerogatives. One of the true puzzles of the new world order is the widespread indifference to the enormous accretion of power by this econopolice ruthlessly enforcing the rules of monetary policy, fiscal policy, trade policy, currency fluctuations and the movement of capital everywhere. In the modern era it has been the nation-state that has acted, on the one hand, to reconcile particular local forms of identification with the larger national identification and, on the other hand, to serve as a boundary membrane regulating exchanges with the outside. The nation-state is now under assault from both sides: global capital already traverses, indifferent to its boundaries, and particularized identifications are reconstituting themselves as 'primordial' against what is increasingly seen as a mere artefact. As a balancing act between different layers of identifications and the extraneous demands of the world market, the nation-state is increasingly being rendered redundant by mobile capital, on the one hand, and the newly reprimordialized identities, on the other. Meanwhile, the imperial economic formations have already consolidated themselves into the emerging superstate. Reclaiming global governance from these formations emerges as one of the most pressing political tasks of the twenty-first century: economics is far too important a matter to be left to the econocrats.

Islam

Ziauddin Sardar

Muslim societies everywhere are caught in a pincer movement: they are being squeezed, on the one hand, by forces of modernity and postmodernism and, on the other, by an emergent traditionalism that often takes a militant form. In the late 1940s and 1950s when most Muslim countries obtained their independence, modernization—or more specifically, development along Western patterns—was seen as a panacea for all social and economic ills. Indeed, most Muslim countries wholeheartedly embarked on a rapid course of modernization. But the strategies for modernization were, on the whole, out of step with the traditional societies they were attempting to change. Thus a rift developed between those who backed modernization and accompanying Westernization and those who were concerned about preserving the traditional culture, lifestyle and outlook of Muslim societies. As modernity loses ground both in the West and the non-West, postmodernism, and its accompanied globalization, is being projected as the new theory of salvation. Traditionalists are reacting against postmodernism just as vehemently, if not more so, as they did against modernity.

The modernist leaders, who took over from the departing colonial powers, maintained their hold on Muslim societies with excessive use of force, and by ruthlessly persecuting the traditional leadership as well as abusing and ridiculing traditional thought and everything associated with it. The economic and development policies these leaders pursued often ended in spectacular failure and allowed for the accumulation of national wealth in fewer and fewer hands. Postmodernism has further marginalized tradition and traditional cultures, creating a siege mentality in historic communities. These factors have contributed to the emergence, throughout the Muslim world, of a new form of militant traditionalism. To a very large extent, all Muslims are 'fundamentalist' in that they believe the Quran to be the literal Word of God. But the fundamentalism of militant traditionalism is of a special variety in that it insists on a single interpretation of Islam which can only be manifested in terms of an 'Islamic state'. In this framework, the integrated, holistic and God-centred world view of Islam is transformed into a totalitarian, theocratic world order, and a persuasive moral God is replaced by a coercive, political one.

The Muslim world thus finds itself caught between an intense struggle between the combined forces of an aggressively secular modernity and a relativistic postmodernism pitted against an equally aggressive traditionalism. This struggle is quite evident in countries like Egypt, Algeria and Sudan, as well as in states which until recently were not attracting media attention: Pakistan, Bangladesh, Malaysia, Saudi Arabia and even in the new Muslim republics of Central Asia. These forces are pulling Muslim societies in two different directions and are thus threatening them with rupture and fragmentation. The West must accept a certain responsibility for this state of affairs.

Modernity sees traditional societies as backward, 'living in the past'. The essential principles of tradition are seen as the cause of 'backwardness', just as their nature is seen to be incapable of change. Therefore the tradition of Muslim societies is a major hurdle towards development and 'modernization'. The classic texts of development, such as Daniel Lerner's *The Passing of Traditional Society* (1958), all argued that tradition must be abandoned, indeed suppressed where necessary, if the 'backward' societies of the Muslim world were to develop and 'catch up with the West'. In the name of development and progress, traditional cultures have been uprooted, displaced, suppressed and annihilated.

Postmodernism simply considers tradition to be dangerous, often associated with 'essentialism'—that is, harking back to some puritan notion of good society that may nor may not have existed in history.

Traditional communities, however, do not see tradition as something fixed in history, but rather as dynamic; they reinvent and innovate tradition constantly. Indeed, a tradition that does not change ceases to be a tradition. But traditions change in a specific way. They change within their own parameters, at their own speed and towards their chosen direction. There is good reason for this. If traditions were to vacate the space they occupy, they would cease to be meaningful. When tradition is cherished and celebrated the entire content of what is lauded can be changed. For example, if Muslims cherish the tradition of 'Islamic Law' (the Shariah), they can change most of its contents—such as various aspects of family law, or laws dealing with issues of crime and punishment to make them more just and humane—without fear of losing what they cherish most: the moral and ethical principles of Islam. Such change is then meaningful because it is integrated and enveloped by the continuing sense of identity that tradition provides. Thus, non-Western traditional communities do not think of tradition as something that will regress to pre-modern times; on the contrary, tradition will take them forward, with their identity intact, to a transmodern future.

What would be a transmodern future? To appreciate what is at issue here, it is necessary to distinguish between postmodernism and transmodernism. Postmodernism is what comes after modernity; it is post in terms of time; it is a natural conclusion of modernity. This is why it is sometimes described as 'the logic of late capitalism'. It represents a linear trajectory that starts with colonialism, continues with modernity and ends with postmodernity, or postmodernism. It is not surprising, then, that postmodernism and tradition are like two fuming bulls in a ring: they are inimically antagonistic to each other. Postmodernism states that all the big ideas that have shaped our society, the master narratives of Religion, Reason, Science, Tradition, History, Morality, Marxism etc., do not stand up to philosophical scrutiny. There is no such thing as Truth. Anything that claims to provide us with absolute truth is a sham. It must be abandoned. Moreover, postmodernism suggests, there is no ultimate Reality. We see what we want to see, what our position in time and place allows us to see, what our cultural and historic perceptions focus on. Instead of reality, what we have is an ocean of images: a world where all distinction between image and material reality has been lost.

In contrast, transmodernism goes beyond modernity; it transcends modernity in that it takes us trans—that is, through modernity into another state of being. Thus, unlike postmodernism, transmodernism is not a linear projection. We can best understand it with the aid of chaos theory. In all complex systems—societies, civilizations, ecosystems—many independent variables are interacting with each other in a great many ways. Chaos theory teaches us that complex systems have the ability to create order out of chaos. This happens at a balancing point, called the 'edge of chaos'. At the edge of chaos, the system is in a kind of suspended animation between stability and total dissolution into chaos. At this point, almost any factor can push the system into one or the other direction. However, complex systems at the edge of chaos have the ability to spontaneously self-organize themselves into a higher order; in other words the system 'evolves' spontaneously into a new mode of existence.

Transmodernism is the transfer of modernity from the edge of chaos into a new order of society. As such, transmodernism and tradition are not two opposing world views but a new synthesis of both. Traditional societies use their ability to change and become transmodern while remaining the same! Both sides of the equation are important here: change has to be made and accommodated; but the fundamental tenets of tradition, the source of its identity and sacredness, remain the same. So we may define a transmodern future as a synthesis between life-enhancing tradition—that is amenable to change and transition—and a new form of modernity that respects the values and lifestyles of traditional cultures. It is in this sense that traditional communities are not pre-modern but transmodern. Given that the vast majority of the Muslim world consists of traditional communities that see their tradition as a life-enhancing force, the vast majority of Muslims worldwide are thus more transmodern than pre-modern.

Most politicians, bureaucrats and decision makers do not appreciate this point. The reason for this is that when traditions change, the change is often invisible to outsiders. Therefore, observers can go on maintaining their modern or postmodern distaste for tradition irrespective of the counter-evidence before their very eyes. The contemporary world does provide opportunity for tradition to go on being what tradition has always been, an adaptive force. The problem is that no amount of adaptation, however much it strengthens traditional societies, actually frees them from the yoke of being marginal, misunderstood and misrepresented. It does nothing to dethrone the concept 'Tradition' as an idée fixe of Western society.

The West has always seen Islam through the lens of modernity and concluded that it is a negative, closed system. Nothing could be further from the truth. Islam is a dynamic, open system with a very large common ground with the West. But to appreciate this, Islam has to be seen from the perspective of transmodernism and understood with its own concepts and categories.

Consensual politics and modalities for adjusting to change are at the very heart of Islam. Consider the fundamental concepts and values of Islam which shape the goals of a Muslim society. These concepts generate the basic values of an Islamic culture and form a parameter within which an ideal Islamic society develops and progresses. These concepts include such notions as tawheed (unity), khilafah (trusteeship), ijtihad (sustained reasoning), ijma (consensus), shura (consultation) and istislah (public interest). Usually, the concept of tawheed is translated as unity of God. It becomes an all-embracing value when this unity is asserted in the unity of humanity, unity of man and nature, and the unity of knowledge and values. From tawheed emerges the concept of khilafah: that persons are not independent of God but are responsible and accountable to God, as well as to the community as a whole, for all their thoughts and actions. Political change in state and society is brought about by the use of ijtihad, which has been used throughout Muslim history to adjust to change, innovate tradition and introduce progressive ideas in the community. The community has to be consulted on the basis of the notion of shura, and its consensus—ijma—is needed to give legitimacy to change and innovation. At all times, change has to reflect public interest—istislah. Given such a matrix of fundamental concepts and values, it is difficult to perceive Islam as a closed system or a negative, regressive world view.

The brutal force with which modernity was introduced in the Muslim world, and the savage way in which tradition was suppressed, has meant that Muslim societies have not been able to practise these fundamental values of Islam. The perennial desire of all Muslim societies is to go forward to the practice of these values and take a quantum leap from instrumental modernity to enlightened transmodernism. Such fundamental concepts of Islam as ijtihad (reasoned innovation), ijma (consensus) and shura (consultation) have to be used to develop contemporary models of governance and social change that are based on the needs and aspirations of ordinary Muslims.

In developing a transmodern framework for discussion, it is important to think of the Muslim world beyond the manacles of governments policies. Most Muslim countries are governed by ultra modernists or ultra traditionalists—neither of whom have any understanding of transmodernism. We need to go beyond decision makers and involve ordinary people—scholars, writers, activists, academics, journalists—in our discussions. We will discover that most people have a critical but positive attitude towards the West. But European analyses of Islam must rise above such one-dimensional theses as the 'clash of civilizations' or 'the end of history'. Transmodernism is not about conflict, or a false sense of aggrandizement, but about a positive symbiosis between Islam and the West. Its aim must be to replace homogenizing globalization with what the Malaysian thinker and statesman Anwar Ibrahim has called 'global convivencia'—that is, a more harmonious and enriching experience of living together.

Knowledge Systems

Frédérique Apffel-Marglin

Postmodernity has put the nails in the coffin of what Bruno Latour has called 'the modern constitution' as far as the humanities and social sciences are concerned. Quantum physics has done the same for the natural sciences. The universe that the public Newton had crafted so brilliantly (while the secret Newton rejected it) has collapsed. We now know that we are not the dominators of an inert mechanistic nature, but part of an interconnected living whole. As many have pointed out, this new cosmology rejoins the visions of many non-modern peoples, and, as Latour has pithily put it, 'we have never been modern', we just dreamed that we were, deluding ourselves that our non-human companions were just inert objects.

The news has not trickled down yet to everyone, by far. Such news is subversive of the status quo and many are suddenly afflicted with partial deafness. The economists in particular tend to blithely go on as they are wont to do, ever refining their mathematical tools to entreat the great God of modernity, 'The Economy', to answer their prayers. The faithful believers continue to pray to development and free trade, finding ever-renewed ways of worshipping these messengers of paradise around the corner. Their faith is ever fanned by their romantic notions of 'the benefits of development, free trade and progress'. The universities continue to be structured by a touching faith in objectivity, value neutrality and rationality. Each discipline jealously defends its turf, preparing the young to be efficient servants of the system. But there are rumblings in the corridors.

Outside, these rumblings are sometimes loud and ominous. Many have responded to the fundamentalism of the modern constitution—which valiantly carried aloft the banner of Europeans' age-old faith in the One Truth, decked out in the newfangled garments of value-free science—with their own brand of fundamentalism, fighting fire with fire. They have found allies in powerful places, since like the fundamentalism of scientific universalism, religious fundamentalism is tailor-made to give strength to the nation-state.

Others turn their sights towards what Foucault predicted as the coming revolt of 'subjugated knowledges'. Many who are not seduced by the siren call of religious fundamentalism are looking in that general direction. As Jit Uberoi reminds us in *The Other Mind of Europe*, subjugated knowledges exist both in the North and in the South. For example, it is well to remember that the mechanistic universe and the scientific method were the winning ticket in the seventeenth century, legitimizing the new nation-state and providing the certainty that most (powerful) Europeans saw as necessary for the re-establishment of social order. However, many other radically different cosmologies, world views and knowledges which blossomed during the Renaissance did not altogether disappear, in spite of the bloody doings of both Catholic and Protestant Inquisitions. Many went underground. Others proposed their own version of science, one that did not separate the knower from the known or relegate experience to the segregated domain of the arts. One such was Goethe, whose writings on an alternative science in the late eighteenth century were more important in his own view than his literary output. Goethe's views have been carried down the centuries to our own days, particularly within the anthroposophy started by the German mystic Rudolph Steiner. The contemporary quantum physicist Arthur Zajonc is a fine example of this alternative Northern way of knowing.

We need to spot the invisible reefs lying just below the surface of the beckoning waters of subjugated knowledges. An obvious treacherous reef is to project on to them the dominant conception of knowledge as an exclusively or predominantly cognitive enterprise. The modern great 'breach of faith towards everything that is'—to borrow the Indian philosopher Gopinath Kaviraj's resonant words—leads to the will-to-think-out the world in which objects are appropriated by rational concepts, the inevitable products of Descartes's thinking thing. The mechanistic universe is a gigantic abstraction: force, shape, mass, motion—a 'Triste (zone) Tempérée' drained of colour, life, feeling or purpose. Full-bodied lived experience must be heroically bracketed to reach the sublime desert of abstract thought. This move, deep-rooted in Western metaphysics, received its fundamentalist twist in the sixteenth and seventeenth centuries. These two centuries, gripped by religious terror allied to political machinations, could not find their way out of the bloody conflicts generated by two equally dogmatic religio-political camps. Social order could not be imagined without certainty. The emerging nation-states needed certainty if they were to inherit the power and legitimacy of the Church. Certainty was reinvented, built from the ground up on new foundations. It was constructed on the arid soil of a radical cognitive individualism and a radical anthropocentrism. Even the paragon of this new era, the much celebrated Newton, lionized in his own lifetime, could not in his heart of hearts, adhere to a totally predictable but de-spirited mechanical universe. In his voluminous alchemical writings, which he kept secret, gravity is a spiritual and moral force.

Full-bodied lived experience cannot, of course, be magically suspended for the purposes of acquiring certainty. It never has been. Universal truth, and with it certainty, was gained at the price of radical decontextualization. Feminists and other critics of science have made abundantly clear that this new knowledge was deeply enmeshed in the time, the place, the gender and class . . . of its creators. The fiction of an unsituated, transcendent mind, unaffected by its body, its historical context and by lived experience in general was useful at a time when talk of religion and politics was a risky business. Most of Europe was engulfed in bloody religio-political conflicts soon after Luther nailed his theses on the door of his church in 1520, until the end of the Thirty Years War in 1648. Talk of religion and politics could be dangerous to one's health. Alternative ways of knowing had become heretical with the fundamentalist turn of both Protestant and Catholic Inquisitions. The new 'natural philosophy' (the word 'science' made its appearance in the eighteenth century) did not threaten the post-Council-of-Trent Christian cosmology—both Protestant and Catholic—which had drained all spirit from this world. The new knowledge was radically materialist, relegating God to an other-worldly transcendental realm. This contrasted with most other knowledges of the time that did not separate spirit from matter. This explains its eventual acceptance by all concerned, as well as Newton's secrecy about his true, but heretical, passion.

Descartes's transcendent *res cogitans*, thinking thing, had to await Robert Boyle to operationalize it. Boyle did so by inviting a select group of educated and trustworthy gentlemen (women, by nature, could not be trusted) to witness his experiments with the air pump in a public space—thus clearly marking it as distinct from the heresy of alchemy, a suspect and maverick science. In that public space they were entreated to freely dispute about what they had seen, and urged to arrive at a consensus concerning the 'matter of fact'. This freedom, however, was carefully orchestrated. It strictly excluded talk of religion, values, politics and personal experience. In the 1640s such topics were just too explosive. The language to be used was to sound as if nature itself spoke through the experiment, since to include the lived experience of even wealthy, educated and trustworthy gentlemen was to risk unmanageable dissension. Voila! the birth of the division between fact and value, objectivity, secularism, the institutionalization of the unsituated transcendent intellect, the seed of the later professions.

In 1660 the Royal Society came into existence—the Academie Française being created around the same time—with Boyle a central member of the former. King James promptly financed the new institution, the forum and support for the new knowledge which had not found favour in the Church-dominated universities. The nation-state, emerging after the Thirty Years War, had found the knowledge to suit its centralizing impetus. In short order, the new science displaced most rivals. This victory conspired to erase the memory of the deeply political nature of grounding this new knowledge in the no-man's land of a carefully crafted, so-called objectivity. The new cognitive individualism synchronized with growing economic individualism and emerging political individualism, all three orchestrated in the emerging bureaucratic organization of state controls.

The very success of the new knowledge has had enormous consequences. One such is the terrible amnesia about our mimetic engulfment in the world of humans and non-humans. Mimetic engulfment refers to that 'primal level of experience in which we are immediately involved as one self in one community of beings with which we identify, and goodness is effective and vital involvement in the world' (Wilshire 1990). The breach of faith with everything that is—in Gopinath Kaviraj's formulation of the ontology of modern science—erases the awareness of the primacy of mimetic engulfment. With the victorious march of materialism, Descrates's arguments for God were forgotten as were his other postulates. The self became only an ego operating a mechanical body. The ego, precariously suspended from the thin thread of the transcendental intellect, had to generate its own sense of strength out of the arena open to it, namely by exerting its power on the 'real world'. This objectified physical and social real world was transmuted into a gigantic arena for intervention, needed by the ego to confirm its own existence and value. Hence the modern mania for 'improving' everything. When the humdrum surroundings have been exhaustively and exhaustingly upgraded, we are unable to rest content and contemplate the fruits of our labours. We must forever discover new and improved things from germ-lines engineering and the 'improvement' of the genes of our descendants to space tourism, all the while shrouding these self-obsessed adventures in the secular nostrums of helping mankind.

Postmodern critiques have deconstructed the real world, the self and even the body. But this move has enthroned the Text, accompanied by the intellect freed from its illusions about Reality.

They sit in a mirrored closet imagined as an endlessly refracted world. The ego continues to be in command, speaking an increasingly sybilline language. To open the door and step outside requires us to lose our minds and be engulfed in the primacy of being and beings. This requires of us a humility, an ego effacement, difficult to attain within the current knowledge forms, whether modernist or postmodernist. To convert objects into beings requires of us a song, requires us to be empathetic, requires us to relate to other beings in a non-exploitative way. It foregrounds the centrality of silence, of contemplation, of reverence, of receptivity, of knowing how to nurture the beings of the world and of knowing how to let ourselves be nurtured by them in turn, as the Peruvian organization PRATEC, the Andean Project of Peasant Technologies, has so movingly put it when speaking of the Andean region. Eduardo Grillo of PRATEC speaks of it thus: 'Here, conversation cannot be reduced to dialogue, to the word, as in the modern Western world; rather conversation engages us vitally: one converses with the whole body. To converse is to show oneself reciprocally, it is to share, it is to commune, it is to dance to the rhythm which at every instant synchronises with the annual cycle of life.'

Further Reading

Apffel-Marglin, Frédérique, with PRATEC. 1998. *The Spirit of Regeneration: Andean Culture Confronting Western Notions of Development*. London: Zed Books.

Berman, Morris. 1981. *The Reenchantment of the World*. Ithaca and London: Cornell University Press.

Latour, Bruno. 1993. *We Have Never Been Modern*, translated by Catherine Porter. Cambridge, Massachusetts: Harvard University Press.

Toulmin, Stephen. 1990. *Cosmopolis: The Hidden Agenda of Modernity*. The Free Press.

Uberoi, J.P. Singh. 1984. *The Other Mind of Europe: Goethe as a Scientist*. Delhi: Oxford University Press.

Wilshire, Bruce. 1990. *The Moral Collapse of the University: Professionalism, Purity, and Alienation.* Albany, NY: SUNY Press.

Zajonc, Arthur. 1993. *Catching the Light: The Intertwined History of Light and Mind.* Bantam Books.

Landmines

Vinay Lal

One might suppose from the American hullabaloo over stealth fighters, Patriot missiles and 'smart bombs', and all the noise over 'weapons of mass destruction', that the greater number of casualties in war ensues when states conduct spectacular air campaigns, unleash the devastating force of modern military technology or otherwise seek to decapitate entire populations. For a brief moment in the mid 1990s, as the Campaign to Ban Landmines won the Nobel Peace Prize and Princess Diana posed alongside victims of landmines, it appeared as though the world had been brought to the belated recognition that in the—often more significant—byways and alleyways of warfare, death takes place slowly, tortuously, with little fanfare and even less visibility, and in steady and alarming numbers. Imagine a farmer who, having gone to sow his land, gets blown to pieces, or a group of children on their way to school who trigger an explosion that takes the life of one of them and removes the legs of another. Or a one-legged Angolan woman, Chisola Jorgeta Poza, who carries on her head a load of 50 kilos of grain and moves at a pace that gives a new meaning to fitness walking.

Even after the weapons have been surrendered, and the soldiers have taken their leave of the land, the sentinel of death still keeps watch. This ever-watchful guard, merchant of destruction, is the puny and seemingly insignificant landmine, once characterized by a Khmer Rouge general as 'the perfect soldier—ever courageous, never sleeps, and never misses'. In a recently published work, *Landmines: A Deadly Legacy*, Kenneth Anderson describes landmines as a 'weapon of mass destruction in slow motion'. As he puts it dramatically, mines 'recognize no ceasefire', and often they 'maim or kill the children and grandchildren of the soldiers who laid them'. Mines were once tactical, primarily defensive, weapons; today, argues Anderson, they are an 'offensive, strategic weapon often aimed deliberately at civilians in order to empty territory, destroy food sources, create refugee flows, or simply spread terror'. They are the most apposite weapons of late modernity: insidious, deceptive, mass-produced, what the United States Army calls 'force multipliers', which bestow unique battlefield advantages upon thinly scattered forces armed with them.

These often long-forgotten mines have been assiduously performing their appointed task, insistently suggesting to us that it is not only flashy items in the arsenal of powerful nations that cause mayhem in the lives of ordinary people and serving as a poignant reminder of the fact that the little things in life might come to haunt us. To gauge the enormity of the problem, and the extent of the complicity of 'civilized' nations in contributing to the manufacture, sale and use of these little merchants of war, consider that at least 110 million unexploded mines lie scattered in over sixty countries. Cambodia, Laos, Vietnam, Afghanistan, Ethiopia, Somalia, Sudan, Mozambique, Angola, Bosnia-Herzegovina, Croatia, Kuwait and Iraq (especially Iraqi Kurdistan) are described as 'landmine disasters', while in numerous other areas, such as the coastal areas of Nicaragua, parts of El Salvador and the border between India and Pakistan, the problem is of acute proportions. In Cambodia and Afghanistan, nearly 25 per cent of the total land area is heavily mined. In most of the acutely affected countries, agriculture still predominates, but much of the arable land is either mined or bordered by mined areas; these are also the countries that, severely hampered by underdevelopment, lack the resources required to tackle the problem.

There may be as many as 30,000 casualties annually from landmines: in Somalia, as many as 75 per cent of the victims have been civilians, while in one hospital along the Pakistan–Afghanistan border 25 per cent of the victims were children under sixteen. Amputation of one or both legs is the most common consequence of stepping on a mine. In the mid 1990s, the ratio of amputees— bizarrely, some by choice—to the general population in the United States was one to 22,000; in Cambodia, one in every 236 people was an amputee, while a more recent estimate suggests a figure of one in 384, and a figure of one in 334 for Angola, another country which serves as a textbook example of the perilous hazards of uncleared mines. In the protracted conflicts in these and some other developing countries, landmines predictably became the favoured weapon. An anti-personnel mine costs as little as $3, a relative pittance even for an insurgent group conducting a guerilla war; the heavier anti-tank mine can be obtained for less than $100. Their detection is difficult, and removal fraught with the greatest risks: therefore military forces are drawn to their usage. Despite the UN Convention governing the use of landmines, these weapons are not used in the 'prescribed manner': both the presence and absence of such standards are measures of our debasement. One favoured form of improvisation by military forces has been 'multiple stacking of mines'. An anti-tank mine requires greater pressure to explode than an anti-personnel mine: to obviate this problem, anti-tank mines are placed below anti-personnel mines, and a mere 230 grams of pressure, caused by the footfalls of a child, can detonate the stack. One protocol might be easily observed, such as marking the location of a mine, while another might be just as easily flouted, such as burying anti-personnel mines two- and three-deep.

The use of mines in warfare has, as is now conceded, vastly proliferated since the Second World War. In the Italian campaign of 1944, the proportion of military casualties attributable to mines was 4.4 per cent; in the Vietnam War, this figure went up to 33 per cent, while in the civil war fought in El Salvador in the 1980s, as many as 90 per cent of the casualties are said to have been caused by mines. Nearly twenty million mines were utilized during the two-decade-old Angolan civil war. The cost of clearing a

$3 mine can run to as much as $1000; worldwide clearance may entail a bill of $400 billion, for which purpose even the wealth of Bill Gates and George Soros will not suffice. Mine-clearing tools are ineffective against mines that require two compressions instead of one: once one has stepped on a mine and nothing has happened, the person behind him assumes it is safe; and when he steps on it, the explosion takes place. Mine detectors, moreover, work only when the metal content of the mine is high enough to allow detection, and manufacturers of mines have in consequence markedly increased the plastic content of new mines. Corporations are quick to innovate; they are triggered to exact profit.

The manufacture and sale of landmines is a transnational, multicultural business in the true fashion of the day, and present and former fascist and authoritarian states rule the roost. The largest manufacturers are Italy, China and the former Soviet Union, though the mines laid in Angola, which is not a manufacturer, emanate from sixty-five countries. The United States, a large producer and exporter of mines in the heyday of the Vietnam War, ceased to be a major player by the late 1970s, but by American government estimates, 15 per cent of the mines buried in the earth today are of American provenance. That seems about right for the quintessential rogue state. The half-a-billion dollars or less spent worldwide on all mines represents an unmentionably minuscule fraction of the annual worldwide expenditure on defence, and explains why the Americans, accustomed to self-aggrandizement and profit-making on a grand scale, withdrew from the trade in anti-personnel mines, though much was made of the conscience of America. The United States remains a hold-out to the new international treaty banning landmines: while condemning chemical and biological warfare, it remains largely impervious to these, equally indiscriminate, forms of slaughter. Indeed, the firm Alliant Techsystems even lobbied for the exemption of its anti-personnel mines from the self-imposed 1992 American moratorium on their export on the grounds 'that they incorporate self-destruct mechanisms'. The unreliability of self-destruct mechanisms aside, an exemption for such mines would confer an advantage upon those American corporations that exercise a near monopoly in pioneering these new landmines. There is the additional consideration that landmines remain an inexpensive way for poorly funded armies in the Third World, who have almost nothing to match American firepower, to hobble American armies on the battlefield. Wounded soldiers, in the modern calculus, are far more disabling to an army than its dead: they require medical attention, disrupt operations and create a detrimental psychological effect on their comrades.

As America's share in the world market for mines began to recede, other countries stepped in to fill the gap: arms manufacturers abhor a vacuum. Italian companies have been pioneers in the production of anti-detectable mines; they have also been the leaders in the market for 'designer' and 'smart' mines, producing mines in 'custom colours to blend into all terrains', and mines booby-trapped with anti-tampering devices. The Misar SB-33 has all these features: it is also blast-resistant, constructed almost entirely of plastic, and can be sown in the ground or scattered from the air; and so it defies all countermeasures. The cool, matter-of-fact attitude with which this business is pursued is nowhere more clearly in evidence than in the marketing of the American Claymore M18 mine, more frequently copied than any other mine worldwide, which bears the useful inscription 'FRONT TOWARD ENEMY.' Even self-destruction must have its limits.

The very companies that manufacture mines also provide, not unexpectedly, expertise and tools for their removal. Conventional Munitions System (CMS), an America-based commercial company specializing in mine clearance, is owned by Deutsche Aerospace, which in turn is a subsidiary of Daimler-Benz; another subsidiary of Deutsche Aerospace, however, is Messerschmitt-Bolkow-Blohm, which manufacturers state-of-the-art scatterable landmines. Such 'cradle-to-grave battlefield services' are not offered by Daimler-Benz alone: the Royal Ordnance, a British firm, manufacturers landmines besides offering clearance services. Their mines were sown in Kuwait; it was also in Kuwait that the company won a $90 million contract in 1991 to help remove those and other mines. The business in mines replicates the general pattern of aid that Western countries have been following in their relations with 'underdeveloped' or 'developing' nations: large amounts of weaponry is sold to poor nations, and when these arms have been used to create havoc and destruction, the Western nations step in to offer aid, a package that includes a generous amount of new weaponry. That is the recipe for repairing economies. The hand that feeds is also the hand that kills.

The clearance of mines, as noted earlier, is an exorbitantly expensive business, and economics dictates that only a few countries can avail of mine-clearing equipment or the skills of experts. Oil-rich and tyrannical Kuwait spent $700 million on clearance experts and numerous squads of lower-paid mine sweepers; meanwhile, in impoverished Angola, where mines outnumber people by a ratio of 2:1, even the location of fewer than 10 per cent of the mines is known. The political economy of mines has its bizarre, even postmodern, features. In Angola, mines are traded for food, and in a portion of the Lunda Sul Province, the presence of a leper colony kept the area from being mined. We may have to be diseased to avoid the modern forms of illness and contamination. Though the sacred and protective verses from Pali scriptures tattooed on the chest of Vorn, a young man living in Beng Ampil in Cambodia, did not save him from having his stomach ripped open and his intestines spilled on to the ground when he accidentally stepped on to a mine, the mine clearance specialists from Conventional Munitions System see themselves as modern-day magicians, 'artists with supernatural powers of survival', risk-takers who walk the thin line between life and death. Sacred texts wither before mines, and it is not the healing power of the shaman but the agility of the athlete to which the anthropologist must give his attention. In the long run, the test of whether we can constitute ourselves as a civilized race of people may be determined less by the large peace treaties—grandiose affairs of state—that the appointed leaders sign than by our active recognition that to neglect the little things is to abandon our deep ecological responsibility to the world.

Further Reading

The Arms Project of Human Rights Watch and Physicians for Human Rights. 1993. *Landmines: A Deadly Legacy*. New York: Human Rights Watch.

Winslow, Philip C. 1997. *Sowing the Dragon's Teeth: Landmines and the Global Legacy of War*. Boston: Beacon Press.

Laughter

Barry Sanders

Do not do it! the rabbis commanded. When you feel the urge to laugh, the fourth-century rabbi Chanina Bar Papa counselled, go read the Torah. Before you get too frisky, let the feeling pass. Get serious. The Church Fathers too urged good Christians to keep it serious, dead serious. 'Truly it is not for us,' announced St John Chrysostom, the most famous of the Greek Fathers, in *On Priesthood* (AD 390), 'to pass our time in laughter.' Christ, he and others pointed out, never laughed. Christ smiled, He may have even teased, but he definitely did not laugh. And Christians should follow Christ's sombre lead. Hence Luke 6:21, instructing Christians on the wisdom of putting off any such urges: 'Blessed are you that weep, for you shall laugh.' Five verses later, Chrysostom temporizes the warning—'Woe to you that laugh *now*, for you shall mourn and weep'—in order to locate laughter where it belongs, as an activity best postponed for much later—in heaven. There, every day, filled with bliss and joy, will pass as a never-ending parade of Sundays. Thus, Christians make a particular mockery of heaven by laughing on the Lord's Day, on Sunday.

Those admonitions against laughter—both Judaic and Christian—may seem odd, since laughter inserts itself into biblical narrative as a miracle. It is given to humankind by a woman. The story unfolds rather early in Genesis: God arrives to tell Abraham and his wife Sarah that they will soon bear a child. Sarah can only laugh in disbelief. After all, she is ninety years old, and her

husband a ripe one hundred years old. God scolds Sarah, promising
to keep His word and convert her scornful laugh into one of joy.
The following spring, Sarah indeed gives birth to a son, Isaac,
whose name in Hebrew, Yitzchak, means 'he laughs'. Sarah's
announcement of the event stands out as the only instance in the
Old Testament of joyous laughter: 'And Sarah said, "God hath
made laughter for me; everyone who hears will laugh with me"'
(Genesis 21:16). Thus Sarah establishes a covenant, a bond of
giddy, optimistic laughter, with every person, friend and stranger
alike, who hears the news of her miracle. A few short verses later,
she will learn something perhaps more important—that in order to
keep this gift of laughter (Isaac), she will have to sacrifice it, offer
it up no matter the dire expectations or consequences.

Patronymic stories play key roles in the Bible; they unravel the
complexities of life in a single word or name. The birth of Isaac
illuminates the basic Judaic attitude towards laughter. Laughter
that wells out of joy, *simcha*, cannot be initiated on earth by
humans. It can only be received, like breath itself, as a miraculous
gift from God. Isaac is truly God's son, but he is not the Word
incarnate. Rather, he is laughter embodied—created out of a
second, more miraculous breath, the breath that exists prior to,
and functions as something more universal than, the artefact of
language.

The holiness of laughter stands out even more clearly in the
ancient world. For Aristotle too, laughter arrives as a divine gift,
bestowed by the gods on to newborns on the fortieth day of their
lives. At that instant the infant produces its first laugh, with a blast
of air so hearty and so hot it animates the infant's soul, moving
that little creature from a mere human into a human being.
Laughter, that noisy pest, separates us from all the other animals
by its power to ensoul us. That's why Aristotle calls us 'animal
ridens', the beast who laughs—laughter is the *only* distinguishing
characteristic that elevates humans, and sets us apart from every
other creature in the kingdom. Since laughter marked animals as
humans and gods as divine, each time we mortals laugh, we forge
a connection with Mount Olympus. Laughter transports us. Joy

marks life as special, different and, most of all, heroic.

The first laugh recorded in the West sounds a harsh and aggressive note. It comes early in Western literature, in the first book of the Iliad. Homer recounts it in a most nasty and annoying passage. Because of his ability to work with clay and metal—to manipulate fire—the gods designate Hephaestus as wine-server. He fabricates the goblets and pitcher and tray. It makes sense that he should serve the wine as well. But he does not always move with a gainly gait, for Zeus once tossed him off Mount Olympus for siding with his wife, Hera, in a domestic squabble. Landing awkwardly on his leg on the Island of Lemnos, Hephaestus forever walks with a limp. And so, Homer describes Hephaestus on one occasion as offering wine to the assembled gods and spilling it all over himself. The gods find his fumbling attempt hilarious and break out into 'unquenchable laughter'—so hard and so loud that poor Hephaestus, feeling the greatest ridicule, runs off to hide in the woods.

Hephaestus's story encapsulates the history of laughter. The gods have snatched laughter away from him—from the man who knows fire so intimately—shaped it into a caustic weapon and fired it back in his face as ridicule. Since Hephaestus has a hard time keeping his balance anyway, the gods have an easy time knocking him down. If only Hephaestus could see that the Olympians have presented him with a test: He can never be regarded as healthy unless he can join his tormentors in their raucous laughter. To withstand ridicule, he must first laugh the attack off. He must turn the situation to his own advantage and allow the caustic laughter to cauterize his own wounds. Fight fire with fire. Get clever in return. Then his attackers might choose to see him as hearty and healthy, that is, as a whole person. The gods turn to their own divine unit, in the desire to reshape a fallen god, and they do it by co-opting Hephaestus's own element, fire—the fire of laughter. At the moment, however, Hephaestus can neither physically nor metaphorically stand up to their abuse. His lameness handicaps him in the most profound, spiritual way.

A lesson from history: breath, that most invisible, most evanescent of things, may be the most powerful weapon we possess. Certainly, joyous laughter, a gift from God and the gods, becomes much more entertaining and interesting as a weapon. And that's why those hostile, aggressive, sometimes nasty, sometimes downright nasty, but always unpredictable volleys of laughter caught the attention of virtually every philosopher and writer and comic. We delight in inflicting pain, in playing tricks, in plotting practical jokes that often spell the humiliating downfall of our neighbours. That agon, between joker and victims, keeps society dynamic. Plato analyses the process. He says that, for our own psychic well-being, we absolutely need to see our neighbours stumble and fall. We take special delight in the misfortunes of our closest, supposed friends, because in our hearts we secretly compete with them. In fact, if those we know did not stumble or fall, we would go out of our way to trip them up or knock them over.

At the same time, it gives us pain to see the grand failures and the small falls of our friends, but the pleasure always outweighs the pain in what Plato calls moments of 'mixed pleasure'. We laugh and cry at the same time, an experience so common we even have a name for those ambiguous emotional outbursts—bitter-sweet tears. (The Indo-European root of laughter, *kleg*, following that same mixed pattern, also produces the word cry.) Every time our neighbour stumbles it makes us feel superior, it elevates us over our rivals. As Thomas Hobbes put it, those stumblers allow us to experience a rush of 'sudden glory'.

What motivates us in the battle to outpace our neighbours is, for Plato, the most lethal emotion—envy. We desire to be taller, stronger, faster, wealthier, more attractive and more established than the person next door. We crave the handsome husband, the beautiful wife, the fancy car. We envy the higher status those things confer. And if we cannot have them, by God, our rivals should not have them either. I pray for their downfall! I demand their ruination! When they do not fall of their own accord, we trip them up, play tricks on them, tell jokes about them, make them the laughing stock of the entire schoolyard, factory, office, neighbourhood.

The greatest fall of all, however, is not physical, but one that we can only call metaphoric. In the absence of divine intervention, of some cosmic act that could set the scales of justice even—that is, a stroke of divine retribution that would destroy our neighbour's new Corvette, for instance—we humiliate and retaliate by cracking jokes about our rivals to their faces in front of a group. And the weapon, instead of the traditional stumbling blocks like the big foot in the pathway or a banana peel on the step, is a grand slap to the victim's psyche: a punchline that reveals to everyone present the victim's deepest, most closely guarded weaknesses. The most sophisticated, literate, most civilized shape of laughter, then, comes in the form of a joke. The joker acts out a ritual murder, in which victims crack up, split their sides, keel over—die laughing.

The model for aggressive joke telling appears as early as the Middle Ages, in Chaucer's 'The Miller's Tale'. The fat Miller, envious that the skinny Reeve has a beautiful wife, tells an elaborate and extended joke in front of the assembled pilgrims, designed to humiliate the Reeve and, as a result, lower his status. At the same time the Miller, by displaying his sharp wit in telling a terrific joke, raises his own status in the eyes of the other pilgrims. Voila: in a single stroke—the punchinesss of the punchline—joke telling sets the pans of justice, so out of balance at the beginning of the encounter, back into equilibrium.

The Reeve tries to laugh it off—finally, *has* to laugh it off, if he hopes to enjoy any status at all with his fellow pilgrims. And that's the point: in the end, laughter aims at leveling all barriers, exposing all hypocrites, righting all inequities. A tall order for this outlander sense, this powerful oddity called a sense of humour. One must take care, though, not to get too cocky, too righteous—remember the rabbis—or too caustic—remember the Greek gods—but with just the right amount of force, against just the right target, laughter can effect great change.

Just try it.

Literacy

Barry Sanders

'Literacy' (from Latin *lettera*) refers to letters. It has nothing to do with television or movies or numbers. Strictly speaking, terms like 'computer literacy' make no sense. One's ability to depress keys, to manipulate programs, to surf the Web with ease and abandon—none of those functions or operations has anything but the slightest and most tangential connection with alphabetic competence. Word processing is the closest the machine comes to embracing letters, and even then putting the two together—computers and the alphabet—stretches the meaning of literacy. Indeed, in order to work, the computer dismantles language by reducing it to a series of electronic bits.

The word literacy has a quite strange and fairly recent history. It first appears in America, and only a relatively short time ago, specifically in 1883, in the *New England Journal of Education*: 'Massachusetts is the first state in the Union in literacy in its native population.' Two years before Mark Twain published *The Adventures of Huckleberry Finn*, America had created a new category of citizen—the non-literate, the person who, like some early medieval peasant, or Huck's pal Jim, has no purchase on the world of letters. In launching this new concept, literacy, the *New England Journal* used two phrases relevant for all future discussions of the idea: 'the first state' and 'native population'.

Literacy cultivates power. It encourages comparisons to determine just who is more adept at inscribing words. Who has read more books; what schools have scored higher on tests; what critics know the most references—preferably the most arcane references? Literacy reduces book learning to a competitive struggle, and thus, even in 1883, New England can raise concerns over which state ranks as number one. Which leads to the second term: 'native population'. In medieval Europe, the Church controlled literacy by owning all the manuscripts as well as all the instruction. In America, the white, notably male population exerted that same control over the disenfranchised—women, Indians and blacks. In 1883, the *New England Journal* needed precise literacy levels because legislatures had already begun to allocate money for reading and writing campaigns in public schools. Cambridge, Massachusetts, the home of the first college and the first printing press in the colonies, could rightly crow about its commitment to the printed word.

Around this same time, both in England and in America, a group of new words found their way into the language—eugenics, race, intelligence, agnosticism—to satisfy a growing nineteenth-century obsession for ordering and measuring. Social scientists could reify abstract ideas of race or intelligence, and rank people along a standard scale that typically placed whites on top and all others, in descending order of the darkness of their skin or inferiority of their genes, running towards the bottom. Literacy belongs to that family of terms. One might well ask, however, how did people refer to the skills of reading and writing—or their lack—before the coining of the new word literacy? Or, to turn things around, what did the word literacy do to alter those two conceptual schemes, reading and writing?

In the West, at least, one can talk about the real beginnings of a lay literacy—that is, an ability to read and write by those outside the Church—around the late twelfth century. And yet, as late as the end of the fifteenth century, reading and interpreting lines of prose still belonged primarily to the clergy—to priests and monks. From the seventh to the seventeenth century, the universities—closed during those one thousand years to women—taught something called Learned Latin, a language only written down and never spoken. The arduous task of writing the vernacular, that is, of listening to dictation and making those words hold fast on parchment, rested with scribes, who would later make copies of their work. Seated in their little carrels inside the monasteries, they recited the lines of poetry or prose out loud to themselves—buzzing and humming like so many bees—in an attempt to more easily copy the words of one manuscript on to another. But no one would ever refer to a scribe, or to a dictator—even to a dictator with patronage, an 'author', like Chaucer—as characters who had moved into some privileged category called literacy. In the sense that any scribe or dictator really knew letters, and there is some reason to believe that the best copiers were illiterate, the medieval world felt content to simply use the term literate, 'educated' or 'learned'.

By the middle of the fifteenth century, a wide enough divide separated the written word from spoken sounds, at least in England, that chroniclers began to use the term literate to designate readers and writers from mere speakers and listeners. An illiterate was one who stood outside this new alphabetic regime, and thus outside any sphere of power. By the early seventeenth century, literate quite specifically means knowing literature of all kinds: a state for the first time not just different from but superior to orality. Witness this line from the English writer and translator George Chapman, from *Caesar and Pompey* (1631): 'The Aegean Sea, that doth divide Europe from Asia. (This sweet literate world from the Barbarian . . .)'

But literacy as a concept disembedded from a group of people, a concept that can be studied and analysed, one to which numbers can be attached, and winners and losers assigned, is wholly American. Literacy makes out of the tremendous power of reading and writing a commodity, a process that can be taught in six or seven or nine easy steps, an instrumentality that spells the beginning, in a real sense, of the death of reading and writing. With hindsight, of course, one might make out in the idea of literacy the early outlines of 'word processing'.

We must remember that America was founded by followers of Protestantism, a religion that relies for its efficacy on a congregation's ability to read the Bible for themselves, without interpretation from some priestly authority. Every country, when it decides to leave orality behind for the world of literacy, does so only at some point well along in its history. From its first day, however, this Protestant experiment called America derived its moral, ethical and certainly its religious success, in great part, from insisting on the importance of the book. In colonial America, it was not enough to simply own a Bible, to walk around with a copy, to riffle through its pages or even to have a few passages by memory. One had to read the Bible—most typically out loud— from cover to cover. Start at the beginning and move to the end and then start all over again. This reading was not a luxury, not a pastime and definitely not an entertainment. This reading was serious business, the most serious of undertakings: It could rescue a person's soul from certain and eternal damnation. One could not hope for anything more from a stack of inert paper. And still, even with such importance accorded to reading—and in some ways to writing, as well—no one in colonial America had the need for a concept so abstract and so fuzzy as literacy.

They did not need it, perhaps, because early Americans could speak of a deep and abiding love of reading. Imagine a country in which one of its principal founding fathers protests: 'I cannot live without books.' Thomas Jefferson made that confession in a letter to another founding father, John Adams, who in turn commented on the unusual commitment the country as a whole showed toward the book: 'A native American who cannot read and write is as rare as a comet or an earthquake.' (Note that the line once again refers to 'native Americans', that is, to white English-Americans.) Even those Puritans who had trouble reading and writing, who could manage letters very little or not at all, still regarded the book as the principal way for every person to acquire knowledge and wisdom. Well, for almost every person.

Protestants, following Martin Luther's instruction, believed in the salvation of the soul through each individual's ability to read the word of God himself or herself. For the Puritans, literacy constituted a kind of moral species. In the colonies, politicians found literacy useful for two major reasons—to keep the lower classes orderly by passing more and more restrictive laws, and to keep all others alert by defining the bedrock on which democracy rested, that is, on literacy, the powerful enabler, the necessary tool for financial success in this New World of opportunity. This economic model clearly did not hold for blacks—free or enslaved—for they themselves constituted capital. But even disregarding the economic liberation that reading and writing promised, slave-masters could not risk letting their charges read, for those poor creatures might come upon something revolutionary, a tract on abolition, say, or scripture or even that primary repository of power, the alphabet itself. Despotism works best when subjects have been denied the possibility of analysis, of reading and rereading the master's statement, extracting from an edict every possible nuance and possibility. Hitler understood the mesmerizing effect of signs and symbols, of speeches and slogans chanted out loud but never written down. One Virginia legislator, commenting on the passage of a law opposing education for blacks, could have been describing a New World version of fascism: 'We have, as far as possible, closed every avenue by which light may enter their minds. If we could extinguish their capacity to see the light, our work would be completed; they could then be on a level with the beasts of the field and we should be safe.'

To understand what was at stake in what we might accurately call 'native literacy', one need only turn to those excluded from the process. Slaves risked their very lives to learn to read. One of them, Thomas Johnson, who later became a missionary preacher in England, learned his ABCs by utilizing to his own advantage his white master's method of reading scripture. Johnson's master would read aloud every day a section of the Bible in the presence of Johnson, who begged his owner to read the same passage day after day, until finally Johnson had it by heart. He would then match up those words and sounds with the printed page. Slowly and quietly, but quite deliberately, Johnson came to learn to read.

It was not always so easy, and the price of getting caught could be steep. One master surprised his slave, Leonard Black, with book in hand, and took the cat-o'-nine-tails to his back so brutally 'that he overcame my thirst for knowledge, and I relinquished its pursuit until after I absconded'. Another slave, Donald Dowdy, reports, 'The first time you was caught trying to read and write you was whipped with a cow-hide, the next time with a cat-o'-nine-tails and the third time they cut the first joint off your forefinger.'

Every person, slave or not, lives a life in orality before she or he begins to read and write. Orality cannot be separated from literacy. Orality serves as the armature, the framework, in which literacy takes its particular shape and fills out its contours. Orality makes social and emotional development possible. As many psycholinguists have argued, people mould their basic perceptions in speech. By swapping stories, a person learns that he does not have to accept things as they are. He can conjure his own world and manipulate it to his own liking. Young people thus talk themselves into a whole and consummate life: they hear out loud how they feel. Without practice in speaking, and in telling stories, without the joy of playing with language, which might include telling a few lies—'stretchers', the semi-literate Huck Finn liked to call them—youngsters quite literally self-destruct. It is not just that they have a weakened sense of self, but that without the formative power of language, the inner life never fills out and takes shape. That leaves nothing, no substance, for literacy to embrace.

When a slave learned to read a sentence or two, he or she might exclaim, 'I am literate.' And he was. She was. And so were Jefferson and Adams. Worlds separate them, but who cares? Each of them feels the same wonderful exhilaration of freedom that reading and writing bring into a person's life. If you need to measure their levels of understanding—of supposed commitment (and worse, supposed intelligence)—then America has provided the term: literacy.

Maps

Sankaran Krishna

A n essay on 'The Politics of Maps' would lead one to expect a synoptic and totalizing description of maps and their politics. Let me disengage myself from such an ambitious and somewhat self-aggrandizing venture by proposing instead to selectively draw our attention to certain aspects of maps over the centuries, especially since the advent of a modernity which I date to 1492 when Columbus sailed the ocean blue.

Making and interpreting maps are representational practices. Most cartographers would like to assert a strict correspondence between the map and a ground reality that it purports to depict, a correspondence so true in their thinking that the mechanisms of representation supercede and replace reality. However, the history of cartography, and its ongoing practices, are replete with contestations over every aspect of maps. In other words, the cartographer's claim to a final and settled depiction of reality through his map has to be regarded as a hegemonic and hubristic act as with all representational practices. It is nothing less than an audacious claim to power/knowledge—and consequently has to be challenged and disputed at every turn.

Political maps are invariably inscribed from up on high. They are not eye-level but literally drawn from above. Long before Nietzsche officially pronounced the death of God, His viewpoint had been usurped by humans. This was not always how it was: a more natural perspective to adopt towards the landscape is one that is roughly five feet above ground—from the eye-level. The modern view from above comports rather well with our self-arrogated power over, and knowledge about, our reality, and of our ability to adapt our realities to suit our conveniences.

Concomitant with the move from eye-level to the I-level is a process of violent abstraction. A giver of directions in the countryside is wont to gird his information around natural landmarks—flora, fauna, a bend in the river, a rock formation, and the like—while the gaze of the modern falls unto an eviscerated landscape: 'Go fifty yards straight up this road and take the third left turn.' Fifty, straight, road, left turn and third are the markers of an enumerated, two-dimensional and linear world view in contrast to the sinuous, sensuous and approximate metrics of the pre-modern gaze. The violence inherent in this abstraction of space into a mere container can and does germinate into carpet-bombing, napalm, ethnic cleansing and partition. These are possibilities that await realization within the modern cartographic dispensation—they are not the aberrations or accidental by-products of an otherwise progressive, rational and scientific procedure, as one is vociferously reminded at every turn.

The modern map is legible only because of the boundaries that encompass it and the borders that criss-cross it. Every border on the political map (that so precisely and finally seeks to separate peoples, plants, cultures, rivers, air and various other things that cannot be separated) should be read as a desire, not as a depiction of reality. Borders are the open wounds of a suppurating global body politic.

The modern map is a metaphor that has run amok. Maps do not represent ground realities—rather, once the modern map came to be, it has demanded that ground realities be changed in order to conform with the requirements of the map. As Thongchai Winichakul brilliantly demonstrates, the map of Siam preceded the arrival of the nation-state of Thailand—and the premature map decided where and how the borders of the new nation-state would be drawn, once it was created. The strenuousness with which this demand to conform with the map is made increases in intensity as one moves from the First World to the Third World, from the older nations to the newer ones, from the poorer classes to the richer ones and from those with no 'education' to those with advanced degrees. Its intensity is, moreover, felt most strongly by peoples and other beings on the borderlines of the inter-nation-state system. The story of the twentieth century can be written in terms of the millions of people who have been slaughtered in order to maintain the integrity of a metaphor.

Conformity with an idealized map is regarded as the telos of postcolonial development. Nearly all boundaries and borders within the Third World are contested spaces. This consequently produces acute degrees of cartographic anxiety in such societies, and many of them wage systematic wars of cartographic aggression on their neighbours. Actual physically violent encounters are mere punctuations in a more continuous form of representational wars that unite most neighbour countries across the Third World.

The modern cartographic world view is enthralled by the fiction of homogeneity—the belief that each and every bounded piece of territory ideally ought to be occupied by a people with a singular sense of national identity. The multicoloured political maps in the atlas, with their clear boundaries, are the benign, etch-a-sketch versions that conceal a deeper inability to deal with ambiguity, overlapping or plural identities and the possibility that sovereignty might be a matter of degree, something that waxes and wanes in both space and time, rather than an either-or matter. When such desired neatness runs aground of a historical reality rich with the miscegenation of races, the commingling of cultures, civilizations and languages, the diffusion of religious faiths, the fusion of architectural or musical forms, the ordinariness of those loath to embrace the counterfeit newcomer called the nation-state, the stubbornness of nomadic peoples with a vastly different relationship to space—in other words, when the modern, static, cartographic sensibility encounters all that has been true of human civilizations and histories—the response is predictably one of xenophobia, introversion and the kitsch construction of national purity. All too often the inability to deal with social existence outside the map-as-metaphor culminates in the merciless and annihilatory project of forcibly producing a singular identity for each enclosed space. Annihilation in the name of a simulacrum (a model based on a real that does not exist anywhere) captures the essence of what passes for progress in these times—nation-building, economic development, modern agriculture, freeing the market, to name but four. What allows the annihilators to rest easy with their consciences at night, and allows most of us to still reckon we live in a sane world, is ultimately a faith in the redemptive project of modernization—a project whose telos is where the map and reality coalesce as one.

In a hilarious scene from Chinua Achebe's *Things Fall Apart*, two bemused natives deep within the Dark Continent are watching a Western missionary in full flow, raving and ranting about the superstitious sloth of the Africans and their stupid unrepentant lives. Finally, one man turns to the other and says, 'I don't think our local wise-man would travel ten thousand miles to another place to tell those people that everything they believe in is nonsense.' The modern map, by laying before us a picture of the entire planet, invites us to think of it as property, of something that can be possessed, something that we have a right to enter, to decipher, to decode—and all on our own terms. The modern map invites the moment that Joseph Conrad recollects in his autobiography:

> ... looking at a map of Africa of the time and putting my finger on the blank space then representing the unsolved mystery of that continent, I said to myself, with absolute assurance and an amazing audacity which are no longer in my character now: 'When I grow up, I shall go there.'

Simply put, the conviction of Achebe's missionary is greatly energized by his possession of a map of Africa and of the world, places that are now legible and translucent for him. The Africans, in contrast, are still awed by distance and humbled by difference, and that humility contains the possibility of a respect for the other, rather than a desire to remake him in an image of the self. Maps are the stolen title deeds of lands that belong to others.

The ecumene of the modern cartographic imaginary is increasing in geometric proportions. Carrying a map of one's country in one's head was the privy of the educated elite early in the twentieth century. The advent of a truly mass media in the intervening decades has meant that billions of people have now become accustomed to thinking of themselves as inhabiting a bordered piece of land adjacent to other, adversarial, bordered lands. Modern geographical education and the decline of the possibility of a humane world civilization would thus appear to be simultaneous and related processes.

Within the discursive universe of the geographer, the belief is common that a solution to the all-too-prevalent slippages between representation and reality inherent in mapping will disappear due to advances in technology. The arrival of computer-imaging techniques and of the vast computational power of the latest information processing technologies (now coalesced under the geographic information system or GIS) is touted as the solution to bridging the wretched gap between signifier and signified. From this viewpoint, the ultimate Borgesian map that replicates reality in all its plenitude is alluringly within reach. Such a narrow view of mapping is remarkable for its political innocence, and for its understanding of technology as completely abstracted from society and issues of power. It is deeply dangerous for precisely that reason. Maps should always be read as an effort to disguise the particular interests and knowledges of some as the universal and only story that can be said about all. Maps will ever be the insignia of domination.

If maps are the insignia of domination, do they also contain the possibility of resistance? I was once interviewing a general in the Indian army who had seen action in Sri Lanka as part of the Indian Peace-Keeping Force. He remarked that the Liberation Tigers for Tamil Eelam (LTTE, a nationalist guerrilla organization fighting for a Tamil homeland in Sri Lanka) had integrated the most sophisticated information and communication technologies within their mode of operation—fax machines, global satellite positioning systems, wireless communications, encrypting techniques, computers, radars, etc. They had a familiarity and skill with these technologies that made him realize he and his army were outdated and flat-footed. The LTTE's adeptness at such deterritorializing technologies is supremely ironic given its own antiquated quest for a territorially bounded homeland and its inability to think outside that framework of belonging. Yet in a larger sense the example shows that even if maps represent a violently fractured world of nation-states, the very technologies for their production and dissemination may yet unwittingly empower us to reimagine our moral cartographies along other trajectories.

Further Reading

Anderson, Benedict. 1991. *Imagined Communities: Reflections on the Origin and Spread of Nationalism*. Rev. ed. London: Verso.

Lefebvre, Henri. 1991. *The Production of Space*. Translated by Donald Nicholson. Oxford: Blackwell.

Shapiro, Michael. 1997. *Violent Cartographies: Mapping Cultures of War*. Minneapolis: University of Minnesota Press.

Winichakul, Thongchai. 1994. *Siam Mapped: The History of the Geo-Body of a Nation*. Honolulu: University of Hawaii Press.

Marley

Charles Carnegie

There can be little doubt of Jamaican-born reggae superstar Bob Marley's pre-eminence as a global cultural icon. His dreadlocked portrait—brooding, clairvoyant, defiant—is perhaps more recognizable, beyond the Americas and within, than that of either Che Guevara or Malcolm X. Taking stock at century's end, two of the most authoritative traffickers in transnational images proclaimed him one of the legendary voices of our age: the BBC declared Marley's song *One Love* the anthem of the twentieth century, and *Time* magazine named *Exodus* album of the century. How, one might ask, can we best situate Marley's inimitable voice? How do we account for its haunting urgency, its undying popularity? In short, how is Bob Marley to be read? Is the endurance of the Marley sound merely an instance of nostalgia, say, on the part of local elite ('bald head') forces on one hand, allied with successful appropriation by international consumer capitalism on the other? While not denying these tendencies, I suggest that Marley's music continues to resonate with ordinary folk worldwide because it proclaims a necessary reckoning yet to be fulfilled. It holds out the graspable promise of a world distinctly at variance either with the dispositions of ruling elites or with the postmodern scepticism of contemporary liberal thought.

Certainly, one abiding feature of Marley's music is its agile multivocality. Social outrage is joined with transcendent hope, damnation with regeneration, assertions of blackness are coupled with a broader, catholic sentiment, tenderness alternates with sharp-edged defiance, mystical detachment with disarming practicality, 'Rudie' combines forces with 'Rasta'. These seemingly disparate tendencies stand inseparably riveted together in the polysemic Marley oeuvre. What is striking in Marley's lyrics, moreover, is the ease with which local, homespun referents can be equally convincingly interpreted as directed at bigger culprits. There is an unmistakable universality here, yet one at variance with, and critical of, the platitudes of secularist Enlightenment universalism that for so long has passed itself off as the only legitimate register of universalist thinking. Ordinary people worldwide can certainly identify with Marley's rise from underprivileged circumstances to international fame, but they also intuitively understand and celebrate his giving voice to an alternative universal agenda that includes and speaks for them.

The singer positions himself as a medium of communication between oppressors and oppressed; between factions of the dispossessed; between past, present and future; between an unseen world of ancestors and the divine, and that of the living. Marley's address is conversational, always phatic, and engages its audience as interlocutors ('Yes me frien' / We de a street again'; 'Get up, stand up / Stand up for your rights!'; 'Won't you help to sing, these songs of freedom'). The addressee is alternately admonished by an all-seeing observer ('I say you are working iniquity / To achieve vanity'; 'If you are the big tree / We are the small axe / Ready to cut you down / Well sharp, / To cut you down') and roused for collective action ('Emancipate yourselves from mental slavery / None but ourselves can free our minds'). There is a stark, judgmental accounting of history, with 'Babylon', 'preacher man', 'old pirates', 'illusions', 'evil men', 'you', heedlessness/forgetfulness on one side of the ledger, and 'Jah', 'the Almighty', 'survivors', 'Zion', 'Natty', 'man', 'we', mindfulness on the other. Ominous warnings are sounded ('Total destruction, the only solution'; 'The way earthly things are going / Anything can happen'), even as the promise of redemption awaits ('Natty keep on coming through'; 'Why do you look so sad and forsaken / When one door is closed / Don't you know another is open').

Bob Marley, thus, *is engaged in a prophetic work*. Credentialed with mystical powers, he claims a capacity to overcome obstacles deliberately set in his path ('Propaganda spreading over my name / Say you want to bring another life to shame . . . And then you draw bad card . . . / I make you draw bad card'; 'The bars could not hold me / Force could not control me now / They try to keep me down / But Jah put I around . . . So if you're a bull-bucker / Let me tell you this / I'm a Duppy Conqueror'). His is a calling ('One bright morning when my work is over / Man will fly away home'). The bard proclaims, exhorts, foretells with an authority that speaks through him unbidden ('These are the words of my Master / Telling me that no weak heart shall prosper').

Marley's oracular, revelatory tone confronts and confounds Western modernity's disavowal of the prophetic. Prophetic discourse was one of the casualties of the Enlightenment. Like 'religion', it was banished or else compartmentalized (say, in the allowed eccentricities of artists operating in their circumscribed sphere), to be replaced by inductive forecasting. Yet we are poorer off for this near banishment of the prophetic mode. Evidentiary habits of mind on which we have become so singularly dependent nowadays lead to cautious prediction at best. Possibilities for transformation large and small tend to be unthinkable in the forecasting mode. For example, although prudent adulthood often follows a reckless adolescence, this sort of turnaround generally happens unpredicted. Similarly, historic transformations on an even grander scale, though unanticipated, have been known to occur, sometimes envisioned by seers and prophets. The loss of the prophetic voice and the corresponding loss of the ear to heed it has robbed us of a capacity to recognize and to act on the possibility of such transformations.

Contemporary postmodernists, who instinctively dismiss projects of large-scale redemption, have inherited this intolerance of prophecy. There is now more cynicism than celebration about secular modernism's boldest social initiatives—the prospect of realizing a socialist society, for example, or the idea of a United Nations. Great society expectations have been scaled down, while the ironclad reign of the free market, race and nation continue.

The mid-twentieth-century euphoria over sovereignty in the former colonial world, and hopes for a meaningful alliance of the non-aligned, have quickly given way to bitterness in the face of state terror and interpersonal violence, official corruption and even more widespread complacence. And while in the liberal academy the popular is now in vogue, it is mostly its fragmentary, recombinant, fleeting qualities that get noticed. Faced with undeniable evidence of the oppressions of the Western universalist project and its excessive hubris, the voice of reason has become the voice of despair.

Belying the current fatalism of the talking heads, and their contentment with the discovery of mere play in popular culture, Marley names injustice for what it is and offers larger dreams of restitution. No matter that in the decades since his passing an idealized 'Africa' can no longer be looked to in its postcolonial condition as warrant for a righteous future. Nor that the international absorption of the Marley project meant that articulation of the local condition from whence it sprung receded from view. Nor that the romance of an imagined transcontinental blackness has proven illusory. Nor even that the stubborn patriarchy of the Rastafari world view that so animates Marley's music has been exposed. The largeness of Marley's prophetic summons endures in spite of these admitted qualifications to its conceptual foundations. Rather than being displaced by his musical successors, Marley now occupies a position of unquestioned, timeless authority. The continued freshness of his appeal has audiences listening not out of nostalgia but in anticipation. There is more than ever a sense of yearning in the world for those such as he who would champion the cause of justice. The prophetic voice still resonates in the hearts and minds of those who live from day to day outside the orbit of the Western academy's self-satisfied though despondent halls.

Marley took possession of the global stage unselfconsciously, as though he were born to it. Though he was perhaps the first musician from the so-called Third World to achieve such celebrity, several other oracular figures from the Caribbean have commanded a similarly uncommon international presence before him: Marcus Garvey, C.L.R. James and Frantz Fanon among them. Admittedly, his global stature owed much to the technological and marketing innovations of a capitalist recording industry. Certainly, those studios did invent a 'world music', of and for the 'other', to market the cache that Marley's quick success made plain was there to be exploited, but the story does not end there.

The impact of Marley and his oeuvre tells us that an incipient transnational cultural circuitry is available to be used, built on and extended. Even though Marley's rise to local popularity coincided with the early years of Jamaican independence, his message is strikingly not nationalist. That message reverberated with local audiences even then because it cut through the veneer of nationalist mythology. The state was recognized not as a vehicle for liberation ('None but ourselves can free our minds') but of violence against its citizens ('This morning I woke up in a curfew / Oh God, I was a prisoner too', or again, 'Babylon system is the vampire / Sucking the children day by day'). Rejecting the state's concerted efforts to shape acceptable liberal democratic citizens, Marley spoke back: 'We refuse to be / What you wanted us to be / We are what we are / That's the way its going to be / You can't educate I / For no equal opportunity'.

While the music is rooted in the proverbial wit of the Jamaican peasantry, it links and articulates the rural directly with the urban and the transnational. Out of conceptual habit or limitation we persist in calling this 'Jamaican' music when in fact it is at once more parochial and more transcendent than that. Indeed, the discourse of 1960s' reggae, to which Marley contributes, is deeply sceptical of the containments of the nationalist project. Its tropes draw on the biblical Old Testament language that has long been used to give voice to black diaspora political aspirations. Marley sets his sights on 'Mount Zion, the highest region', not only, perhaps, as a longed for homeland for diasporic return but as a space allowing for greater plurality and a more expansive conversation and sharing of ideas than has proven possible in the democratic nation-state modelled on the West. This is a discourse that enables a political/economic critique at once old and new, timeless yet fresh and current in its appeal both locally and transnationally ('Oh it's a disgrace to see the human race in a rat race'). In this music we can detect a sound and a language that voice and enable creation of a transnational political consciousness. Marley, along with others, sketches out a border-transgressive imaginary ('Africa unite / 'Cause we're moving right out of Babylon / And we're going to our Father's land', 'Zion train is coming our way'). This music, then, confirms the inadequacy of our models, cautions against both the limitations of conceptual tropes like community, race, nation that still inhibit social inquiry and viewing an emergent global culture as the mere residual product of global consumer capitalism.

Social scientists who collectively put their analytical buckets down with the national project in the 1960s and 1970s tuned in to this music, if at all, only as recreation. They generally missed its counter-national address just as postmodern sceptics now overlook or discount its larger, prophetic appeal. Sadly, the interpretive sound detectors seem to adjust only to take in the fragmentary, or else to entertain the louder, more phonetically recognizable though hollow sounds of national/racial reclamation. Notwithstanding their deafness, Marley's music echoed (and still does) across the borderlands. It cleared new paths and crossings, and still gives warning, vision, voice and hope. That the border zone is still an open frontier, unregulated, without overarching systems of meaning or democratic governance, and teeming with liminal confusions, does not imply that it always will be, nor that when the time comes the old hegemonies will necessarily set the grid for the new order.

Further Reading

Cooper, Carolyn. 1993. *Noises in the Blood: Orality, Gender, and the 'Vulgar' Body of Jamaican Popular Culture*. London: Macmillan.

Edwards, Nadi. 1998. States of Emergency: Reggae Representations of the Jamaican Nation-State. *Social and Economic Studies* 47(1): 21–32.

Marxism

C. Douglas Lummis

Karl Marx left us with one of the greatest philosophies of work ever formulated, and with what is certainly the most profound analysis of the capitalist economic system. A century and a half after he wrote his manuscripts on estranged labour, they can still help to explain to us why we feel the way we do about our jobs today. What he saw as the iron laws of capital, which would systematically mobilize the whole world into the capitalist system, and inevitably generate a steadily increasing gap between the rich and the poor, seem not to have worked that way if you look just at the rich countries, but if you look at the world economic system as a whole, you can see them operating quite according to prediction. Moreover, the corruption and collapse of what was called socialism in the Soviet Union and other countries does not refute Marx's hopes. No revolution of the sort he envisaged—that is, a revolution in the most industrially advanced country, at the moment that capitalist development had reached its completion and deadend—has ever so far occurred.

On the other hand, Karl Marx also left us with some knotty problems. Being human, he had his blind spots—a fact that he tried unsuccessfully to communicate in his famous statement 'Anyway, I am not a Marxist'—therefore, when Marxism gained hegemony as the ideology of the opposition, his blind spots became the blind spots of countless dedicated political activists. Here I will mention only several important examples.

Marx and Machines

Marx famously believed in the liberating potential of technology; in this he shared the faith of his most naive bourgeois enemies. According to Jacques Ellul, it was Marx who finally persuaded the European workers to give up their Luddite machine-breaking and to believe that it was the capitalist system, not the new technology, that was their enemy—a conclusion that Ellul believed to be profoundly wrong. This left Marxists with no intellectual equipment for thinking about such things as nuclear weapons (so we would hear from them in the 1950s that the Soviet and Chinese bombs were 'forces for peace') or nuclear power (so we heard that nuclear plants would be safe in socialist countries—until Chernobyl) or environmental destruction. It took the longest time for the Marxist community to get it into its head that these things are horrors in any system.

Moreover, Marx was never entirely persuasive in his argument that estranged labour had everything to do with the system of ownership and nothing to do with the machinery. For example, in *Capital* he wrote:

> Factory work exhausts the nervous system to the uttermost; at the same time, it does away with the many-sided play of the muscles, and confiscates every atom of freedom, both in bodily and in intellectual activity. Even the lightening of the labour becomes an instrument of torture, since the machine does not free the worker from the work, but rather deprives the work itself of all content.

I have never found where Marx successfully explained why the same machine would treat the worker differently in a workers' state. If he means that in a workers' state the workers would never build such machines (and indeed, why should they?), then his lavish praise (for example in *The Communist Manifesto*) for the technological achievements of the bourgeoisie seems misplaced.

Marx and the Non-West

Like virtually all Western political and economic writers of his time (and many today), Marx was Eurocentric. When he said 'the world' he tended to mean Germany, France and England. When he wrote of what would happen when 'the whole world reached full capitalist development' he was still thinking mainly of those three countries, which is why his predictions were off by more than a century. But unlike many of his contemporaries he did not simply ignore the non-Western world, or dismiss it as barbaric: he had a theory.

The Iron Law of History, the law of class struggle which carried 'the world' forward from feudalism to capitalism and would carry it further to socialism, did not operate in the non-Western world. This was because the village-centred economies there operated under what Marx called the Asiatic Mode of Production. With their 'economic' activity buried deeply under layers of custom and tradition, with much of their property held in common, or worse, with ownership not clearly fixed at all, these societies simply did not generate the economic competition that would supply the fuel for the Engine of History. What was to be done?

Here we come to one of the worst moments in Marxism: there was nothing for it but to stand aside and allow the European bourgeoisie, in its colonial guise, to smash those societies to smithereens. Writing of India at the time of England's bloody response to the Indian Rebellion of 1857-58, Marx tells us:

> [W]e must not forget that these idyllic village communities, inoffensive though they may appear, had always been the solid foundation of Oriental despotism, that they had restrained the human mind within the smallest compass, making it the unresisting tool of superstition, enslaving it beneath traditional rules, depriving it of all grandeur and historical energies.
>
> The question is, can mankind fulfil its destiny without a fundamental revolution in the social state of Asia? If not, whatever may have been the crimes of England she was the unconscious tool of history in bringing about that revolution ('The British Rule in India').

Let me direct the reader's attention to the word 'whatever'. One would like to believe that Marx didn't know the extent of the horrors he was including in this blanket forgiveness, but probably that is too much to hope for. And what about this puzzle: suppose you were an Indian who had read this essay in 1857 and been persuaded by it, what would have been the 'correct line' for you to take? Take up arms with the British against your own people? Throw yourself off a cliff? (It is alleged that Marx changed his mind about this late in life, and came to believe that such traditional villages might not after all have to be smashed by the bourgeoisie and suffer the agony of a capitalist stage, but might instead be coaxed directly from their 'primitive communism' to the 'scientific' communism Marx envisaged [see Shanin 1983]).

Marx and Action

This leads to another peculiarity of Marxism, its conception of action. What does it mean to be the 'tool of history'? Suppose you were a British infantryman who had helped massacre a lot of sepoys, read Marx's essay in 1853, and been persuaded by it— should you feel guilty? Should you feel proud? Suppose you were a dedicated Marxist who had the opportunity to join the British army and go to India to help destroy Indian society—should you go? If not, why not? I knew a young Marxist in Japan who came to the conclusion that Japanese capitalism had not yet developed to the revolutionary level, so in order to help develop it to that point he quit the movement and went into business. The decision is perfectly logical.

If history has a determined course, and the political actor is the tool or agent of history, this leads to a peculiar notion of responsibility. On the one hand one has the duty to act (no one is more insistent on this than the Marxists) but on the other hand one bears no responsibility for the consequences of one's acts. 'History', like Yahweh and the modern state, has a right of legitimate violence; if it commands you to act, you must, but if your acts turn out to be atrocities, that is history's doing, not yours. This form of responsibility-without-responsibility (which was shared by the Nazis and, more recently, by promoters of 'modernization' and 'development') has enabled people to carry out the most monstrous of crimes, while believing themselves sublimely innocent.

Marx after the Cold War

Having said this, it remains true that Marx's analysis of capitalism is still the best. Ironically, after the collapse of 'socialism' in the Soviet Bloc the world looks far more like the world he described than it did during the cold war. With 'socialism' no longer a factor, capitalism is reverting to type, dusting off those old Iron Laws, and getting down to the business of bringing every corner of the world under the free market, proletarianizing all work, commodifying every human product and service, demoralizing the working class everywhere and expanding the gap between the rich and the poor. Marx's writings may be out of fashion, but today may be the best time to read them.

Further Reading

Avineri, Shlomo. 1969. *Karl Marx on Colonialism and Modernization: His Despatches and Other Writings on China, India, Mexico, the Middle East and North Africa*. Garden City, New York: Anchor.

Marx, Karl, and Friedrich Engels. 1972. *On Colonialism: Articles from the* New York Tribune *and Other Writings*. New York: New World Publishers.

Shanin, Teodor, ed. 1983. *Late Marx and the Russian Road: Marx and 'the Peripheries of Capitalism'*. New York: Monthly Review Press.

McDonald's

Vinay Lal and Ziauddin Sardar

Ever had what McDonald's calls a 'total experience'? If one hasn't had a meal at McDonald's, one cannot count oneself among the fortunate many, though perhaps a visit to the toilet at one of the many outlets of this restaurant chain brings one halfway to heaven. When McDonald's isn't selling fattening burgers, carcinogenic French fries or testosterone-enhanced chicken nuggets, it's selling clean toilets. 'Given the lack of public toilets in Korea,' writes one anthropologist, 'the relatively clean and convenient facilities provided by McDonald's encourage heavy traffic.' McDonald's toilets are bound to please, even when their burgers are found wanting. McDonald's should have been flourishing in India, which Naipaul a few decades ago declared a cesspool of shit. And Gandhi, who devoted as much time to keeping toilets clean and trying to devise some that would not be a drain on scarce water resources as he did to delivering India from British rule, might have appreciated McDonald's—if one can overlook the cows. McDonald's devours cows; Gandhi advocated a ban on cow slaughter. Still, Gandhi at McDonald's: the name for a new skit in the mode of Samuel Beckett.

From its humble beginnings in Des Paines, Illinois, nearly five decades ago, McDonald's has grown to become the most recognizable brand name around the world. Following the attacks on New York's World Trade Center and the Pentagon on 11 September 2001, the American military presence extended to

140 countries. But McDonald's set the trend: the military is there to enforce the supply of burgers as much as the flow of oil. Burgers and oil are the two engines of American life. In 29,000 outlets—a number well over 30,000 by the time this book arrives at bookstores—in 121 countries, serving over forty-five million customers a day, McDonald's restaurants sell much more than fast food. They sell the American consumer lifestyle all over the world. Or, as one recent study, *Golden Arches East*, tells us, McDonald's sells a 'system' called 'total experience'. It takes people out of the drudgery of their daily 'ordinary routines'—never mind the fact that in the mid 1990s breakfast at McDonald's had become part of the daily ritual of 11 per cent of Americans. It may be a standardized, controlled and mechanized experience, but the consumers in East Asia, anthropologists assure us, find it richly rewarding and spiritually meaningful. The new class of yuppies, who patronize McDonald's in Beijing, where the world's largest franchise restaurant with 700 seats and twenty-nine cash registers opened in 1992, serving 40,000 customers on its first day of business, 'assume that something profound is happening to them'. Swallow a Big Mac: enter into the entrails of bovine America, and elsewhere create a famine.

Indeed, McDonald's has imparted many positive values to its customers. People everywhere have been taught how to queue and become 'proper consumers'. McDonald's might profitably be enlisted in the cause of 'law and order': one too many fracas in the developing world has taken place because people step out of lines. The Japanese have, thanks to McDonald's, learned how to eat with their hands. The Chinese have discovered that there is a big, free world outside; they also savour McDonald's because they experience a moment of equality. Communism's promise is no longer deferred. Children in Hong Kong have found that McDonald's provides a perfect substitute for youth clubs. Taiwanese youth have realized that French fries are a 'dietary staple' for a healthy person. And everyone has discovered birthdays. 'Prior to McDonald's entry into the local scene,' the authors of *Golden Arches East* tell us with a sense of real discovery, 'festivities to mark the specific birthdates of youngsters were unknown in most part of East Asia.' Today, teenage cognoscenti would kill their parents if they refused a birthday party at McDonald's—particularly when parents get presents too! So McDonald's, the creator of fast food in its modern incarnation, is the paragon of inventiveness: it introduced standardization into the food industry, opened up the world to the idea of the drive-in restaurant, dispensed with the idea of the chef, made self-service perfectly respectable and, if all this were not enough, it pioneered the modern trend of children as consumers.

We are all, then, indebted to this wonderful multinational corporation for spreading 'egalitarianism' throughout the world. McDonald's is the perfect corporate exemplar, a living repudiation of ageism and sexism, marvellously attentive to ordinary human needs, sensitive to those who are physically and mentally challenged. It is the shining example of the laissez faire spirit, since more than 70 per cent of its restaurants are independently owned. In cultures where the open expression of romantic love, much less sexuality, is frowned upon, McDonald's has given a fresh lease of life to frolicsome youth, furnishing 'lover's corners' in many of its restaurants. There lovers may implant kisses on ketchup-stained lips. The ketchup lipstick still awaits a patent. Above all, McDonald's is good for, and to, women. Its 'Social Responsibility Report' reminds us that it is the business leader in advancing the welfare of women: 20 per cent of McDonald's US franchises are women-owned, 56 per cent of its US restaurants are managed by women and 30 per cent of the company's top executives are women. In 2001, McDonald's was named among the 100 best employers for working mothers. Nor is this all: in Beijing, Taipei, Seoul, Hong Kong, Mumbai, New Delhi, Jakarta, Bogota and elsewhere, it is a sanctuary to women 'who wish to avoid male-dominated settings'. Nearly synonymous with 'family values', McDonald's keeps away bad men. Indeed, almost everywhere women linger on at McDonald's longer than do men.

And yet, for all its hard work, its 'People Vision' and its 'People Promise' to be the 'best employer in each community around the world' and people oriented, even anthropologists cannot entirely rescue McDonald's from its dominant image among some as the 'unambiguous symbol of evil'. The company provides assurance, and anthropologists give their eager assent to its claims, that McDonald's gives due respect to local cultures and provides a familiar, homely atmosphere to its Oriental (and doubtless Occidental and African) patrons. Can anyone doubt that it is spreading good cheer, generous smiles and free-market ethics around the world? The cultured elites in the West deplore the deadening of taste associated with McDonald's, but they have not adequately grappled with the 'fact' that ordinary folks in China think of burgers and shakes as high cuisine, and that even the elites of ancient civilizations will readily describe the 'total experience' at McDonald's as a social event. More to the point: when anti-American sentiment surfaces anywhere, McDonald's is the first business to be pelted with stones. Think Big Mac, think beef; think Big Mac, think imperialism.

But we mustn't be facetious. McDonald's cannot be described with such a nasty epitaph as 'Multinational Corporation'. It is, in fact, 'a federation of semi-autonomous enterprises' that is not 'multinational' but 'multilocal'. McDonald's always works with local cultures to meet the requirements of their customs and traditions. So, in Beijing, the company's mascot, Ronald McDonald, has acquired a wife, Aunt McDonald. In India, McDonald's serve vegetable McNuggets and mutton-based Maharaja Macs to please Hindus, Muslims and the strictly vegetarian Jains. These are pork- and beef-free McDonald's, the equivalent of the vegetarian circus (the Cirque Soleil) for the fastidious and the sensitive. The 'religious sentiments' of the people, McDonald's India website reminds us, prompted the company to innovate and develop an eggless mayonnaise, a McAloo Tikki Burger and Veg Pizza McPuff. In Malaysia and Singapore, their burgers are halal. In Israel, Big Macs come without cheese, respecting the separation of meat and diary products required by kosher laws. All meat, in kosher and non-kosher restaurants, is '100 per cent kosher beef'. In Turkey, McDonald's serve chilled yoghurt drinks (*ayran*), and in the

Philippines they serve McSpaghetti. The Japanese eat teriyaki burgers, and espresso and cold pasta is the common fare in Italy. In the macho culture of Caracas, McDonald's provides a waitress service; and, in Rio, where there are no wimps and festivity is in the air, the Big Macs are served with champagne. And for the health conscious, salads, fresh celery and carrot sticks are always available. To understand 'unity in diversity', do not turn to the platitudes in political science books, or pay much attention to the slogans generated by the United Nations and other well-meaning bodies. It is enough to study McDonald's. James Watson tells us, with less than anthropological objectivity, that though the main fare at McDonald's varies around the world, 'the signature innovation of McDonald's—thin, elongated, fries cut from russet potatoes—is ever-present and consumed with great gusto by Muslims, Jews, Christians, Buddhists, Hindus, vegetarians (now that vegetable oil is used), communists, Tories, marathoners, and armchair athletes'.[1] French fries freaks of the world, unite!

All of this goes to show that McDonald's is not a foreign imposition on long-suffering non-Western cultures. It is a local company, doing local business, in a local way. That's why it has blended so much with the local scene in Japan, a country perennially suspicious of foreigners. That is why the Chinese in Hong Kong would rather have their breakfast at McDonald's than at the traditional tea-houses and hawkers' stalls. In every country, the vast bulk of its employees are locals. At most, if one is tempted to think in the imperialist vein, one could argue that eating Big Macs is a way of rendering tribute to the US and inserting oneself into a globalized world. In today's globalized society, we are certain to be told, it is simply not possible to distinguish between 'local' and 'foreign'. So, 'who is to say that Ronald McDonald is not Chinese?' Children in Hong Kong are 'more familiar with him

---

[1]This was written before Hindus and vegetarians successfully sued McDonald's for failing to reveal that its French fries and hash browns were, in the words of the company's apology, 'improperly identified as "vegetarian"'. See www.mcdonalds.com, Press Release of 1 June 2002.

than mythical characters of Chinese folklore'. To a generation of children in Hong Kong, Tokyo and Taipei raised on Big Macs and milkshakes, McDonald's food is local cuisine. So the future belongs to American consumerism, not Chinese culture.

Having read the anthropologists' account of how each culture moulds McDonald's to suit its own norms, one begins to comprehend how anthropology, once an academic arm of Empire that was deployed to manage and control the unruly native mobs in the colonies, is so easily placed in the service of corporate imperialism. We are inclined, rather, to sympathize with the South Koreans who equate eating Big Mac with cultural and economic treason—as well as with the American commentator Ronald Steel, who declared that, unlike traditional conquerors, Americans are not content simply to subdue others but insist that 'they be like us'. So queue up, grill this baloney over a slow, naked flame, smile, and fight the bastards. And don't forget to have a nice day.

Further Reading

Love, John F. 1995. *McDonald's: Behind the Arches*. Rev. ed. New York: Bantam Books.

Watson, James L., ed. 1997. *Golden Arches East: McDonald's in East Asia*. Stanford: Stanford University Press.

Memory

Sudesh Mishra

The faculty of memory is governed by two operations: the act of remembering *and* the act of forgetting. Whether calculated or instinctual, the act of remembering is sparked off by another time or context and, consequently, cannot offer us an original event in all its purity. This is not to assert that all acts of recollection are brazenly false or fictional, but to suggest that the contours of the original event are subject to (narrative) shifts (sometimes negligible, at other times momentous) during the process of retrieval. To what extent an act of recollection conforms to or deviates from the original event may depend on rhetorical strategy or, more pertinently, on the memory others have of the same event. Truth, in any case, becomes a tricky business. Obviously the act of forgetting, whether calculated or involuntary, is determined by the act of recollection: what is forgotten about an event depends on the procedures of repression—voluntary, historical or neuropsychological—employed in the act of remembering. It follows, then, that memory is related to the exercise of power: conscious or psychic, communal or historical, genocidal or productive.

Remembering

Calculated or voluntary acts of remembering are found in private as well as public spheres. Common birthdays, wedding anniversaries, private jottings in diaries, sympathy cards, snapshots, grocery lists stuck on refrigerator doors, yearly visits to temples or cemeteries: these are random examples of private acts of calculated memory. In the literary domain, this type of remembering has given birth to two genres: the autobiography and the bildungsroman. James Joyce's *Portrait of the Artist as a Young Man*, Marcel Proust's *Remembrance of Things Past*, Nirad C. Chaudhuri's *Autobiography of an Unknown Indian* and Eugenio Montale's *Collected Poems* are acts of private recollection directed towards an aesthetic end. Ironically the public consumption of such 'memoirs' transforms them into visible events of history or, as is the case with Chaudhuri's book, into notorious records of historical events. Where the autobiography resists the lure of art, it may furnish ethnographical or historical 'data' (that is to say, narrative fragments) of much significance. Totaram Sanadhya's *My Twenty-One Years in Fiji*, the only extended first-hand account of *girmit*, is a crucial archival text in any discussion relating to the system of indentured labour.

Public acts of voluntary memory are most visible in the widespread habit of erecting monuments in honour of important figures and events. In every Australian township, for instance, there is a memorial obelisk naming and numbering those who died in the two great wars of the last century. (Significantly, this type of memory forgets the casualties on the other side.) A bronze statue of the poet Byron stands in the middle of Rome. The rock star Jimi Hendrix has a brass plaque recalling his sojourn in London. Conquering heroes on prancing metal stallions are routinely stranded in the plazas and squares of all major cities. Not infrequently, the ubiquity of their presence has a reverse impact on pedestrians: instead of remembering, they forget them.

Public holidays are habitually used in managing this type of calculated memory. Christmas marks the advent of Christ, Diwali the return of the exiled Rama. Special holidays hark back to watershed moments, such as a nation's independence, or pay homage to national heroes: Lenin, Mao or Martin Luther King. (Of course what events or which figures qualify in this regard is largely determined by those with a purchase on hegemony.) Occasionally, when the political barometer shifts radically, national heroes turn into embarrassing villains and lose their place in the roll of honour. At different times in history, and to varying degrees, calculated memory of the public type has been made to serve ideological interests: right (Nazi), left (Soviet) and liberal (American). Be that as it may, modern nation-states have built civic shrines to promote and protect a culture's memory of its past. Museums, libraries and archives are the repositories of calculated memory of the public variety.

Instinctual or involuntary acts of remembering are mostly confined to the private sphere, although they may and do have serious social implications. It has been discovered, for example, that adults who have been victims of child abuse suddenly call up 'repressed' memories of their trauma. While in most cases what the adult recalls may 'approximate' to the childhood experience, it has also been found that, in a few cases, the memory may yield an outright fabrication. Manipulative psychiatrists, internalization of media effects and transference via empathy: these and other explanations have been offered to account for the syndrome. In effect, then, narratives of repression may be artificially implanted in a subject without the subject's active knowledge or consent. Something of this sort happens in the 1990 film *Total Recall* where the protagonist, caught in the spiral of memory effects, is unable to say whether he is Hawser, the morally justified revolutionary, or Quaid, the brutal infiltrator acting on behalf of colonial corporatism.

Involuntary acts of recall may display a degree of randomness but they are not independent of the present time of recollection: contextual cues play a crucial part in triggering the memory. Perhaps the best way to illustrate this is to think of nostalgic memories. Usually the cues for nostalgic memory are supplied by the five senses of sound, smell, taste, touch and sight. A well-known example of this type of sensory trigger may be found in the writings of Marcel Proust. In his novel *Remembrance of Things Past*, the texture and taste of his mother's tea-soaked madeleines transports Marcel, the mature narrator, to childhood Sundays spent in his aunt's bedroom at Combray. Diasporic subjects are frequently exposed to such nostalgia-inducing cues as they go past culture-specific restaurants, movie theatres or music outlets. Interestingly, poets of memory, such as George Seferis and Agha Shahid Ali, see nostalgia as a faculty that shrinks the original experience to the point of inaccessibility.

Forgetting

Acts of forgetting can be individual or communal, as well as voluntary or subconscious. Repression and amnesia are two common ways of forgetting; generally speaking, they are neuropsychological reactions to traumatic episodes of one kind or another. In Tony Morrison's novel *Beloved* the protagonist, Seth, forced by the degradations of slavery to kill her own child, reacts to this trauma by lapsing into amnesia. The clouds of amnesia lift only when the child returns as a revenant to prey and gorge on the love she was cruelly denied. Morrison uses the term rememory for a past whose potential future is brutally terminated but which remains a parallel possibility to the one that exists as history. Significantly, she sees rememory in individual-subjective as well as objective-historical terms.

Amnesia and repressive forgetting are themes running through fiction certainly, but also through the history of the twentieth century. Many victims of the violence that erupted after the partition of India were either reluctant or unable to recall their trauma. Again, the reasons for this are manifold: the failure of language in the face of intense horror is one; another is repressive forgetting of the Freudian variety. A third sociological reason relates to inhibitions introduced by culturally defined codes of honour and shame. It is also possible, however, that silence and amnesia are therapeutic strategies (conscious or involuntary) adopted by victims to enable themselves to 'live' beyond the line of trauma.

When sponsored by an autocratic state or hijacked by communalist interests, acts of forgetting can be highly insidious, as well as overt and even fascist and genocidal. The destruction of

Buddhist rock sculptures in Afghanistan is an example of the Taliban regime's desire to erase all non-Islamic reminders of Afghan history. Not too long ago, to cite a less dramatic instance, the state governments of Madras (Chennai) and Bombay (Mumbai) replaced the colonial names of the two cities with vernacular designations. Cheap political motives aside, one could view this as an attempt either to retrieve a pre-colonial memory rudely suppressed by colonial history or, alternatively, to forget the foundational 'imperial' history of these stubbornly modern cities. Many brutal dictators and regimes, aiming to preserve a mythical homogeneity, have tried to erase the signifiers of difference from their societies. The extermination of Gypsies and Jews in Germany during the Holocaust, the 'ethnic cleansing' of Muslims in Bosnia and the slaughter of Tutsis in Rwanda are examples of attempts at refashioning a national memory purged of 'racial' difference. The perpetrators may choose to forget or actually forget the atrocity, but the victims remember. In Australia, for instance, when members of the Stolen Generation (consisting of aboriginal children forcibly taken from their parents as part of a state-sponsored assimilation policy) requested an apology for the outrage, the prime minister declined to take up this responsibility. Japan has yet to say sorry for its brutal role in the last War (despite requests), the United States has shown little remorse for its military intervention in Vietnam, while Indonesia has washed its hands of East Timor without the slightest penitential murmur. Such modes of forgetting, which rely on selective memory, are strategic denials of culpability.

Memory, however, is rarely the preserve of one player or culture or point of view. Since it is subject to complex acts of inscription and erasure, the truth behind a memory is frequently contestable. We remember and forget *differently*. This is exactly why memory is so painfully susceptible to acts of power and ideological scripting, even while it is also wonderfully subversive of these.

Further Reading

Chaudhuri, Nirad C. 1951. *Autobiography of an Unknown Indian*. London: Macmillan.

Joyce, James. 1967. *Portrait of the Artist as a Young Man*. London: Thames and Hudson.

Montale, Eugenio. 2000. *Collected Poems 1920–1954*. Bilingual edition. Translated by Jonathan Galassi. New York: Farrar, Straus and Giroux.

Morrison, Toni. *Beloved*. 1990. New York: Penguin.

Proust, Marcel. 1934. *Remembrance of Things Past*. New York: Random House.

Sanadhya, Totaram. 2003. *My Twenty-One Years in Fiji and The Story of the Haunted Line*. Translated and edited by John Dunham Kelly and Uttara Kumari Singh. Fiji: Fiji Museum.

Military

C. Douglas Lummis

Upon retiring as President of the United States, General Dwight Eisenhower warned against the danger of the growing 'military-industrial complex'. The warning gives the false impression that the military's infiltration into civil society is a 'danger', not a fact. But the military—at least in those states formed on the Western model—is not merely a 'branch of government'. It is an economic organization, a political entity, a legal entity and a bearer of culture. (William Blackstone [1768] called it a 'jurisdiction'.)

The Military as an Economic Entity

In ancient times (for example, under the Roman Republic) the army contributed to the economy by sacking the cities it conquered, and exacting tribute ('contribute' once meant 'to levy tribute upon' [OED]). In the age of colonialism the Western militaries brought foreign lands and peoples under their control, and provided the force by which wealth could be systematically extracted from the conquered territories. Today this unequal economic system (renamed 'economic development') is well established on a world scale, and (especially after the demise of the Soviet Union) to defend this system is the job of the Western militaries.

At the same time, as wages replaced booty as support for the soldiers, the military itself became an important economic body. In the US it is the hidden Keynesian pump-priming system that keeps the capitalist economy afloat. It was not the New Deal, but the military spending after 1941 that pulled the American economy out of the Depression of the 1930s, and the US has, on various pretexts, stayed on a war economy ever since. Hundreds of thousands of people are paid salaries though they do no productive labour, and billions of dollars are spent to research and manufacture products that have, with occasional exceptions, no social value. If this make-work spending were suddenly cut off, the US-led economy would surely fall back to 1929. The military, like other economic organizations today, protects its existence by actively creating demand for its product, that is, war.

The Military as a Legal-Political Entity

In many states today, the military is *the* governing body. But even in republics, the military stands alongside the constitutional government as the state's 'other body'. This means, first, that the military is a system of rule over its own members ('regiment' originally meant 'rule or government' [OED]). Military organization arranges people in an ascending hierarchy of groupings with a direct line of command connecting the commanding general with the foot-soldier. This rule is based on a code of law different from that which governs civilians. Here there is no freedom of action: orders are commands; refusal to obey is a criminal offence. There is no social equality: ranks are established by law. There is no freedom of speech. And soldiers don't have workers' rights: an attempt at collective bargaining would be mutiny, and an attempt to quit, desertion. At the same time soldiers have a right that civilians do not have: when they kill people in accordance with the laws of war, they cannot be treated as murderers.

Moreover, the military is not only a jurisdiction in itself it also aims to create new jurisdictions. That is, war seeks to bring a people under the rule of the government on behalf of which the military is fighting. Though today it is illegal to engage in old-fashioned wars of expansion, all wars fought since 1945 have been either attempts to replace the jurisdiction of one state with that of another or else to force a state to accept the political demands of another state—that is, to accept its 'rule' at least partially.

Third, the military also has the capacity, and in most countries the operational plans, to place the citizens of its own country under its rule: martial law. Martial law does not mean that citizens are placed under the legal system of soldiers; that would be totalitarianism. It means that the legal system is suspended, and the citizenry is placed under the arbitrary rule of the military, that is, treated as a conquered people. Martial-law commanders will generally not be interested in suspending, say, traffic law, but rather the laws protecting the rights of accused persons. Martial-law regimes typically arrest and execute people according to their whim. But a martial-law regime could suspend traffic law, if it so decided. A martial-law regime is the 'return' to a pre-political, pre-legal state of war between the government and the people.

Why Are Armed Forces Forceful?

Why do militaries win? Of course they don't always. In war, for every winner there is a loser, an average success rate of 50 per cent: not that good, considering the cost. But what is decisive is the advantage militaries have over civilians. This has three aspects: resources, training and organization, and state-granted legitimacy.

Concerning resources, it is unnecessary to elaborate, especially in the case of the modern militaries of the great powers. These control fabulous wealth, which supports huge numbers of personnel. Moreover they have access to weapons and technologies available to no one else. This is a great difference from the days when wars were fought with swords and arrows.

But even then, militaries had the advantage of their training ('drill') and organization. Drill means to turn round and round, but also used to mean 'to turn', as on a lathe. 'Drill', under which soldiers are turned this way and that on the 'drill field', shaves away bumps and idiosyncrasies and creates a homogenized body of individuals conditioned to respond instantly to commands. 'Soldiers' (from the Latin *solidare*) are drilled in unit-solidarity, and that is the secret of their strength. They are drilled in ranks, and in battle it is the side that breaks ranks that loses. Civilians have no 'ranks' in the first place.

A third advantage militaries have is state legitimacy. Soldiers know that they will never be condemned as murderers. It makes it easier for them to kill with no moral or interest-based qualms, sleep well and kill again. This is a great advantage, especially when fighting civilians.

What Do Militaries Do?

The answer has two aspects: what military organizations are supposed to do (under the laws of war) and what they actually do. Put differently, what soldiers do when they hold ranks, and what they do when, after prevailing, they break ranks.

These two faces of the military are well illustrated in Shakespeare's *Henry V*. In this play's description of the Battle of Agincourt, said to be historically accurate, the English and French armies line up at opposite ends of a field where no non-combatants are present, begin the battle at an agreed-upon time, end it before sunset, show great concern for the laws of war and accept the verdict of the heralds who had watched the battle from the adjoining hill, as to who is the victor (it is the English, who never break ranks). This is a classic model for Just War.

In the same play there is a description of the English siege of Harfleur. On the verge of victory, King Henry tells the Governor: If you surrender now, I will grant you 'our best mercy'. If not, 'I will not leave the half-achieved Harfleur / Till in her ashes she lie buried.'

> Therefore you men of Harfleur,
> Take pity on your town and of your people
> Whiles yet my soldiers are in my command;
>
> . . .
>
> If not—why, in a moment look to see
> The blind and bloody with foul hand
> Defile the locks of your shrill-shrieking daughters;
> Your fathers taken by the silver beards
> And their most reverend heads dash'd to the walls:
> Your naked infants spitted upon pikes,
> Whiles their mad mothers with their howls confus'd
> Do break the clouds.

Here is a prophecy of the carnage that ensues when the laws of war are suspended. The soldiers are 'unleashed'. An old term for this scenario is 'Military Execution': 'delivering a country up to be ravaged and destroyed by the soldiers' (OED).

Today such actions are forbidden by international law and by the internal regulations of most armies. This puts modern militaries in a difficult position. War carried out under strict discipline, especially ground war, is an activity that leads naturally to a collapse into mob violence once victory is assured. This is also built into military culture and, as in the above example, is an effective tactic: a commander can terrorize an enemy by threatening to release his troops from discipline, or by actually doing so. The fact that it has been outlawed does not mean that it has disappeared as a phase of military action, a potential that all ground armies carry. The pervasiveness of military mob action throughout history is testified to by the rich vocabulary for describing it: we speak of rapine, of laying waste, of sacking a city, of taking spoils, or booty, or plunder. One of the definitions of 'rape' also refers to this form of military action: 'to rob, strip, plunder (a place)' (OED), for example, the Rape of Nanking. At the same time, the actual raping of women seems to be an inseparable aspect of military rapine, as can be seen in the most ancient wars of which we have record, and the most recent.

Who Does the Military Kill?

The task of soldiers is to kill. According to the rules of just war, they should try to kill only enemy soldiers, and avoid killing civilians. But in most wars, more civilians are killed than soldiers. This is understandable: civilians are easier to kill. Untrained, unorganized and unarmed they don't know how to take cover, don't act according to a plan, and can't shoot back. It is much more dangerous to try to kill soldiers; you might get killed yourself.

More surprising is the fact that in the twentieth century military organizations killed more of their own country people than they did foreigners. This goes against the fixed idea that militaries are established to protect the citizens of a nation-state against foreigners. It is less surprising if one remembers that the chief function of the military in most states is to establish and protect the government's power over the people. Most of the wars going on in the world are between governments and their people, and most militaries have no other purpose.

Can Women Achieve Equality in the Military?

Most of the debate on this issue misses the point, because it falsely assumes that only legal warfare will be fought. Certainly women can do all the things that legal warfare entails. No doubt women are even capable of long-distance war crimes, such as are carried out by aircraft. The military Old Guard, who argue that women can never be soldiers in the way men can, can't publicly state the real reason. They know that there is more to warfare than legal operations. They know that an army that does not carry with it at least the tacit threat of rape and pillage is no army at all in the traditional sense. 'Yes,' they want to say, 'you can fire a machine gun and drive a tank, but how are you going to participate the rape and pillage?' The question is probably unanswerable, but certainly unaskable.

Further Reading

Blackstone, William. 1979. *Commentaries on the Laws of England: A Facsimile of the First Edition of 1765–1969*. Chicago: University of Chicago Press.

Bourke, Joanna. 1999. *An Intimate History of Killing: Face to Face Killing in 20th Century Warfare*. New York: Basic Books.

Lummis, C. Douglas. 1996. Democracy's flawed tradition. In *Radical Democracy*. Ithaca: Cornell University Press.

Rummel, R.J. 1994. *Death by Government*. New Brunswick and London: Transaction Publishers.

Mystery

David Punter

Mysteries: originally a plural rather than a singular. Relating to rites, rituals, secrets that can never be told. In the service of these secrets, initiates come to take part in a certain etymological closure; at root, 'mystery' refers to the closing of lips or eyes. The absence, therefore, of what is seen, or the absence of narrative, the vanishing of an account even in the moment when it is to be transmitted. To participate in a mystery is to act and at the same time to withhold that action: it is to enter fully into the structure of the secret, whereby every secret is withheld but simultaneously told—for if it were not told, then we would have no evidence that there was a secret. As with children saying, 'Mummy, I have a secret,' we are left dumbfounded, grounded in dumbness (the closure of the lips); we cannot request that the secret be told, for that would breach decorum and trust, but neither can we remain outside the charmed circle for in that way the secret in the child's possession would remain painfully valueless. The secret, then, is a commodity, whose value is activated only in the instant of its trading, its commutation; asserted only in the moment of its disappearance as it resigns itself to the patina of common wear. 'A religious truth long kept secret, but now revealed through Christ to his Church'; without mystery there can be no revelation, without the secret there can be no apocalypse, no unbinding of the book in which all secrets are written, displayed and hidden at the same time in complex tiers of augmentings and accretions.

In these etymological terms, then, we might state the 'history of mystery': from the apparently 'classical' (in the West—the silence, for example, of the dramatic chorus) to Freudian theories regarding the psychic mechanisms behind impulses to secrecy. But now, in the twenty-first century, we find—or lose—ourselves on the terrain of other mysteries. Plurality, for example: what is now the mystery of plurality? Let us take it to be, for example, the 'mystery of the uncounted vote'. Who would have guessed, as one commentator recently put it, that the future of the US presidency would be decided, not on votes cast, but on votes uncounted, precipitating, apparently, an unprecedented legal interposition in the 'political' process? Who would have guessed, in particular, that this could occur on the terrain of the 'policeman of the world', whose strictures have so often been handed down (rarely through any alternative notion of plurality known as the 'United Nations', more usually through the violent weapons of economic and military ascendancy) to those 'remote' corners of the world in which votes may be (unaccountably) lost? Let us be clear, and not succumb to the lure of the 'mystery'; any pretension the US has ever had (not so considerable, after all) to democracy is now irretrievable.

The further mystery remains this: it has made no difference. Black voters were disenfranchised by the thousands, but the WASP establishment does not consider this worth pursuing. Democracy fatally, mysteriously damaged; but the oily white man returns to power, so business can proceed as usual. And the final mystery remains unanswerable: what skeletons in their own closet so terrorized the Democrats that they abandoned all hope of justice at the earliest convenient stage?

We should not ask such questions; to do so would be to probe the mysteries of political mastery, and luckily much education is now geared to prevent us from acquiring the tools with which we might construct such disturbing queries. Let us turn instead to the mystery of the singular. The 'I' of capitalism for example, which is the consumerist 'I', the apparent singular which is at the mercy of the statisticians of the many. What a great mystery there is, for

example, in the pseudo-conflict of the colas (Coca, Pepsi, Virgin)—
how shall we find a mechanism to arbitrate between these subtleties
of taste, between the future effects of indistinguishable deadly
concoctions whose own composition is a jealously guarded mystery?
Where might the (residual) 'I' reside amid the blandishments of so
many indistinguishable pleasures?

Or we might dwell on the thought of rituals—freemasonry, to
take one example, the age-old state within a state. As Edgar Allan
Poe knew though, such unaccountable brotherhoods can conduce
to a lethal immuring; and we see every day within the judiciary—
spread from the UK and the US, through various colonial courts
(Hong Kong, Puerto Rico) and courts of appeal—a 'brotherhood'
of privilege held together in the moth-eaten robes of a presumed
'universal' justice. There are, of course, difficult, liminal, cases. We
have, perhaps, no powerful individual 'case' to make against a
courageous white Zimbabwean Chief Justice, except for this: how
mysterious it is that he was there in the first place. 'In the first
place': what greater mystery could there be than who occupies the
first place . . . But really there is no mystery here: the 'first place'
is occupied, settled, by reason of pre-eminence—not, that is, of
prior rights over the territory, but by right of dominance or
occupation, from Zimbabwe to Ireland, from Papua New Guinea
to Hawaii.

The closing of lips—and eyes—may also be seen as a question
of silence in the face of brutality. The mystery of silence, of
compliance, of non-complaint. Mystery, we might say, is a
conspiracy, but there we come upon an important political and
discursive weapon. For conspiracy, we are told, always comes
from below; it is the way in which the discourse of the dominant
reconfigures the organization of resistance, from Algeria to Vietnam.
In the corporate boardrooms (where they plot the trajectory of, for
example, the colas and other weapons of mass destruction) there
is, we happily notice, no talk of conspiracies: the discourse is
instead of strategies, of tactics, of market penetration, of sales
trajectory. Campaigns without bloodshed, vampirisms without
substance. In Shanghai, as I have seen, children dyed white and

shaking from accumulations of lime and the residue from poisoned factory floors complete their Stakhanovite tasks by sewing labels on to the fashionable clothing they will never wear. Sears Roebuck, the labels said; how mysterious are the consumptive ways of capital.

Boardroom discourse is nonetheless military in nature: and what the military (the arch-conspirators and Caesars through the ages) most hates and acknowledges it cannot tackle is a . . . well, let us call it a conspiracy. We might put it out on the broadcast channels thus: here is your army, the army you are paying for, and it is as transparent as a pane of glass (or the pain of a 'glassing'—or as the pain of class, if we were to mysteriously mishear), but over there, hiding in the jungle, or festering in the housing estates and barrios, in the Walled Cities of the imagination, or at any rate deep underground, is what we need to call a conspiracy. What a pity, we might later be told, that it turned out to have only a few dozen rusty rapiers at its disposal as we covered it in protective napalm. How dreadful it is that the few thousand 'anti-capitalists' of Seattle actually dared to use the Internet as a mode of organization, thus aping the manners of their superiors; how doubly dreadful when we consider that they were thus using a weapon invented by the Pentagon itself for use in precisely such civilization-threatening circumstances.

A further mystery, then, is why overwhelming power conjures its own paranoias so swiftly, and with such dire consequences. Were the cultists of Waco really a threat to the nation-state? Did the Unabomber's lonely, crazed campaign really menace the foundations of society? Did he really, when finally placed before the all-seeing camera of 'justice', really seem more out of touch with the real than Lieutenant Calley, than Stormin' Norman, than the bronze generals and adventurers who still strut high on horseback along avenues in most of our major cities? What is more insane: to suppose that one can suppress, infiltrate and control an entire people or to hope that one might be able to carve out a small area of freedom within the all-encompassing panopticon of capitalist triumph? Mystery is, perhaps, really a hall of distorting mirrors.

Then again, there is the mystery that appears to flow from the absence of narrative. Let us consider, for instance, the cases of Pinochet (no other tribunal seems interested in hearing the evidence) and Milosevic. As soon as we think of their names and of the unfortunate situations that have recently come their way, we have to realize that narrative is crucial. For without narrative, who can make connections? Perhaps these sad, sick men, presenting their doctors' notes as though they were students trying to avoid an essay deadline, really had no idea what was going on. Perhaps, like Macavity the mystery cat, they were somewhere else at the time. Perhaps they were badly served by acolytes and minions who overstepped their instructions, like those who killed Thomas à Becket believing they were carrying out their monarch's wish. Then again, perhaps this is all really the rubbish we know it to be in our heart of hearts; these are perversions of narrative, the invocation of mysterious subversions of communication that never really existed. To believe that Pinochet and Milosevic (and the French generals of Algeria, and the European destroyers of Indochina) should suffer for their crimes is no doubt an offence against the concept of a liberal conscience. If it were not for the workings of mystery, then the obvious next stage would be to interrogate the origins of the universalist claims of such a notion as the 'liberal conscience'; but to bring such a matter before a 'higher court' would be to risk upsetting the fictions of a new world order, to roll back the pleasing plenitude of Western commercial and military dominance.

A quick checklist of further mysteries. Evidence itself is now a mystery—on what can one rely? The signature, as we have always known, is falsifiable; its replacement, the PIN number, is unreliable—or at least the machines that feed on it are. Video evidence can be tampered with, remade differently. As Bret Easton Ellis chillingly says, to place an axe in anybody's hand is the work of a moment, the merest movement of a mouse. We no longer need grand tyrannies; the record can now always show us to be, or to have been, different from ourselves, in a different place, doing different things; our memories are subordinate to a different register of arrangement.

In the dark light of this vanishing of evidence, it becomes impossible to trace the trajectory of the commodity or of currency or of identity itself. The fiction used to run that it was the criminal mind that invented means of deception, fraudulent systems, forgeries of all kinds. What we have to know in the twenty-first century is that it is (as, in truth, it always was) the state apparatus which displays its mastery in the control and proliferation of precisely such devices. These may include the plethora of false records surrounding the death of John F. Kennedy—a plethora that has grown so large, we may reasonably suspect, that it now even confuses those state officials who constructed it in the first place. Is there, then, any other public death of which we can feel truly certain, any circumstance in which the hand of a mysterious remarshalling of evidence cannot be detected?

Under such circumstances, we might ask to be shown the body, but here we find ourselves again on a terrain of mystery: the mysteries of the body and of mortality. We are now told, for example, that the human body need not age. The obvious question would be (were we not blinded by mystery): *where* need it not age? In Cambodia? In Niger? In the Philippines, where the remains of a heroic struggle against US hegemony has left a population with the prospect of endlessly expanding in a catastrophically diminishing economy? Of course not. This is the politics—and the medicine—of Paradise, as ridiculously irrelevant in the current world as the notion of children's rights. Let us be clear: children do not *have* rights—to say so is merely to contribute to a further utopian level of mystification. Children *should* have rights; but the fact remains that in most of the world they do not, and they are not about to have rights conferred upon them by fiat—at least partly because the only global bodies that could have any feasible effect on the situation are fatally compromised by their (mysterious) relation with the US.

As I write, there is news of a potential embargo of Exxon, whose products may kill children: more mystery. It is as though it is supposed that, if we stop buying Exxon products (even supposing we know what they are, which we do not), then somehow Exxon would suffer. What is not grasped here is that multinational corporations are invulnerable: they cannot suffer. They can see their profits reduced, certainly; in extreme cases (but not, I think, in the case of Exxon) they might cease to trade. But this, apart from reducing some shareholders' savings, has no real effect. The members of the board, or at least those few insufficiently rich and old to retire (who are probably also the least intelligent), merely pop up elsewhere, making more money. Profits continue, even if the name under which they are reaped changes.

So at the moment, we might say that the most apt name of mystery is the multinational corporation. Elusive, always able to vanish and reappear under another name, demanding staff and customer allegiance without any return, it seeks the attributes of an unresponsive divinity and makes (holy) fools of us all. The question then becomes: how to rid ourselves of this monstrous parasitic growth that threatens to cover the planet? This is the real mystery; it is the one that we should be plumbing. It is even, we might say, the task of the twenty-first century, the old Marxist task of ideological demystification still with us, still haunting us, still as demanding as ever of our energies.

Nuclearism

Ashis Nandy

Nuclearism is the ideology of nuclear weaponry and nuclear arms-based security. It is the most depraved, shameless and costly pornography of our times. Such an ideology cannot be judged only by the canons of international relations, geopolitics, political sociology or ethics. It is also a well-known, identifiable, psychopathological syndrome, as identified by a series of studies, conducted by psychologists, psychoanalysts and psychiatrists, of genocidal mentality in general, and nuclearism in particular. The following is a brief summary of its clinical picture, epidemiology and prognosis, as they emerge from these studies.

Nuclearism does not reside in institutions, though it may set up, symbolize or find distinctive expression in social, political and scientific institutions. It is an individual pathology and has clear identifiers. Many years ago, Brian Easlea argued in his book *Fathering the Unthinkable* that nuclearism was associated with strong masculinity strivings. Isley was no psychologist, but the works of Carol Cohn and others have endorsed the broad contours of his analysis. They show that not only the language and ideology but the entire culture of nuclear weaponry is infiltrated by hard, masculine imagery, and those participating in that culture usually suffer from deep fears of emasculation or impotency. Indeed, that is the reason they participate in that culture with enthusiasm.

Such strivings for hyper-masculinity are usually linked to various forms of authoritarianism. Even people ideologically committed to democratic governance may vicariously participate in subtler forms of authoritarianism associated with nuclearism. Robert Jungk's work on the nuclear state, *New Tyranny* (1979), shows that secrecy, security, surveillance and police-state methods invariably accompany the nuclear establishment in every country. In that sense, the culture of nuclearism is one of the true 'universals' of our time. Like Coca-Cola and blue jeans, it does not permit much cultural adaptation or many edited versions. It is the same in Paris and Pokhran, Lahore and Los Alamos.

Nuclearism is framed by a specific personality type, the spread of which at some points of time may acquire epidemic proportions in a society. Eric Markusen and Robert J. Lifton have systematically studied the links. In their book *The Genocidal Mentality* they make a comparative study of the psychology of mass murderers, in Nazi Germany, in Hiroshima and Nagasaki and among the ideologues of nuclearism today. The authors find remarkable continuities. In the genocidal person there is, first of all, a state of mind called 'psychic numbing'—a 'diminished capacity or inclination to feel' and 'a general sense of meaninglessness'. One so numbs one's sensitivities that normal emotions and moral considerations cannot penetrate one any more. Numbing 'closes off' a person and leads to a 'constriction of self process'. To him or her, the death or the possibility of the death of millions begins to look like an abstract, bureaucratic detail, involving the calculation of military gains or losses, geopolitics or mere statistics. Markusen and Lifton may not agree, but such numbing can be considered the final culmination of the separation of affect and cognition—that is, emotion and thought—that the European Enlightenment sanctioned and celebrated as the first step towards greater objectivity and scientific rationality.

The genocidal mentality also tends to create an area protected from public responsibility or democratic accountability. Usually such responsibility is avoided by re-conceptualizing oneself as only a cog in the wheel, advancing one's own bureaucratic or scientific career like everybody else, by taking and obeying orders from superior authorities faithfully, mechanically, without thinking about the moral implications of the orders. The Nazi war criminals tried at Nuremberg at the end of the Second World War all ventured the defence that they were under orders to kill innocent people, including women, children and the elderly, and could do nothing about it. Hannah Arendt's *Eichmann in Jerusalem* (1963) is a classic study of the evil that masquerades as banal, harmless, everyday conformity to bureaucratic norms.

The other way of avoiding accountability is to remove it from individuals and vest it in institutions and aggregates, as if institutions by themselves could run a death machine without the intervention of individuals! After a while, even terms like the military-industrial complex, fascism, imperialism, Stalinism, ruling class or American hegemony become ways of freeing the actual, real-life persons from their culpability for recommending, ordering or committing mass murders. In a society where genocidal mentality spreads, intellectuals also find such impersonal analyses soothing; they contribute to the creation of a business-as-usual ambience, in which institutions are ritually blamed and the psychopathic scientists, bureaucrats and politicians who work towards genocides move around scot-free and are even celebrated as national heroes.

This is not surprising in a world where the persons responsible for the genocides in Rwanda, Cambodia and Bangladesh—to give only a few recent examples—face no serious threat of prosecution today. Sometimes they are protected by the lethargy of, and loopholes in, the operative regime of international criminal law, sometimes by the fact that the killers enjoy the protection or patronage of the powerful and the wealthy. The Indonesian massacres of 1965 and the Bangladesh massacres of 1971 are two of the least studied genocides of our times and have not attracted the attention of too many activists. Their perpetrators also look perfectly safe. Perhaps because both the genocides were made possible by the political establishment of the United States of America, including Henry Kissinger, a recipient of the Nobel Peace Prize.

In acute cases, the genocidal mentality turns into necrophilia, a clinical state in which the patient is in love with death. Indeed, he or she wants to sleep with the dead, in fantasy and, in some cases, in real life. Saadat Hassan Manto's famous story *Thanda Gosht* (Cold Meat) is, unknown to the author, the story of an 'ordinary' murderer and rapist who, while trying to satiate his sexual greed during a communal conflict, confronts his own necrophilia and is devastated by that. Those interested in more authoritative case studies can look up Erich Fromm's once-popular *The Anatomy of Human Destructiveness.*

Nuclearism does not remain confined to the nuclear establishment or the nuclear community. It introduces other psychopathologies in a society. For instance, as it seeps into public consciousness, it creates a new awareness of the transience of life. It forces people to live with the constant fear that, one day, a sudden war or accident might kill not only them but also their children and grandchildren, and everybody they love. This awareness gradually creates a sense of the hollowness of life. For many, life is denuded of substantive meaning. The psychological numbing I have mentioned completes the picture. While the ordinary citizen leads an apparently normal life, he or she is constantly aware of the transience of such life and the risk of mega-death for the entire society. Often this finds expression in unnecessary or inexplicable violence in social life or in a more general, high state of anxiety and a variety of psychosomatic ailments. In other words, nuclearism begins to brutalize ordinary people and fragments everyday life.

Studies by researchers, such as of William Beardslee, J.E. Mach and Eleonora Masini, show that these traits express themselves even in adolescents and children. Even children barely eight or ten years old begin to live in what they consider to be a world without a future; they are fearful and anxious about their life, but unable to express that fear and anxiety directly, because in a nuclearized society the fear of nuclear death is made to look like an abnormal psychoneurotic state.

The situation could become worse in countries or societies where despair stalks the landscape, where life and the future have already lost much of their meaning. A good example is Peter Landesman's chilling description in the *Atlantic* monthly of his conversation with a politically influential Pakistani army officer casually talking of a nuclear war with India:

'We should fire at them and take out a few of their cities—Delhi, Bombay, Calcutta,' he said. 'They should fire back and take Karachi and Lahore. Kill off a hundred or two hundred million people. They should fire at us and it would all be over. They have acted so badly toward us; they have been so mean. We should teach them a lesson. It would teach all of us a lesson. There is no future here, and we need to start over. So many people think this. Have you been to the villages of Pakistan, the interior? There is nothing but dire poverty and pain. The children have no education; there is nothing to look forward to. Go into the villages, see the poverty. There is no drinking water. Small children without shoes walk miles for a drink of water. I go to the villages and I want to cry. My children have no future. None of the children of Pakistan have a future. We are surrounded by nothing but war and suffering . . .'

. . . He told me he was willing to see his children be killed. He repeated that they didn't have any future—his children or any other children.

Many neurotics and psychotics at first look like charming eccentrics. To start with, nuclearism may appear a smart game and the partisans of nuclear weaponry may look like normal politicians, scholars or defence experts. Many psychopaths, too, have attractive, charismatic, almost seductive personalities. Apart from that, in modern societies there is ample scope for keeping double ledgers. As we all know, the Nazis killers too were usually loving fathers, connoisseurs of good music and honest, tax-paying citizens. However, beneath such façades lies a personality that is insecure, doubtful about its masculinity, fearful of the interpersonal world and unable to love. The mindless violence such a personality anticipates or plans is a pathetic attempt to fight these inner feelings of emptiness, and the suspicion and the fear that one's moral self might already be dead within. You father the unthinkable because you have already psychologically orphaned yourself. Like the Pakistani army officer, you make contingency plans to kill millions because you fear that your innermost core has already been cauterized against all normal feelings and human relations. Acquiring the power to inflict death on millions, or by living with the fantasy of acquiring that power, you pathetically try to get some confirmation that you are still alive. However, that confirmation never comes. For, in the process of acquiring that power, you may not be not dead physically, but you are already morally, socially and psychologically a corpse.

Further Reading

Cohn, Carol. 1996. Nuclear language and how we learnt to pat the bomb. In *Feminism and Science*. Edited by Evelyn Fox Keller and Helen Longino. New York: Oxford University.

Easlea, Brian. 1983. *Fathering the Unthinkable: Masculinity, Scientists and the Nuclear Arms Race*. London: Pluto.

Lifton, Robert J., and Eric Markusen. 1990. *The Genocidal Mentality: Nazi Holocaust and Nuclear Threat*. New York: Basic Books.

Peasant

Ashis Nandy

The peasant is a multivalent idea in our times. It arouses strange passions and often brings out the worst and the best in human nature—from genocidal rage to cultivated apathy to dissenting moral visions. The idea is often autonomous of the social sector or vocation it is supposed to describe. As a result, while the proportion of peasants in the world population has dramatically declined in the last 300 years, their importance as a cultural-psychological category has not. Indeed, the social sector or occupational group has been often forced to bear the brunt of our tortuous, love-hate relationship with the idea. The peasants have been the target of virtually every form of radical social engineering during the last three centuries. They have defined most utopias and visions of desirable societies that continue to shape our lives—directly or indirectly, either as constituents of a utopia or that of a dystopia. Indeed, only in recent decades have we tried to break out of the nineteenth-century visions of desirable societies that almost invariably defined progress and social evolution with reference to the movement from a peasant lifestyle to an urban-industrial culture. At least some of the new analyses of the shape of things to come seem to avoid entanglement in a debate on the sustainability or moral stature of a peasant lifestyle. However, such theorizing is a recent trend and none of these new intellectual exercises has as yet caught the public fancy or become influential among the policy elite.

All modern societies and all industrial societies—modern or partly modern—have emerged by explicitly repudiating peasant lifestyles and the state of mind reportedly associated with the peasantry, whether the association is true or false, real or imaginary, natural or unnatural. Industrialization began in Europe with the enclosure movement, which, whatever might have been its stated goals, was basically an attempt to re-engineer the peasants into an industrial proletariat. Singapore, one of the last states in the world to complete its industrialization, saw its peasants, along with their pigs and poultry, being huddled into apartment buildings as part of an attempt to convert them into a developmental resource, that is, an industrial working force. Such projects acquired a murderous look in despotic, self-righteous regimes. During the twentieth century, in Soviet Union and Maoist China, the peasants were victims of state-mentored genocides—in the first case, in the name of equity through collectivization; in the second, in the name of a state-designed, non-exploitative society through man-made, avoidable famines. According to the relatively conservative estimates of the political scientist R.J. Rummell, in 1932-33, about five million Ukrainian peasants were more or less deliberately starved to death and, during 1930–37, six and a half million better-off peasants or peasants resisting collectivization were slaughtered. In 1943, in the man-made Bengal famine, the three million victims were all peasants. They died for the sake of the British war effort in the eastern sector, when there was enough food in Bengal. For the moment I am ignoring the case of the man-made Irish famine during 1845–50, mainly because they targeted not so much the Irish peasants as the Irish people as a whole.

Such exterminations were not widely condemned—indeed, they were often condoned or whitewashed by well-meaning, thinking people, partly because the idea of transformative politics that must be paid for in blood satisfies some deep-seated human need and helps us to grapple with some of our core fantasies. The fantasy of fighting for a just cause or bringing about radical social change by meting out death to hundreds of thousands has a peculiar appeal for social engineers. It seems to bestow omnipotence upon insecure rulers and millennial political movements.

However, organized exterminations are often not condemned also because, during the last two centuries, most progressive thinkers have thought poorly of peasants. Peasants have been seen not only as irrational and traditional, but as specifically steeped in stereotypes and prejudices, superstitions and magic. Politically, the peasants have looked irredeemable, perhaps because they have been notoriously tough to organize along modern lines. Not surprisingly, during the nineteenth century, a century of a certain innocent, uncritical commitment to modernity and social evolutionism as the final index of progress, there were systematic efforts to redefine all peasants as redundant and disposable—as useless burdens on societies, a population which should be ideally supplanted by a new agricultural working class given to industrialized farming and driven by technological innovations. This theme has recently staged a comeback under a new guise as part of the package called globalization. Until Gandhi and Mao Zedong began to insist otherwise, the peasant was popularly perceived as an impossible target of social engineering and transformative politics. Karl Marx called the peasants a sack of potatoes and spoke of the idiocy of village life. The great Eastern civilizations that he held in contempt as prehistoric and static entities were, predictably, agrarian societies. He accepted colonialism as an agent of history, despite recognizing the oppression and violence it unleashed, because it opened up such societies for historical changes.

That idea of the peasant lasted a very long time. In the poor societies—now euphemistically called developing societies—that constituted the so-called Third World after the Second World War, the peasants appeared to be the main stumbling block to social change and agricultural innovations. Literally hundreds of papers in journals of social sciences and dozens of books were written on the subject and on the strategies to change the peasant attitudes to time, leisure, money, occupation, family and, above all, agricultural practices in general and agricultural innovations in particular. Strangely, when new seeds and pesticides and irrigation systems were introduced in these societies, the peasants took to them rather quickly, though often with a clear touch of scepticism. Today, in retrospect, it seems that they sometimes accepted the innovations a bit too eagerly. Often living at the margins of survival, oppressed and exploited by unjust land-ownership patterns and land relations, and targets of rulers and local tyrants eager to extract surplus from them, the peasantry perhaps saw in the new agronomy an escape from poverty and drudgery. In some societies they were already rendered vulnerable by famines, wars and other major social and political upheavals. Yet, few states were impressed by that adaptability. To most, the peasants still looked incapable of handling modern agronomy, cash crops meant for the global market and scientific farm management. These states were convinced that development had to be defined as the means of siphoning off resources from the agrarian sectors to the cities. Many Third World regimes particularly resented what looked to them like peasant obstinacy in matters of social change, and peasant cunning that apparently aimed at subverting major state projects in what some psychiatrists might call a passive-aggressive manner.

However, just when the image of the peasant began to look less recalcitrant and more versatile, just when the Green Revolution began to spread in South and East Asia and in parts of Latin America, and the re-imaging of the peasant as a major tool of history, initiated by Gandhi and Mao, began to seep into popular consciousness, the Soviet Union collapsed. And an astonished world found the famous, near-mythical, valourized Russian peasant of Leo Tolstoy and Fyodor Dostoevsky pathetically waiting, without a clue, for instructions from the now-extinct Soviet policy makers— the agricultural bureaucrats and the laboratory agronomists who had come to set the pace of Russian agriculture after asserting their dominance through a series of particularly cruel, genocidal interventions. Evidently, progressivism had done its job. The Russian peasants had obviously lost some of their traditional, crafty, robust scepticism and their self-confidence in their own lifestyle, practices and beliefs.

Even the formidable Indian peasants today seem to be caught in the same rat trap. They have modernized themselves enthusiastically and at breakneck speed. In the process, they have become more, not less, dependent on forces outside their world. During the 1990s, an epidemic of suicides broke out and has continued more or less unabated among farmers in three of the most prosperous states in India, where modern agricultural practices are triumphant. And to spike our ideas of what constitutes progress and healthy development, the poorest states in the country, still ill governed and mired in exploitative land relations, have seen virtually no instance of suicide. According to some estimates, the total number of farmers who have killed themselves is already double the number of those killed on 11 September 2001 in New York City. Indeed, the number of suicides may in the end exceed the total number of those killed by what India's power elite calls cross-border terrorism in Kashmir. The news of the self-destruction of farmers is usually reported in the inside pages of newspapers as minor misfortunes and as sad but accidental by-products of the process of modernization.

The epidemic of suicides, in exactly those parts of India that are most progressive and responding to the forces of globalization most efficiently, could turn out to be the final denouement of the fate of the traditional peasantry in Asia. Agribusiness and industrialized farming by multinational corporations have arrived. A lifestyle and a vocation at least 4000 years old is finally facing extinction.

Further Reading

Gay, Peter. 1995. *Irish Famine*. New York: Harry N. Abrams.

Polanyi, Karl. 1944. *The Great Transformation: The Political and Economic Origins of Our Time*. Boston: Beacon.

Rummel, R.J. 1994. *Death by Government: Genocide and Mass Murder since 1990*. West Hanover, Massachusetts: Christopher Publishing.

———. 1997. *Power Kills*. New Brunswick: Transaction.

Place

Roby Rajan

In 1974 the Congress of the United States passed the Navajo-Hopi Land Settlement Act to end a 'land dispute' between the Navajo and Hopi tribes over approximately 1.8 million acres (7285 square kilometres) of land in north-eastern Arizona. The act called for the land to be equally divided between the two tribes; a Navajo-Hopi Relocation Commission was created to oversee the removal of nearly 10,000 Navajos from their ancestral homelands, to construct a barbed-wire fence demarcating the lands apportioned to the two groups and to provide modern mobile or modular homes in nearby towns to relocated Navajos. Until the passage of this Act, the land had been classified in official US government documents as a 'Joint Use Area' used by the sheep-herding Navajos and the agriculturist Hopis.

Shortly after the relocation had begun, officials with the federal Indian Health Service noticed a sharp increase in the incidence of violence, divorce, crime, alcoholism, depression and suicide among the relocatees—findings that were subsequently corroborated in studies. Loss of memory, inability to concentrate, partial paralysis and other symptoms of psychoneurotic and psychosomatic deterioration were found to be widespread. Scholars have since tried to understand the psychological problems that suddenly surfaced among the Navajo as a result of a loss of 'identity', identity grounded in sacred places. Paul Shepard, for instance, describes in *Nature and Madness* how place is an integral part of the indigenous unconscious, enhanced by mythology and ceremony and generating a network of deep attachments that cements the self. Place acts as a mnemonic, integrating component of sacred history, with the whole region becoming a hierophantic map for time, memory, relationships and home. Relocation from sacred place, according to Shepard, can lead to loss of orientation, loss of community and ultimately loss of self.

But might the symptoms manifested by the Navajo have something more to teach us than the psychological ill effects of being uprooted from sacred place? After all, there is today an aggressive new kind of resurgent indigene who is laying claim to sacred place, and is willing to go to any length to annex and defend it—even if it means mutilating and annihilating. The most spectacular recent demonstration of this was staged by certain Hindus on 6 December 1992, when they set upon a sixteenth-century Muslim mosque in Ayodhya in northern India with pickaxes, shovels and bare hands, reducing the medieval monument to rubble in a matter of hours. It was alleged, in defence of this wrecking orgy, that the mosque stood on the site of an ancient temple commemorating the birth of their god Rama on that very spot.

One should therefore be careful not to confuse two very different kinds of claimants to sacred place: the Hindu indigene is best understood as a neo-primordialist who—even as he swears by his primordialism—is fiercely wedded to all the latest in social engineering. His motto is identical to that coined by Erich Fromm for the sadomasochistic character type: 'deference to superiors, contempt for inferiors'. This was seen most clearly when India's Hindu nationalist regime detonated the country's first nuclear device. After this fiery demonstration of might, the first act of the prime minister was not to consult the leaderships of the smaller neighbouring countries (who might have the most reason to be concerned about his new-found virility) or the non-aligned movement to which India had historically been committed. No, his first act was to get on the phone to the US president, seeking affirmation and approval, even citing to the Master the 'strategic threat' from neighbouring China as jeopardizing their collective security. In the Hindu indigene, we can see in stark form the elements that make up the ideological universe of the neo-primordialist: a history that can be traced back to the very dawn of time; the outsider who broke the fabulous temples and palaces of his Golden Age; extreme technological mobilization; and the wiping out of any recalcitrants—especially powerless ones—that stand in the way of his prestige projects. The idea of purified place underpins this universe: within days of the destruction of the mosque at Ayodhya, anti-Muslim violence had spread to numerous urban centres. During this period, according to Arjun Appadurai, 'Bombay's Hindus managed to violently rewrite urban space as sacred, national, and Hindu space'.

It is in this drive to rewrite space through cleansing and segregating that the hidden compact between the neo-primordialist and his counterpart in the West—the suburbanist—comes clearly into view. Both are convinced they have arrived at total self-definition: the neo-primordialist after having pinned down all the attributes that make up his ethno-religious 'identity', the sub-urbanist after having attained full-blown normalcy as the generic 'individual' fully adjusted and responsive to the competitive demands of today's global market. The one wants to cleanse his place of ethno-religious enemies, the other of sundry aliens, indigents and deviants.

Recent history has seen both categories simultaneously and rapidly on the ascendant, but it is suburban man who is definitely senior partner and pacesetter. Although the past few decades have seen him convincingly lock up his supremacy, they have also brought his habits, needs and predilections into sharper relief. On a typical day he moves between various privatized interiors: home to office complex to shopping centre to health club back to home, all of which are separated by distances that can only be covered by car. In the housing subdivision or condominium complex where he lives, every activity must be demonstrably purposeful. If walking, then it must not be mistaken for loitering, else it would immediately invite suspicion. Anyone not readily identifiable is experienced as upsetting and uncomfortable. Sharp demarcation lines separate residential area from business district, high-income neighbourhood from low-income neighbourhood to make sure the least possible strangeness is encountered. Enclaving and exclusion are his dominant principles of place-making, and security agencies his preferred form of group protection. Everything must be patrolled and surveillanced. His cities can be mapped as a series of zones first settled, then exploited, finally discarded as ghetto. Housing subdivisions, shopping malls, office parks sprawl farther and farther out, but when he is finally at a safe enough remove from the ghetto, he finds that everybody he encounters in his living space and during his activities outside that private space is just like him: they are all comrades in flight.

Unrestrained consumption and interest-group politics are the two principles of social organization most dear to him, and he is convinced that the rest of the world is in such sorry shape because they have not taken to these principles as readily as he has. He must therefore be ever alert to defend himself from rogues who are conspiring to wreck his domestic happiness and prosperity. Not content with the most advanced nuclear arsenal, he has now embarked on a scheme that would throw a protective anti-missile shield around himself and his 'allies' (in which ranks, incidentally, the neo-primordial Hindu has also eagerly enlisted); counter-missiles would be deployed in space, over land, air and sea that would intercept and destroy anything the rogues may fire at him.

On the face of it, this recurrent need for 'additional security' may seem like a universal one, but there is a specific feature of sub-urban man that lends to all his manoeuvres a certain air of menace. Over the years, he has gradually managed to pry himself loose from any form of moral economy and successfully become a free-floating maximizer of satisfactions, operating with a dangerously naive conception of freedom. In his everyday life, he may continue to be a friend, a son, a nephew, a church volunteer—but only so long as he 'freely chooses' to be so, only so long as he deems that these roles enable him to realize his 'true self'. One could, in a Lacanian idiom, say that the unsettling feature of sub-

urban man is that he has broken away from any ego-ideal that still
calls for the integration of a symbolic law. But this movement
away from an ego-ideal only heralds his entry into the kingdom of
rules and should in no way be mistaken for a release into some
realm of 'pure freedom'. Rules on how to eat healthy, rules on
how and when to exercise, rules on how to relax, rules on how to
dress for success . . . in short, rules and manuals for everything
that had in an earlier time seemed self-evident.

But being thrown into a field saturated with rules without an
ego-ideal, suburban man is left without any symbolic mandate
other than that of role playing, and ends up libidinally over-
invested in upholding the rule. It is therefore futile to try to
measure any threat 'objectively' and reassure him that his worry
is unfounded. His fear was always attached to breakdown of the
form of the rule, never to any moral or existential content behind
it. The fear is that if the rogue is allowed even a single violation,
the entire edifice of rules may come crashing down, resulting in
extreme self-humiliation. Psychoanalysts have described such a
condition as a reaction formation, to a situation in which no
paternal law has been internalized, and the subject is left in harsh
pre-Oedipal dependence on the rule. Hence the most common
affliction of the suburban man: the 'borderline personality disorder'
that displays a combination of both psychotic and neurotic
symptoms.

Let us now return to the symptoms of the relocated Navajo and
try to read the symptoms of suburban man through those of the
Navajo. The Navajo was forcibly removed from the land
circumscribed by the four sacred mountains which shielded him
from danger, the land where he obtained the earth to make his
medicine bundle offered during prayers, the land which kept him
close to his gods, ancestors and myths. Needless to say, this
'relocation' was unimaginably disruptive to his way of life. But
what is often overlooked even by the cultural anthropologist
sympathetic to the Navajo's plight is that the Navajo had lived on
the same land with the Hopi (who has different gods, different
histories, different myths), and had even intermarried and attended

the other's ceremonies for hundreds of years without any serious conflict over 'land use', without any need for partitioning or security patrols. In short, the Navajo had always been cosmopolitan in his dealings with the Hopi. And perhaps the loss of his land, his mountains and his sacred places only became unbearable trauma upon coming face-to-face with the terrifying parochialism of sub-urban man.

As for suburban man himself, the farther he flees and the more he arms himself, the more his fears seem to multiply. Every day brings news of superfluous violence that only inflames his anxiety: disgruntled office worker showers bullets on fellow employees; student goes on rampage in school with automatic weapons; sharp rise in number of random drive-by shootings . . . Could it be that place was never just 'merely physical', as the sub-urban man imagined it to be? That perhaps in the externality of place is always also another topos? And it may even be—just may be— that in the symptoms that are striking back on their bodies, both neo-primordial man and suburban man are today harvesting the bitter fruit of the malignant seeds they first planted together on the cosmopolitan place of all the world's Navajos.

Further Reading

Appadurai, Arjun. Spectral housing and urban cleansing: Notes on millennial Mumbai. *Public Culture* 12(3): 627–51.

Shepard, Paul. 1983. *Nature and Madness*. San Francisco: Sierra Club Books.

Plague

Ashis Nandy

Plague activates anxieties and imageries that few other diseases do. Tuberculosis invokes images of dissipation and waste, occasionally even of nineteenth-century romanticism and self-destruction. John Keats suffered from tuberculosis; so probably did Saratchandra Chattopadhyay's hero Devdas, the archetypal Indian hero. Syphilis has usually been a simultaneous marker of decadence, masculinity and moral transgression in the old world, and a symbol of intrusive civilizations, conquests and changing times in the margins of the world. Cardiovascular diseases have become associated in recent years with mindless overconsumption and the stress of modern living. Cancer smacks of the revenge of nature; it is often seen as a disease of the rich and the powerful who have to find, after getting the best of healthcare, some excuse to die. There are many in Asia and Africa who would rather die from the afflictions of the rich and powerful, such as the heart diseases and cancer, than from such lowbrow predators as cholera, typhoid and dysentery.

Plague is a different kettle of fish. Like cholera in South Asia, it activates more primitive fears, particularly in Europe. Annually, ten to fifteen people are infected with plague in the United States and at least another 1000 scattered cases occur in the rest of the world, but they hardly arouse any public interest. Such deaths are reported in the inner pages of newspapers, sometimes not even there. But once plague breaks out in an Afro-Asian country, there is panic in Europe. There are countries in Europe that have lost more than half their populations to plague in the past. The continent as a whole has lost, at some points of time, as many as one-fourth of its inhabitants to different versions of the Black Death. That historical memory survives in the European consciousness.

The primeval European fear of plague has become entwined, over time, with a fear of the Third World. There may no longer be a proper Second World any more, to guide the poor and the dispossessed towards a proletarian heaven, but the Third World survives as an area of darkness for the First World and for the modern elite of Asia and Africa, breathlessly running to catch up with their Western big brothers. Beneath all the compassion and philanthropy directed towards the Third World, there persists an image of it as the abode of the third-rate, where a surplus of obsolete or redundant people, living in dirt and penury, provide a fertile breeding ground for pestilences of all kinds. The unacceptable thought that poverty is a crime and a proof of one's worldly failures and sinful ways is constantly encroaching upon Western awareness. The ungodly are also the godforsaken and, therefore, pestilence-prone. The most recommended rational and protective course to take, by this logic, is to avoid contagion at all costs.

Moral and public hygienes intersect in the Third World. Albert Camus's 1947 novel *The Plague* is set in Algeria, and its French doctor-hero, working among Arab victims of plague, symbolizes a person seeking existential meaning in a battle against an epidemic that did not have a known cure when the novel was written. The protagonist acts out the philosophy of life spelt out in the author's *Le Mythe de Sisyphe* (1942). As is well known, in Greek mythology Sisyphus was condemned by the gods to roll a stone uphill for all eternity. *The Plague* is the story of a modern Sisyphus battling the arbitrary suffering of a people and, in the process, giving meaning to an otherwise meaningless existence. This idea of randomness is, of course, a negation of European Christendom's tacit theory of causality, with plague as the central metaphor in Camus's vision.

The fear and the fantasies associated with plague, particularly in Europe and its apparently forgetful progeny in North America, cannot be contained by any discovery of plague vaccines or antibiotics effective against the disease. Most Europeans are not impressed that the mortality rate in plague has reportedly come down to below 5 per cent the world over. In well-equipped West European or North American hospitals, that rate cannot but be even lower. As Ingmar Bergman shows so elegantly in his film *The Seventh Seal* (1956), plague is located in a melancholic, grey, mental landscape where it cohabits with ideas of sin, moral responsibility, death and death-defiance, repentance and expiation. That landscape remains, but has become invisible in recent centuries, thanks to the overdone festive style of contemporary capitalism. Europe's post-medieval prosperity promises perpetual happiness in a deathless society. In such a society, death is an accident. When it strikes somebody nearby, one must try to quickly forget it as a disturbance in one's normal daily rhythm. Ideally, one must pretend that it has not taken place.

Plague, which is remembered in Europe primarily as a medieval disease, is a reminder that death *does* come, even in a world of plenty, dominated by mega-science, superdoctors vending magical cures, including permanent youth, and foolproof rationality, packaged in narcissistic overconsumption. Plague is a reminder of the mortality that cannot be sanitized, beautified or passed off as a deviation from the cycle of normal life.

The fear of plague in Europe, however, is not only the fear of death. It is the fear of death that comes as the biblical wages of sin. That fear of one's own imagined Hobbesian past—when life was nasty, brutish and short—is often projected on to the Third World. The Third World living in abject misery—because that is what it merits in God's scheme of things—is also Europe's past that survives and haunts the modern, desacralized Europe and its godless ways. The Third World visits Europe as plague when the European Christendom fails to maintain its purity—of body and of mind—and its moral high ground.

Plague also gives ample scope for heroism. The knight who plays chess with Death in *The Seventh Seal* is no mere cinematic figure. He lives in the European unconscious as the crusader who has risked his life for his faith. His decision to take on Death in a death-defying game of chess in plague-ridden Europe cannot but acquire heroic proportions. Likewise, the doctor in *The Plague* becomes the ultimate symbol of heroic resistance to the vagaries of fate. As befits an existentialist hero, he thinks he creates his personal morality out of the essential meaninglessness of life. But to many European readers, Camus's doctor probably looks like another version of Bergman's knight, a crusader fighting larger Satanic forces in the cosmos.

The fear of plague in the tropics is of a different kind. For instance, in South Asia, too, plague connotes moral waywardness and divine retribution, but the disease does not invoke the inner demons that haunt European consciousness. Roughly the same can be said about Africa. The great epidemiological fears of Africa centre around sleeping sickness and, increasingly, AIDS. This despite the widespread belief of Western historians that the originating grounds of plague were Africa and Asia, that Europe got its first great plague epidemic from Egypt and that the last epidemic of plague spread from China through a number of popular trade routes and reached Bombay before reaching Europe.

For South Asians, smallpox and cholera remain the prototypical afflictions of the tropics. No student can graduate from a school of tropical medicine even today without a thorough grounding in the study of these two extremely contagious diseases. Even tuberculosis has acquired a mythic status over the last hundred years in the region. Plague, though it has sometimes been a *mahamari* or great killer, remains for many Indians, rightly or wrongly, an imported epidemic. Most Indians, probably overexposed to Western historiography, consider plague to be a disease that thrives in cold weather, not in the torrid summers of India. Nor does it usually have any goddess presiding over the course of the epidemic or the fate of its victims, the way Shitala presides over smallpox and Olaichandi or Olaibibi does over cholera. One of the only two goddesses associated with plague, Pilegamma, belongs to coastal Karnataka, which was for centuries one of India's major windows to the world; the other one's geographical coordinates are not clear.

Plague certainly does not have any distinctive, traditional ritual to accompany it. Generally, you do not acquire mastery over plague by appeasing or establishing a contractual relationship—through a *manta, mannat, manat* or any other kind of ritual compact—with any particular deity, despite the presence of a couple of goddesses of plague. Perhaps there is no felt need to have that sense of mastery over fate through a steady compact with divinity in the case of plague. Like malaria and unlike smallpox and cholera, plague is an outsider trying to get naturalized in South Asia.

This is implicitly admitted by many Indians. Plague is viewed mainly as a scourge of urban India, a terrain marred by its dirty streets, mixed populations drawn from diverse and often unknown sources, unhealthy lifestyles and crowded slums. Public hygiene and modern preventive medicine, combined with some degree of precautionary measures, are supposed to take care of plague. Hence, even at times of great pilgrimages like the Kumbh Mela, which can attract as many as fifty million pilgrims, efforts to inoculate the pilgrims against plague are rare; they are mostly inoculated against smallpox and cholera.

Yet, plague has been visiting urban India on and off to take its toll. Last time, in 1994, Surat and to a small extent metropolitan Bombay and Delhi were its main victims. I do not know how the residents of Surat in Gujarat explain the epidemic—as a failure in civic management, government apathy towards warnings given by experts or as the natural fate of a particularly filthy city that had no time to build a civic culture because it had lost its soul entirely to the profit motive and never looked beyond commerce.

However, I have a fair guess what the greatest Gujarati of all time might have said on the plight of Surat when plague struck the city. Mohandas Karamchand Gandhi would have almost certainly invoked his notorious theory of collective karma, the one that he had coined at the time of the Bihar earthquake in the 1920s. As we know, he blamed the earthquake on the practice of untouchability, to the utter chagrin of rational humanists like writer and humanist Rabindranath Tagore. Perfectly comfortable with the moral universe of pre-modern Europe, Mohandas Karamchand Gandhi would have, I am quite sure, held the particularly cruel religious riots of Surat in 1992 responsible for the outbreak of plague in the city.

Pollution

Sudhir Chella Rajan

Since the early 1990s, a newly liberalized television industry in India has been producing a weekly environmental show called *Living on the Edge*, a saucy and popular programme that boldly wades through (actual and metaphorical) slime in search of (mostly real) poachers and corporate intrigue. The show's rather extraordinary success, given its unhappy tales and characteristically unsavoury images, seems oddly allied with the giddy excitement of the times, whose prevailing sentiment is that humanity is being pushed towards a new millennium by forces that are barely within reach and perhaps beyond all control. Indeed, much more than its polysemous title reflects the distinctive thrill and anxiety of a non-stop MTV party to celebrate Y2K: hand-held cameras, visual montage, clever sound bites, droll scripts of ridicule and dread, and, not least, the startling youthfulness of its producers and correspondents.

The association is perhaps less fortuitous than one might think. After all, if the new millennium's most reckless celebration is evinced in its ever-innovative packaging of 'alternative' youth culture, nothing connotes its proximate danger more acutely and accurately than environmental pollution. Pollution is, of course, not merely a modern phenomenon, in the sense of simply being the evil twin of capitalism. To be sure, it acquired universal significance only when it became linked with the worsening health of a nineteenth-century 'public' in the course of industrialization; and, since then, has become imprinted in the modern imagination as the upshot of bourgeois society's enduring desire for mass-produced goods. Even so, today's pollution is quite different, in real and imagined ways, from what our great-grandparents encountered. It reflects, if only circumstantially, modernity's own struggle to retain its identity as avant-garde, or indeed to exist 'on the edge' of the eternally new.

In any case, there are even longer genealogies of pollution whose traces regulate, and undoubtedly will continue to haunt, its modern meanings. One of these strains is the fairly common cultural experience of visceral shame and disgust that surface in an unexpected encounter with another's bodily fluids and odours. But even such apparently universal forms of anxiety towards polluted and polluting otherness are not indiscriminate, as ethnographic accounts portray several distinct cultures and conditioned responses of disquiet relating to alterity. Thus, pollution appears as fear and loathing in several conditions: when the social order is defiled by human displacement, for instance, by the pariah crossing the Brahmin's threshold; the anomalous natural occurrence, such as physical deformity or an ill-timed rain-shower; and various bodily states themselves, including menstruation, possession by spirits and the fact of death. Notably, it is incongruity and the danger it represents that causes pollution to be viewed with foreboding.

The modern sense of pollution also evokes notions of opposition and displacement: a pollutant is seldom harmful in itself, but jeopardizes one's existence only when it overflows into spaces where it doesn't belong or is generated in excess within a domain where it is otherwise useful. Thus, mercury is safe under the ground, but dangerous when spilled into streams and rivers that are used to irrigate crops and are home to countless forms of marine life. Likewise, carbon dioxide is necessary for the growth of plants and essential for maintaining the temperature of the atmosphere at a level that supports life. When human intervention raises its concentration significantly, as it has in the past century through rampant fossil-fuel use and deforestation, the planet is at a heightened risk of climate change that could have catastrophic effects on all life.

One direction in which to explore the pollution fears that preoccupy our time is to review contemporary purification rituals, their shamans and the ways they gain legitimacy. In some ways these rituals have become fixed; in others, they are still in the process of formation. But primarily, all modern pollution practices operate along a gradated scale of risk, so that a pollutant's damage is scaled in terms of the measurable human or ecological injury it is expected to cause. This is consistent with the methodology of contemporary science, whose primary means of theory formation is through data collection. With several complex phenomena affecting the ways in which actual pollutants will cause physical harm to humans, environmental assessment has predictably become the first line of attack in the battle against pollution.

Paradoxically, while science has managed to provide very extensive and convincing grounds for estimating a pollutant's quantifiable harm at any given level of exposure (for instance, the excess cancer risk in humans caused by a given concentration of a pesticide in drinking water), it typically cannot decide what a 'safe level' would be, because there is generally no threshold below which zero harm would take place. Removing modern pollution is therefore a serious challenge even in methodological terms. Instead of pollutants being completely proscribed, they are given dimensions based on their concentration and toxicity, and ranked accordingly. Pollution control is thus managed through concepts like 'acceptable risk' that refer to implied consensus for blanket standards, whether or not there are institutional arrangements to legitimize them.

There is a significant literature whose ethnographic lenses attempt to demystify the enterprise of environmental control and the public science it calls for (for instance, see Douglas and Wildavsky 1988 and Jasanoff 1990). There is also the suggestion in such analyses that environmental risk is a cultural concept, so that the degree of 'acceptability' varies with cultural context. Yet, this is not to deny that the effects of modern pollution, which include ill-health and destruction of habitat and biodiversity, are indeed universal. The broader question, therefore, is really a pragmatic one: How must we now recognize things that are dangerously out of place and identify the actions that will restore some sense of collective security? Most earlier traditions of pollution control have confronted clear-cut problems relating to the clash of beliefs and events, for which pathways for recovering from the threat of consequent harm are almost always available. The modern task, by contrast, is to recognize at exactly what point a pollutant becomes dangerous and needs a response, which creates normative difficulties for it has to do with the way the danger itself is specified. This very helplessness, in being unable to locate true harm, may characterize the frisson of our environmental 'edge'.

The lack of clarity about what constitutes impurity and its hazard is obviously indicated in a general qualm about how to respond to risk. But 'risk management' is further complicated by several practical constraints relating to natural phenomena, space, technology, money and institutions. Take, for example, the problem of dealing with industrial plastics, whose low costs and enormous versatility have institutionally 'locked in' their application for a vast range of everyday products and services. Plastic waste cannot be broken down quickly or, in some instances, cannot be broken down at all by the action of organic or inorganic forces. When concentrated within any one area, it interferes with organic life, creates accumulations of trash and leaches chemicals into groundwater, causing several immune function problems as well as cancer. If burned, it generates dangerous airborne chemicals that cause cancer and respiratory disease. Only certain types of plastics can be recycled or reused, and doing so on a meaningful scale implies dealing with thorny and expensive organizational arrangements of waste collection and separation, not to mention the costs of new reprocessing technologies. Additionally, any proposal to change the nature of plastic use itself must confront the weary discourse of social transformation.

Modern pollution's massive scale of disruption is perhaps the strongest indication of its unique place in history. With unremitting logic, local, regional and global ecosystems have been seriously endangered by human activities and, in too many cases, been destroyed beyond repair. Fresh water, land and the air in cities are now polluted to such an extent that further abuse in several locations will almost certainly result in catastrophic conditions of illness or death. And, by threatening the futures of rich and poor alike through a web of physical and institutional interactions, the trans-boundary character of pollution is finally refuting liberal claims of sovereignty and safe refuge. Rather than becoming an overt confrontation with conventional social and economic institutions themselves, much of the formal engagement with pollution in the twentieth century has minimally tried to cope with the rude interruptions caused by environmental damage to the 'normal' practices of states, markets and other movers of capital. It is only of late, with the widespread recognition that environmental pollution has global dimensions and impacts, that a more systematic approach to pollution control has been invoked in international forums, involving actual proposals for institutional change.

In fact, in a somewhat chagrined response to the growing crisis, mainstream environmental discourse now entertains talk of the 'earth's carrying capacity', signalling either a macabre endgame to pollution within hitherto accepted customs of risk management or, more optimistically, a paradigm shift towards new and practical solutions. Concurrently, the notion of 'sustainability' is also emerging as a dominant metaphor, with its own contradictions and possibilities for redeeming humanity's future. Sustainable development expresses the broad requirements for long-term economic development as follows: resource consumption ought to be managed in such a way that social equity and empowerment are promoted, and present needs are met adequately, without jeopardizing the needs of future generations (WCED 1987). Implicit in this definition is an ideal set of preconditions of equity, empowerment and environmental soundness for long-term human prosperity, rather than a precise programme or methodology to achieve this end.

To the extent that the trendiest sustainable development initiatives ignore the political labours and institutional transformation needed to reach their objectives, they are bound to repeat the sterile gestures of risk management, whose efforts have hitherto only rearranged the various dimensions of environmental pollution into compact administrative operations. In contrast, there already are resistances to pollution that proliferate in local attempts to realize sustainable development's momentous paradigm shift in the form of innovative institutional arrangements and, sometimes, the use of advanced technology adapted to local needs. These more modest ventures may perhaps soften the edge of anticipation of catastrophe within restricted spheres, but are not likely to constitute the broader cultural transformation that is needed to shake off modernity's engagement with pollution. That problem, and a final cultural and political rapprochement with regard to the perpetual lack of control over our environment, remains our legacy to the next millennium.

Further Reading

Bradby, Hannah. 1990. *Dirty Words: Writings on the History and Culture of Pollution*. London: Earthscan Publications.

Douglas, Mary, and Aaron Wildavsky. 1993. *Risk and Culture: An Essay on the Selection of Technological and Environmental Dangers*. Berkeley: University of California Press.

Jasanoff, Sheila. 1990. *The Fifth Branch: Science Advisers as Policymakers*. Cambridge, Massachusetts: Harvard University Press.

Redclift, Michael. 1987. *Sustainable Development: Exploring the Contradictions*. London: Methuen.

WCED. 1987. *Our Common Future*. Report of the World Commission on Environment and Development. Oxford: Oxford University Press.

Postmodernism

Ziauddin Sardar

Postmodernism is not just a buzzword but a key term of our times. It conditions our thought and politics, shapes our art and architecture, frames much of the entertainment industry and is actively shaping our future. We can watch it, hear it, read it, shop within its precincts, be awestruck by it—in short, we live and breathe it. It is a theory, a contemporary practice and a condition of the contemporary era. Slowly but surely postmodernism is taking over the world we inhabit, the thoughts we think, the things we do, what we know and what we don't know, what we have known and what we cannot know, what frames our nature and our being. It is the new, or perhaps not-so-new, all-embracing theory of salvation.

Given its multifaceted temper and character, postmodernism is not an easy beast to pin down. The nature of postmodernism is further complicated by the fact that it seems to be for everything and against (apparently) nothing. If postmodernism did have a motto, it would be 'anything goes'. The eclectic nature of postmodernism has been used by its champions and apologists to mystify it: to present it as a mythical and mystical intellectual and pragmatic force that cannot be fathomed, let alone resisted.

So what defines postmodernism? The principles that define postmodernism also pit it against tradition and modernity. Postmodernism, as the label suggests, is *post* modernity: it transcends modernity, which itself surpasses tradition. Thus the first principle of postmodernism is that all that is valid in modernity is totally invalid and obsolete in postmodern times. Modernity was framed by what are called, in the technical jargon of cultural studies, Grand Narratives: that is, Big Ideas that give sense and direction to life. Such notions as Truth, Reason, Morality, God, Tradition and History, argue postmodernists, do not live up to analytical scrutiny—they are totally meaningless. And all world views that claim absolute notions of Truth, for example, Science, Religion, Marxism, are artificial constructions that are totalitarian by their very nature. Truth is relative, contingency is everything: or as Richard Rorty, the one-time American guru of postmodernism, put it, nothing has an intrinsic nature which may be expressed or represented, and everything is a product of time and chance. Thus postmodernism rejects all forms of truth claims; it accepts nothing as absolute, and rejoices in total relativism.

When Truth and Reason are dead, what becomes of knowledge? Postmodernism considers all types, as well as all sources, of knowledge with equal scepticism. There is hardly any difference between science and magic, as Paul Feyerabend took so much pain to demonstrate. For postmodernists, knowledge is acquired not through inquiry but by imagination. As such, postmodernism contends, fiction rather than philosophy, and narrative rather than theory, provide a better perspective on human behaviour. The philosopher Ludwig Wittgenstein argued that all we have is language, even though its representation of reality is, at best, approximate and faulty. Rorty asserts that we should even 'drop the idea of language as representation'. Irony, ridicule and parody are the basic tools through which this postmodernist goal is to be achieved.

The second postmodern principle is the denial of Reality. Postmodernism suggests that there is no ultimate Reality behind things: we see largely what we want to see, what our position in time and place allows us to see, what our cultural and historic perceptions have conditioned us to focus on. Thus, even in science, the easiest thing to find is what we are looking for.

Instead of Reality, what we have, contends postmodernism, is simulacrum: a world where all distinction between image and material reality has been lost. This is the third principle of postmodernism. Postmodernism posits the world as a video game: seduced by the allure of the spectacle, we have all become characters in the global video game, zapping our way from here to there, fighting wars in cyberspace, making love to digitized bits of information.

In a world without Truth and Reason, where no knowledge is possible and where language is the only tenuous link with existence, where Reality has been drowned in an ocean of images, there is no possibility of final meaning. Everything is meaningless: this is the fourth principle of postmodernism. As Umberto Eco tries to show in *Foucault's Pendulum*, the world is nothing more than an onion: once we have 'deconstructed' the world layer by layer, we are finally left with nothing. Deconstruction—the methodology of discursive analysis—is the norm of postmodernism. But once deconstruction has reached its natural conclusion, we are left with a grand void. This fourth principle of postmodernism thus takes us back to the first, reconfirming the total arbitrary nature of truth and morality, science and religion, physics and metaphysics, while generating a fifth principle: doubt. Doubt, the perpetual and perennial condition of postmodernism, is best described by the motto of the cult television series *The X-files*: 'Trust No One'. In postmodern theory, this is extended to include no theory, no absolute, no experience: doubt everything.

There are two further defining characteristics of postmodernism. It is concerned with all variety of multiplicities: it emphasizes plurality of ethnicities, cultures, genders, truths, realities, sexualities, even reasons, and argues that no particular type should be privileged over others. In its concern for demolishing all variety of privileges, postmodernism deliberately seeks a more equal representation for class, gender, sexual orientation, race, ethnicity and culture.

Postmodernism, therefore, can be understood in terms of its seven defining principles: No Truth, No Reality, Only Images, No Meaning, Multiplicities, Equal Representation, and Total Doubt. It offers a rather TRIMMED view of life, the universe and everything: neat, without dogma, but ultimately totally nihilistic!

As postmodernism seeks to give voice to all cultures, decentres the 'centre' while making the 'periphery' the centre of all cultural action and gives 'voice' to the 'voiceless', it is projected as a new and great force of liberation. However, far from being a liberating force, postmodernism is a totalistic project that seeks to subsume all non-Westerns cultures into the fires of liberal secularism and nihilistic consumption. In trying to deny privilege to everyone and everything, postmodernism only privileges itself. It becomes an arch-ideology to beat all ideologies. Far from being new, it is, in fact, a natural extension and continuation of colonialism and modernity. It is new in comprising the new imperialism of Western culture.

Colonialism was all about physical invasion and occupation and exploitation of the non-West through war and military power. Modernity was about the mental invasion and occupation of the non-European cultures through such notions as 'development' and 'progress'. Both these ideas prepared the ground for the final uteral and epistemic assault: the actual consumption and total absorption of the non-West in liberalism, secularism and Western consumerism through postmodernism.

The idea of the sacred is central to all non-Western cultures—from China, India and Islam to the indigenous cultures of America, Australia and Africa. The notion of sacredness, through religious or nature-oriented world views, is the source of the basic identity of all non-Western cultures. The sole aim of postmodernism is to destroy the particular traditions of the non-West and negate their history. The objective of the postmodern project, Rorty states, is 'to de-divinize the world'. 'The best way to cause maximum pain to someone,' he declares, 'is to demonstrate that everything they hold dear is without meaning and totally powerless.' The West has already been almost totally secularized; so only the non-West can be the real target of postmodernism.

Since colonialism and modernity have already drained much of the wealth of the Third World, postmodernism appropriates the last resources of the non-West: its traditions, spiritualities, cultural property and ideas. While postmodernism celebrates difference, it allows no space for difference to actually exist—thanks to such postmodern notions as 'globalization' and 'free markets' (which are free only for the West). The postmodern thesis that everything is relative is incapable of suggesting that anything is in some distinctive way itself, with its own history. Under postmodernism, distinctive cultures are hybridized, ethnicities are appropriated, sacred spiritual practices are turned into mass products, local cultures are arrogated by the global entertainment machine. The cultural subjects of difference, the non-Western cultures, are venerated solely for their difference but denied the right to negotiate their own conditions of discursive control and to practice their difference as a rebellion against the hegemonic tendencies of postmodernism. Thus American Indian sacred (and secret) ceremonies suddenly become the property of every New Age reveller. Traditional non-Western music is now owned by record companies! The cadences of African Pygmies go postmodern on the musical album *Deep Forest*! Qawwali, the devotional music of India, Pakistan and Bangladesh, becomes funky, so what was meant to be sung to the simple rhythm of traditional drums and hand-clapping in praise of God and Prophet Muhammad is sung to a syncopated rock beat generated by synthesizers. What was originally designed to induce mystical ecstasy is now used to generate hysteria for rock music. Even indigenous flora and fauna, like the neem tree in India, is now being claimed as the property of multinational corporations. The Body Shop regularly appropriates the traditional products of indigenous cultures, repackages them and sells them back, through its international outlets, to non-Western societies, while claiming to be helping the indigenous people! By collapsing all kind of cultures and traditions in a single space, postmodernism creates a façade, a simulacrum, of multiculturalism. Postmodernism constructs and disseminates the seductive allure of pluralism while ensuring that the oppressive and unjust structures of power remain intact.

How can postmodernism be resisted? The non-Western cultures need to do more than simply offer cultural resistance—they have to become cultures of resistance. The non-West has to promote and enhance indigenous culture in all its forms and variety and jealously safeguard its traditions. However, passive traditionalism and militant formalist traditionalism are both easy prey to postmodernism. Postmodernism induces panic in all forms of passive and militant outlooks, and thus not only renders them ineffective against its all-pervasive nihilism but makes them self-destructive. In other words, postmodernism co-opts passivity and fundamentalism to promote its own goals. Thus, unthinking and simplistic reactions, which shuffle the blame entirely on to the Western world while seeking to best the Western demon with its own tools and rationales, lead to further entrapment. The only cultural survival kit for those who would choose to remain alive within living traditions, retain their identity and distinctive moral and ethical vision of themselves and the purpose of their existence is to understand postmodernism, to see through the limitations of passive minimalist tradition and the futile trap of militant fundamentalism. For the world views of the non-West, the only option is to transcend meaninglessness through living consciously, creatively making and mending. This is a difficult and complex agenda, yet it is the only worthwhile enterprise that can offer us any kind of sustainable future.

At the heart of culture and its traditional forms is a distinctive moral and ethical understanding, a world view. Traditional culture in all its forms is about expression and communication of this moral vision, about working out its contemporary significance and relevance for a people with a strong historical identity. It can only remain alive when it becomes the living language through which contemporary questions, problems, choices and decisions are articulated. For the non-West, history will really end, the project of modernity will be complete and postmodernism will rule unassailed, unless its world views become the medium through which economy, politics, social, industrial and ecological conventions are negotiated. Culture is not an optional extra that can be indulged in privately after work, or indulged in only on certain high days and holidays. If that is what culture becomes, then it is the rotting corpse of a dead system of thought and understanding, the dried husk of a world view that no longer interacts with the real world we inhabit. It is not just one world view but every world view comprising the rich mosaic of the non-West that must be brought back to life if the non-European cultures are to defy and resist postmodernism and the seductive path into total dependency and ever-expanding decay that it so magnanimously offers.

Moral and ethical considerations are never easy: they are the greatest challenge to our humanity and our intellect. Becoming centred in the moral and ethical concepts of non-Western world views cannot mean renouncing old interpretations or abandoning all that is of the West. It does, however, require recognizing and transcending the limitations of both as part of the process of taking responsibility for the present and creating a future that answers to, and is a function of, what non-Western cultures really believe to be of enduring value and meaning.

Further Reading

Eco, Umberto. 1995. *Foucault's Pendulum*. New York: Hartcourt.

Sardar, Ziauddin. 1997. *Postmodernism and the Other: New Imperialism of Western Culture*. London: Pluto.

Poverty

Majid Rahnema

Poverty has as many meanings as there are human beings: it is a social construct, built upon a combination of external factors and the ways each subject, or social agent, interprets these subjectively.

Historically, the word has been used, more often than not, to describe a particular mode of living with and relating to necessity. Many of the 'lacks' presently listed to define the so-called poverty line—that is, the line of unmet 'needs' below which a person is officially pronounced as 'poor'—were traditionally considered parts of an inescapable necessity that had to be respected. Some saw that necessity as part of one's 'fate', 'qismat' or 'karma'; some, as a call for attaining one's inner freedom from material enslavement. Yet, as life on earth was generally thought to be a gift of the Creator, adversity was perceived as a challenge aimed at receiving one's share from the ever-living source of the Creation's unlimited baraka and ni'ma ('abundance' and 'boon' or 'bounty' in Arabic and Persian). Living was a way of sharing and using with others one's God-given gifts with a view to bringing together the two worlds of necessity and baraka.

For all these reasons, to be poor had not always a negative connotation. For Christ, blessed were all the poor who lived their predicament with dignity. By contrast, he said, 'It is easier for a camel to go through the eye of a needle than for the rich to enter the Kingdom of God.' In many a vernacular society, the only forms of destitution and indigence to be depreciated and reprimanded were those that expressed the moral demise of their authors. For similar reasons, the rich and the powerful, who lived on and profited from the fruits of other people's labour, were seen as despicable creatures.

Three Main Categories of Poverty

Properly speaking, vernacular societies knew of two major forms of poverty: spiritual or voluntary poverty and convivial poverty. The first was perceived as one of the highest forms of self-realization, of freedom and of true riches. It was the type of poverty shared by exceptional humans such as Socrates, Jesus, Rabi'a al Adawya, Saint Francis and Mahatma Gandhi. It is the same to which the prophet of Islam referred when he said, 'Poverty is my glory.' The second, convivial poverty, was a mode of sharing together the common gifts of a community and, consequently, of enhancing its collective potentialities.

An unprecedented category of poverty accompanied the advent of economized societies, often referred to as modernized poverty. The poor suffering from this predicament could be characterized by an ever-increasing gap between their socially generated needs and their inability to find the necessary 'resources' to meet those needs.

Poverty versus Material and Moral Destitution

None of the three categories of poverty should, however, be confused with the various states of destitution or imposed indigence. The poor and the destitute are both subject to harsh external conditions. Yet only those persons belong to the latter condition who are no longer in a social or personal position to actively cope with necessity. The destitute or the indigent are thus persons who have lost the social or the individual 'bed' or 'hammock' that prevented them from falling into destitution. In vernacular societies, the need to maintain and protect these poverty 'beds' often helped the poor in transforming their 'lacks' into assets or boons.

The destitute are persons who generally suffer from a double misery. Socially and outwardly, they live in a state of extreme solitude and isolation. They are the *bi kass* (in Persian, those who 'do not have anyone' to take care of them), with no bed or hammock in which to lie down. Inwardly, they have lost the inner strength or the regenerative powers of the voluntary or semi-voluntary (convivial) poor. This double misery sometimes reaches such proportions that the destitute lose even their abilities to think and act intelligently in defence of their own interests. The last thirty years have witnessed the corruption of some very important social movements, particularly in times when destitute masses are more prone to be manipulated and misled by unscrupulous politicians. When the deprived lose their 'poverty beds', and fall into destitution, they become easy prey to manipulative populist ringleaders or abusive social systems.

From Simple Life to Addiction to 'Needs'

There is enough historical and anthropological evidence to suggest that earlier human societies lived in 'a kind of material plenty', and 'adapted the tools of their living to material which lay in abundance around them' (Marshall 1961). Their lack of interest in innovating or adopting more productive tools reflected only a different philosophy of being and relating with each other. They did not think that they *had* to divert *all* their energies to producing or making more 'profit'.

In vernacular societies, people considered it natural and normal to produce enough for meeting needs that were considered both limited and culturally constituted. Living in a convivial fashion was thus a semi-voluntary choice imposed by necessity and common sense. To have few possessions was, for most people, 'a matter of principle' and not a sign of misfortune. *Homo oeconomicus* was not yet born to teach them how to trade their freedom against material possessions.

The gradual emergence of the individual as a person achieving one's ends, independent from one's community and, later, as one motivated mainly by increasing one's economic assets brought about a substantial change in the perception of poverty. The inability to meet socially induced and established needs became the main criterion for defining the poor. The pressure on everyone to adapt appropriate personal lifestyles in the process of becoming addicted to the fulfilment of these needs became a major reason for transforming most of the poor into destitutes, in constant need of assistance.

Wars against Poverty or against the Poor?

The so-called wars against poverty have thus often acted as subtle ways of permanently converting the poor into modernized destitutes.

Three key assumptions underlie these campaigns: first, that the poor suffer from a worldwide scarcity of goods and services required to meet their socially defined 'basic needs'; second, that they are unable to meet them on their own; and, third, that their integration into a modern economy can help them meet these needs and provide satisfactions, as is the pattern in a normal consumer society. These highly questionable assumptions have been responsible for transforming 'poverty alleviation' campaigns into indirect wars against the poor.

Economy as the Main Producer of Scarcity

What is totally concealed by these assumptions is that the modern systems of production, being geared to profit, are themselves the main producers of the scarcities from which the poor suffer. Economy does indeed produce many unprecedented goods and services. Yet it does so only for those who can afford to pay. It acts as a double-faced Janus that systematically creates scarcities wherever socially created needs grow faster than the people's ability to pay for them.

Agricultural production, an area of vital importance for the physical survival of the poor, is a case in point. It is true that the introduction of new technologies has produced an unprecedented increase in food production; rice production, for instance, has increased by 240 per cent in the last forty years. Yet this phenomenal productivity has mostly benefited the privileged. For the poorer peasants, this increase has only increased their dependency on the richer and the more powerful. The Green Revolution has actually been instrumental in dispossessing the poor of their own means and ways of producing and exploiting land. Their natural and social environment and their traditional knowledge and indigenous technologies have been destroyed, together with the possibilities of finding their own solutions to the problems created for them.

Major modern economic institutions manipulate their audiences by using one-sided statistics to conceal the scarcity-producing aspects of economy. The World Bank's latest poverty eradication programmes are a prime example. A number of carefully selected projects are highlighted to show how these have improved the lot of a few among the 'targeted' populations. Yet nothing is said about the overall effects of the Bank and IMF policies that have systematically destroyed the endogenous capacity of the poorest populations in addressing their problems, in particular the new socially generated scarcities. Neither are these institutions ready to accept their responsibility for the modern processes of pauperization, including policies of 'granting' loans that end up by making the poor nations totally subservient, both to their foreign 'donors' and to their national recipients.

Economic growth and its globalization *cannot* therefore be the answer to the socially generated scarcities from which the poor continue to suffer. At best, it could be a temporary and divisive answer to the 'winners' in societies entirely geared to individual profit. A compelling example of this type of 'performance' is the United States, where the number of millionaires has increased from two to five million only in the last five to seven years, while the number of persons living below the 'poverty line' is still around thirty million. As a whole, no solution could be imagined to the increasing risks of destitution threatening the 'losers', so long as they remain within the prevailing economic paradigms.

Towards New Modes of Interaction Enhancing the Riches of the Poor

Victims of socially generated scarcities are however, ultimately, the only ones who are in an ideal position to reverse the processes triggered by economy.

Over the past few decades, many grass-roots movements have emerged everywhere, with a view to defending the poor against the globalizing trends of market economy. These movements— some as tiny as the CHODAK in Senegal, others as massive and powerful as the indigenous resistance in the Chiapas region of Mexico, or as numerically important as the multifarious local movements in India—are a testimony to the worldwide resistance against such trends. In the search for new alternatives, millions of the world's poor are using their imagination and creative capacities with a view to finding their own ways of thwarting destitution. Although their efforts generally take place in adverse and non-supportive political environments, they constitute the only rays of hope for the underprivileged victims of economic growth.

Political, economic and social forms of power, originating from state or market forces (autocratic and institutional, invisible and 'elegant', violent or 'participatory'), try to stop, alter or co-opt such movements. Yet, people's resistance to such forms of power continues, sometimes peacefully, sometimes violently. The manifold encounters between these two forms of power seem to have resulted in new forms of awareness. Increasingly, socially conscious populations seem to be set on the search for local and substantive alternatives to such questions as dependency, suffering and socially generated scarcity. They could well be the signifiers of totally new approaches to poverty.

One important lesson of the twentieth century's social adventures is that any concerned community (or person) can become its own powerful agent of change by regenerating its own potential riches. Every single person can do this, through small, yet meaningful daily activities in his or her own location and circumstances.

The Real Issues

A final point that comes out of the latest social adventures is that poverty or riches, as abstract ideas and definitions of lack, are not the real issue. What is at stake is, first, the search for a 'good life' for everyone without impinging on lives or destroying the social and natural environment; second, the organization of society in such a way as to give each of its participants the full possibility of nurturing each person's unique gifts to the greatest benefit of all.

In present-day class-based societies, the have-nots are systematically expected to choose between the binaries of material destitution or acceptance of the market rules, traditional hardships or modern comfort, 'progress' or 'regress', advanced technology or primitive tools, high-tech medicine or second-rate shamans, school systems or illiteracy. The more socially conscious among the poor of the world are opposing these tyrannical binaries with insights and wisdom of a different kind, based mainly on the full use of the untapped riches of the poor.

Searching for new approaches, the wisest among the poor seem to have rediscovered two lost truths. The first is that no political or social intervention can be fruitful if it does not stem from an inner revolution and a radical change in one's own perception of reality. The second is that self-knowledge and awareness have to find their own languages, their own ways of locating and interacting with each other and finally their own methods of eventually using a host of carefully chosen modern techniques for assimilating the best traditions of the past. For the 'poor'—whose number worldwide may now be more than four billion—the two classical verses of the great Persian poet Hâfiz could be an inspiring light. Referring to the *Jâmi jam*, the crystal ball of King Jamshîd that could show him all the secrets of the world, the poet had this to say: 'For years, my heart was asking me to provide it with the *jâmi jam*. [He was not aware that] it was asking from others what it already possessed.'

Further Reading

Elgin, Duane. 1981. *Voluntary Simplicity: Towards a Way of Life That Is Outwardly Simple, Inwardly Rich*. New York: William Morrow.

Kothari, Rajni. 1999. *Poverty*. London: Zed Books.

Lappé, Frances Moore, et al., eds. 1998. *World Hunger: Twelve Myths*. New York: Grove Press.

Marshall, Lorna. 1961. Sharing, talking and giving: Relief of social tensions among Kung bushmen. *Africa* 31(3): 231–49.

Rahnema, Majid. 2001. *La richesse des pauvres: Une archéologie de la pauvreté*. Paris: Éditions Fayard.

Sachs, Wolfgang, ed. 1993. *Development Dictionary*. London: Zed Books.

Prison

Barry Sanders

Prison. The word terrifies. No other image affects the daily life of each and every citizen the way the idea of prison does. The architectural brutality of the prison establishes it as a presence in every person's mind—no matter what one's gender, ethnicity, social position or economic class. Everyone has a vision of what a prison looks like. The youngest child can produce a rendering of one—high walls, steel bars, striped clothing, tall towers, guards with guns, a threatening sky, and so on. In the West, at least, prisons, like cars, have become fairly common, recognizable appliances of both fully advanced technological societies and those striving to belong in that elite group. Prisons carry a no-nonsense public relations message. They signal to the world that a nation has arrived: it now produces enough consumer goods that its citizens will risk stealing both large and small amounts of desired commodities. The presence of prisons also means that the market economy has generated a new category: the impoverished, with enough desperate people in that category.

Prison just may be the most potent metaphor holding modern society together. Nations in the West, in various constitutional declarations of civil liberties, offer the promise of unfettered personal freedoms; charters and documents enumerate and describe in detailed language the scope of those freedoms. At the same time, however, the awful prospect of liberty spinning out of control, of personal freedom collapsing into anarchy, prompts political leaders—founding forebears and subsequent legislators—

to write into law myriad variations on imprisonment and punishment. To govern efficiently and effectively, politicians know that both the image of the prison and the threat of punishment must be firmly entrenched in the people's lives.

The American Dream gains its strength from that American Nightmare. In any society, the list of what a citizen cannot do far outstrips the list of possibilities. 'Thou Shalt Not' guides people's lives, keeping their wilder dreams and schemes in tight harness. How well citizens incorporate those sanctions into their everyday behaviour reveals the degree to which they have agreed to abide by the social contract.

But there's a problem. Prisons, of course, need clients. Beds must be filled. Criminal justice, however, behaves like no other business. Instead of trying to attract customers, the criminal justice system creates them. While social scientists point out that the level of crime remains fairly constant over time in any society, America, for instance, builds prisons at a rate that outpaces crime. The criminal justice system scoops people off the street, and turns them into deviants—not just any people, it turns out, for the overwhelming majority of those in prison are people of colour, most of them young and convicted of minor, non-violent drug-related offences. With a higher and higher percentage of the young adult, black population locked down, the definition of deviance narrows dramatically, while that of normalcy becomes both more sharply defined and more tightly constrained. More and more, to be a person of colour in America is to be on the fringe. So-called racial profiling is more than a matter of racist thinking. It's a result of imprisonment thinking. Nowadays, it takes a great act of will for the average American to imagine any brown or black citizen out on the open road as free and innocent, and uninterested in committing some nefarious deed.

In the United States, the number of people in prison as the new century opened stood at close to two million, 85 per cent of them men—the highest per capita prison population in the world. Add to that number those awaiting sentencing, probation or parole, those in boot camps, reform schools, Youth Authority holding compounds of one kind or another, or in court-mandated facilities, and the figure approaches a staggering five million. (The incarceration rate for young black men in the United States exceeds that of South Africa during even the worst years of apartheid.) The system does not exempt women, whose number in US prisons and jails has more than tripled from 39,000 in 1985 to 150,000 in 2000. Again, the authorities have locked up more than 75 per cent of them for non-violent offences (200,000 children live out their formative years behind bars with their mothers).

Shocking as these numbers may seem, we should not stop there. We can indeed reach a more socially relevant and meaningful audit. Think of all the husbands and wives, sisters and brothers, relatives, older children, friends and loved ones of those imprisoned who, in their hearts and imaginations—in their spirits—suffer dramatically on account of such punishment. Those people outside prison experience much more restricted and contracted lives knowing that someone close to them struggles to stay alive behind bars. This population lives in a kind of purgatory created by the criminal justice system—their salvation in the hands of a system imagined for the most part, centuries ago, in the Middle Ages, with little significant change since that time.

Even though it measures a few scant feet in diameter, the prison cell may be the largest room in the imagination of a population. The cell has the ability, indeed, to fill the imagination and to dominate it. Who has not, at one time or another, sat in a cell, frightened and alone, either in reality or in fantasy, turning over and over key existential questions: Could I actually do it? Could I survive? Would anybody remember on the outside that I am sitting here, hour after hour, day after day? Would they actually work to get me out? The inmate continually wonders, how is my wife or husband or girlfriend doing. What is he or she doing? Doing time—to contemplate that possibility is to immediately descend to Dante's seventh or eighth ring. One can reasonably ask: Just who is being punished in the world of incarceration—the insiders, the outsiders? Both?

Of course, I have moved imprisonment and punishment past its life as a material institution, to a point where it has great symbolic weight—to incarceration and punishment as a state of mind. To be effective, prison must always carry that function. In early Modern Europe, or earlier still, say in the seventeenth century, court officials carried out executions in the town square, high on the scaffolding of a public stage for everyone to see—a spectacle—in an attempt to punish the imagination and tame the spirit, not merely of the victim but also of those who persist in thinking the accused may be innocent, as well as casual bystanders witnessing the ritual by chance. Those performances drove home an essential truth: everyone is guilty. Or, more accurately, perhaps, everyone feels guilty about something, or knows that he or she may very well in the near future be found guilty. Prison, punishment and torture—deprivation in general—simply do not matter unless they, as concepts, imprison and capture not just the body but, more importantly, the imagination. One false step and any one of us, even the most righteous and upstanding, might wind up behind bars.

For things have a natural tendency to fall apart, to fly apart, to spin out of control and fall into chaos. Order, at all costs, must be maintained. This state of affairs describes not just human-made objects but things in nature too. Everything awaits the next disaster—peace and stasis are merely moments between outbreaks of some form of disaster and anarchic revolutions. Every man, woman and, yes, even the youngest child, stands in need of corseting, straightening and chastening. The centre simply will not, and does not, hold.

Love affairs break up; plans fall apart. The list of devices and inventions to hold things together, to repair and make them whole again seems practically endless—pins, needles, baling wire, twine, string, staples, screws, bolts, nuts, rivets, tape, brads, buttons, zippers, Velcro, snaps, rubber bands, buckles, hooks and eyes, thread, rope, bungee cord, chains, clamps, glue, cement, clips, soldering and welding, cartons and containers of all shapes and sizes. Consider the devices used to break and split things apart, and the list grows substantially shorter—crowbars, hammers and axes, wedges of one sort or another, including chisels, scissors and knives and, of course, the most potent divider of them all—the political tool of today's most feared criminal, the terrorist—explosives.

We create more fasteners because things of the world—physical objects as well as social institutions—do not of their own accord remain solid and unified. Law is always followed by order. Even elected officials, paid to lay down the law, exploit social fasteners, such as regulations, acts, laws, bills, constitutions, charters, contracts, decrees, and so on; but the most powerful of these, the equivalent of explosives in the other category, is prison. Blow up a building—most dramatically a government building—and go directly to prison. Blow up a federal building, and you might even move beyond mere corporal punishment—prison—to capital punishment.

Conditions of war, of course, suspend all normal rules. The military can blow up whatever it pleases without fear of imprisonment, an irony since 'prison' first occurs in the English language as a military term. At war's end, governments symbolically reassemble the shards of the defeated by promulgating declarations of peace, and writing new constitutional safeguards, bilateral treaties and pacts. The final act by the victorious government, the statement to the world that its people mean business, takes place when it puts convicted war criminals behind bars.

Prison is the final statement of war, as it is the opening statement of peace. A country richly girded with prisons allows the overwhelming majority of its citizens to sleep soundly because large numbers make them feel safe and secure. And all because the imagination itself has been so thoroughly and so neatly straitjacketed, criminalized and imprisoned.

The political outlaw knows better. The outlaw, perhaps only the self-declared outlaw, realizes that people can never escape the clutches of incarceration, can never escape from prison—except by appropriating the experience itself, removing it from the fringes of society and relocating it right in the heart of political action. So, for instance, both Mahatma Gandhi and Nelson Mandela embraced prison as a way of defusing its hold on the popular imagination. When South Africans welcomed Mandela back to Johannesburg the morning of his release, his supporters assembled as a validation of the organizing strength of exile, and the catalysing power of incarceration. No one could deny the absolutely compelling way Mandela staved off his captors with a quiet but deliberate sense of dignity and honour. Mandela went to prison, Gandhi went to prison, in order to break free its hold on those outside its walls.

The experiences and visions of Mandela and Gandhi are mirrored, even if in a distorted fashion, in another sector of contemporary life. Gang members know that to have any real clout back in the neighbourhood, they must have done time—preferably tough time—defending their local turf even when deep inside the prison. In the modern world, prison becomes part of one's address, one's required background experience. Tattoos advertise the places where one has done time, and sometimes even the kinds of crimes one has committed.

In the 1950s, scientists attempted to eradicate pests by spraying with a new chemical wonder, DDT, guaranteed to wipe out, if necessary, an entire species. For a while the plan worked. But none of the experts foresaw the incredible adaptive abilities of, say, the mosquito, a number of which simply fed on the DDT, grew bigger and stronger, and finally disregarded the poison altogether. That power of immunity spread. Scientists would have to produce some stronger pesticide if they hoped to eliminate the mosquito, or the potato bug, or any number of pests.

Just so the prison system. Mandela fed off it, gained strength and acquired political stature from it, and brought those virtues back into the community. Like agricultural chemicals, prison authorities, too, would have to escalate if they want to, not just collar any political outlaw but imprison the popular imagination again. Indeed, in America, prison technology has evolved the technique of becoming a good portion of the main building, out of sight, almost as a way of erasing the old image of the monolithic, highly visible prison, which, perhaps, has run its course. Prison architects will have to choose to focus on the invisible, secret and daily drama that goes on, quite literally underground, to embark on a self-defeating project to make the prison system more effective.

Records

Vinay Lal

There are many peculiar things to be said about the various records by which we mark the 'progress' or degeneration of civilizations, nations, institutions, organizations and even individuals. Oppressors, for example, have commonly shown a marked interest in leaving behind a detailed inventory of their crimes. They have wanted to record for posterity the manner in which they eliminated their hated foes or subjects. The Nazis were meticulous record-keepers, and their elaborate ledgers of the dead furnish detailed information on the trains in which Jews were shipped to concentration camps, the number of Jews in each train, the number of Jews gassed to death.

The British in India had a similar expansive and administrative conception of records, and numerous departments of the colonial state were charged with the task of recording the diversity of India's races, its flora and fauna, its mineral deposits and natural endowments. Imperial record-keeping was enabling for the state; it constituted the bibliographic version of the panopticon, where the state knew, or thought it knew, nearly everything of vital importance to assure the longevity of British rule. As nationalism surfaced in the closing years of the nineteenth century, records became more elaborate: there was a new-found compulsion to predict the native's behaviour and stop rebels in their tracks. The new nation-state inherited the imperial department of record-keeping, and today every nation-state is characterized not only by a national anthem, a national flag and a national language but also a national archive. These national archives are, in each instance, also the repository of a nation's secrets, its crimes and misdemeanours; each archive holds the record of missed and repudiated opportunities for peace.

To speak of records is, in the modern idiom, also to speak of numbers. Under conditions of modernity, moreover, numbers have become wholly associated with utilitarian, bureaucratic or statistical exercises, but there was a time when numbers played a fecund and playful role in the shaping of many cultures. To be sure, many of the numbers, for instance the number of free throws missed by the Los Angeles Lakers star Shaquille O'Neal in a basketball game, might be viewed as frivolous, but to the enumerators of such records this is a statistic intended to spur O'Neal to renewed efforts at improving his free throws, generate discussion among fans and provide some cues to teams about how they might contain O'Neal. American sportscasters do not reel off numbers in jest, but in utter seriousness: the 60-odd points scored by Michael Jordan in a certain game is celebrated as an instantiation of history in the making, the only kind of 'history' that some Americans know and care to know.

To gauge the sheer play to which numbers lend themselves, one can turn profitably to the cultural cosmology of the Hindus, for whom the taxonomic impulse was a critical component in ritual enterprises such as divination, sacrifice, literary compositions, construction of genealogies, astrology and even sex. The *Kama Sutra*, a record of sexual activity among a people considerably less prurient than their latter-day descendants, is precise about the number of sexual positions possible during copulation, just as the *Atharva Veda* notes that fifty-three kinds of sorceries are possible (with dice) or that there are 101 varieties of death. The Hindu preoccupation with numbers, a trait both ludic and compulsive, filled the English with exasperation, and the Utilitarian philosopher James Mill pointed to Hindu numbers—such as the 15,55,20,00,00,000 years during which the Creator was incubating, or the 1,70,64,000 years during which the Creator transformed itself from 'neuter to masculine, for the purpose of creating worlds', surely records in their own right—as a sign of the 'rude and imperfect state' of the Hindu mind. Hegel, who would be viewed as possessing more lofty mental faculties than Mill, remained similarly clueless. If certain kings were said to have reigned 70,000 years, and Brahma is said to have lived 20,000 years, one had to presuppose, Hegel argued, that the 'numbers in question, therefore, have not the value and rational meaning which we attach to them'. Around the same time that these two giant specimens of the European mind were ruminating on the folly of the Hindus, England was, as the historian of science Ian Hacking reminds us, engulfed by a 'sheer fetishism for numbers'. Bodies were furiously counted, and statistics were accumulated on everything, from the total number of lashes administered in a year to all habitual offenders to the number of drunkards and lunatics contained in prisons and asylums. The way was being paved for what might be called Holocaust record-keeping. Hegel and Mill might have done better if they had pondered the murderous sensibility informing the record-keeping, by which the management of recalcitrants, outcasts, rebels, criminals, deviants, dissenters and those merely different was being attempted.

It would not have occured to European commentators on Indian culture and European 'experts' on Indian knowledge systems that those numbers which Hegel and James Mill derided may not have been without 'meaning', or that they followed a cultural logic impervious to an instrumental rationality. Never mind that no one in Europe was thinking of geological time, and that subservience to the Bible made it inconceivable to think of millions and billions. The present-day obsession with numbers and records among many Indians is, once again, being read as demonstrable evidence of their lack of rationality. Indians are, admittedly, good with numbers; the country remains a world powerhouse in statistics. The most extraordinary 'human computer' in the world is an Indian, Shakuntala Devi. When she was given two thirteen-digit numbers (76,86,36,97,74,870 and 24,65,09,97,45,779) to multiply, Shakuntala Devi, who apparently became known at the age of eight as 'a living wonder', did so accurately within twenty-eight seconds. She has repeatedly performed such feats. 'Some experts on calculating prodigies refuse to give credence to Mrs Devi,' states the 1992 *Guinness Book of Records*, 'on the grounds that her achievements are so vastly superior to the calculating feats of any other investigated prodigy that the authentication must have been defective.'

Few in India have ever tasted Guinness the stout, or even heard of it, but the penchant for *The Guinness Book* runs deep among many Indians: this 'irrational' obsession is more widely known in the West, rather than the country's contribution to statistics. Mastram Bapu, a holy man of a type, as Winston Churchill might have said, well-known in the East, arrived in *The Guinness Book* by remaining seated at a single spot for twenty-two years. Mastram, the 'contented' fellow, appears to have resolved to make every cliche about the unmoving and stagnant Orient resound with truth. The peculiar achievement of Mastram Bapu, with which Hegel would have been pleased, is only one of many like stories as Indians clamour to install themselves in the records of history. Speaking of effeminacy, which the British particularly associated with Bengalis, Brahmins and babus relaxing in portly splendour, it is notable that the world record for needle-threading is held by an Indian man, Om Prakash Singh of Allahabad, in a country where stitching at home is invariably deemed to be a woman's job.

When the Indian was not seen as lazy, effeminate or downright dishonest, he was construed as being bizarre and eccentric, bound to peculiar customs, wild in his looks and wholly obsequious to authority. Much was written in colonial days about the 'Hindu Juggernaut', and of fanatical believers who would allow themselves to be crushed under the wheels of the chariot at the Jagannath festival in Puri. In 1994, over a period of eight months, the sadhu Lotan Babu rolled his body nearly 4000 kilometres, or an average of 16 kilometres a day, from Ratlam to Jammu by way of rendering obeisance to the goddess Vaishno Devi. In a similar vein, during a period of fifteen months ending on 9 March 1985, Jagdish Chander crawled 1400 kilometres apparently 'to propitiate his favourite Hindu goddess, Mata'. Students of Indian history might recall that the notorious General Dyer, perpetrator of the Jallianwala Bagh massacre in Amritsar in 1919, and of the even more infamous 'crawling order', which required Indians to crawl on a particular street where an Englishwoman had been assaulted, when asked to explain his conduct replied that some 'Indians like to crawl'. It may be poetic justice that the record for the longest continuous crawl is held by an Englishman, who traversed 45.8 kilometres in a mere nine and a half hours. India's yogis and rishis have long been viewed as capable of the most bizarre or absurd acts, and Swami Maujgiri Maharaj of Shahjahanpur, Uttar Pradesh, took it upon himself to engage in the most unusual form of penance by continuously standing for seventeen years, thereby establishing a world record that no one is likely to break too soon. But stagnation was not the only leitmotif of the British idea of India; the country had, it was argued, regressed from an earlier state of comparative efflorescence. Thus, it is perfectly fitting that while Rajiv Gandhi as prime minister was striving to take India forward, through acts such as inaugurating the Shatabdi (or Twenty-First Century) Express train as a mark of his commitment to propel the nation towards modernity, Arvind Pandya of India was setting the world record for 'backwards running'.

Though middle-class Indians, who fancy that their country could become a world power, are eager to embrace the achievements of their countrymen and women, the records which push Indians into *The Guinness Book* shame the nation. The immense breast-beating and wailing that accompanies the return of every failed sports team from the Commonwealth Games or the Olympics is a sight to behold. Indians wonder why a country of one billion people can never win more than one bronze medal in the Olympics, or why some 'lousy' African country racked by coups, starvation and mayhem on its streets wins more gold in the Commonwealth Games than all of India's runners, weightlifters and wrestlers put together. The drought of medals afflicts the aspiring classes with much pain, but they are generally much less bothered by the other droughts that ruin the lives of millions. Accustomed to viewing triumphs in beauty contests—a near-monopoly of Miss World and Miss Universe titles in the mid and late 1990s has cheered Indians—and Olympic Games as the true measure of a nation's greatness, these modernizing Indians are anguished that their country should be held up to ridicule by record seekers intent on setting achievements that are not merely outlandish but positively useless.

A certain anxiety over the manliness of a people, no less of a nation, may perhaps account to a great degree for the quest among Indians to have their names etched in *The Guinness Book*. Part of the ethos of manliness consists simply in gaining recognition, in being acknowledged as supreme in one's chosen field of endeavour. One long-lasting effect of colonialism has been that the Indian continues to look up to the white European male, who confers recognition upon inferiors, and who has established the standard that the Indian (like other formerly colonized people) must meet. *The Guinness Book* is there to remind them that such recognition is possible and desirable, but the politics of this 'recognition' also demands that we read this form of record seeking not merely in the idiom of mimicry. The freakish activities that perturb the modernizers in Indian society represent, indeed, a counter-hegemonic force to modern orthodoxies about development, production, competition and modernity. It is precisely the narrative of competition and progress, which modernity has claimed as its very own, that is being defied—even in the act of emulation and the rendering of profound homage. If the 'competitive spirit', which stands behind the quest for records, leads to the drive to excel, or to raise productivity, why not do so by setting records in activities and achievements where the disutility is all too apparent? The 5 metres of fingernails on Sridhar Chillal's left hand, the 3.4-metre-long moustache of Kalyan Ramji Sain: these have their political economy, not measured by any stock index. The previous record holder in the moustache department, the life convict Karma Ram Bheel of Delhi, must have had prison personnel assigned to help him in keeping his moustache groomed, or in preventing his fellow prisoners from tampering with so seductive an appendage to a man's body. While the city was facing acute butter and milk shortages, Bheel, *The Guinness Book* informs us, used 'mustard oil, butter and cream to keep it in trim'. And, since India meets its petroleum needs largely through imports, Har Prakash [later Guinness] Rishi thought it apposite to keep a motor scooter in nonstop motion for 1001 hours, covering a distance of 80,195 kilometres at Traffic Park, Pune, between 22 April and 3 June 1990. We are at a considerable remove from the scenario of world wars over oil.

In the Indian engagement with *The Guinness Book*, modernity is at once both emulated and defied, honoured and parodied, celebrated and mocked. If the scientific spirit and the competitive ethos appear to be enshrined, it is also unequivocally clear that the achievements which have enabled Indians (in the most cliched phrase of the times) 'to make history' scarcely redound to the credit of the nation-state, or do modernity proud. If the Indian obsession with *The Guinness Book* is construed as constituting irrefutable evidence of Indians' feelings of inferiority or their emulation of the 'achieving races', and their commitment to modernity and the nation-state, perhaps one should also begin to view the records set by them as markers of the resilience of a complex civilization against the homogenizing and deleterious effects of modernity. Resistance in an era of globalization and totalization will perforce enact both homage and parody. The bureaucratic exercises of record-keeping will perhaps have met their match in the more absurd, idiosyncratic and whimsical forms of record-seeking.

Refugees

Imtiaz Ahmed

The UNHCR, United Nations High Commissioner for Refugees, has an interesting poster which says, 'Einstein was a refugee.' The purpose of this poster, one imagines, is mainly to educate its viewer that a 'refugee' may turn out to be as creative and great as Einstein and therefore must not be abhorred and neglected or treated as a socially undesirable element. From that standpoint, the poster does carry a strong message. But then, there are very few Einsteins in this world, and few of them end up as refugees outside their homeland. Moreover, Einstein was already a Nobel laureate before he became a refugee. Put differently, Einstein-like refugees hardly face any problem in settling down in refugee-receiving nations. In fact, such Einsteins are welcomed with open arms and fanfare by their hosts, sometimes almost to the point of personal embarrassment. The same, however, cannot be said about the Budu Mias and Sakeenas—the poor, unknown, mostly illiterate, semi- or unskilled millions—who end up as refugees in other nations. In fact, out of the 22.3 million refugees 'cared for' by the UNHCR, a majority come from the world's poorer countries. And there lies much of the 'problem' with the refugee population today.

A classic definition of the term 'refugee' is found in the 1951 UN Convention on Refugees. Set against the backdrop of the devastation following the Second World War, the convention, which was later extended by the 1967 protocol, defined a refugee as follows:

Any person who owing to a well-founded fear of being persecuted for reasons of race, religion, nationality, membership of a particular social group or political opinion, is outside the country of his nationality and is unable, or owing to such fear, is unwilling to avail himself of the protection of that country; or who, not having a nationality and being outside the country of his formal habitual residence, is unable, or owing to such fear, is unwilling to return to it.

Two critical features are central to this definition. First, the state in question has failed to protect a section of its population and in the process has transformed itself into a refugee-producing nation. The use of coercive force, mainly the biased policing of and political and social discriminations against the aggrieved people, is otherwise a critical factor in the birth of refugees.

Second, the persecuted segment of the population does not technically qualify as refugees unless they cross the national border. But in crossing the national border, the refugees become, and remain so until the end of the resolution of the issue, the jealous 'vocation' of the police and the government of the receiving state. At this point, the policing of refugees by the state varies from utilizing them in national interest to the other extreme of ghettoizing and criminalizing their existence—also, sometimes, in the national interest.

Before further elaborating these points, let me clarify one or two conceptual issues pertaining to the idea of policing. To begin with, the distinction between 'policy' and 'policing' is more apparent than real. In one important sense, policing of things is what 'policy' does. But then, the act of policing does not take place in a vacuum; it operates within a system, forming only a part of the larger order. Michel Foucault opined that the pastoral, the post-Westphalian diplomatic-military techniques and the police (whose specific technologies could be traced back to the 'art of government' in the seventeenth and eighteenth centuries) represented the three key elements that subsequently contributed to the governmentalization of the (Western) state. Put differently, 'policy,' 'policing' and 'police' are intrinsic to the organization of the government, contributing to a state of affairs where the policy of the government is thoroughly governmentalized or, worse, in the hands of the police! The position is no different when it comes to recognizing or understanding governmental policy towards refugees or any other section of the people residing within the boundaries of the state.

Colonial domination, which gave birth to a particular kind of government, one that is practically alienated from the colonized population, further limited the scope and shape of governmental policy. It was through the benevolence of the colonial government that much of public life was organized and reproduced. This ranged from public education to public transportation (roads and railways) to the postcolonial enactment of citizenship or nationality laws. In the wake of the exploitative policies of the colonial government, however, a fundamental change took place in the nature of the state. The state ceased to have a vibrant and consenting civil society. Much of it became polarized and violent, which further eroded the power of civil society while further empowering the government. Governmental policy, under the circumstances, could not help but turn rigid and unimaginative, if not tyrannical. In this context, the failure of civil society to carry out a consistent, independent and protracted policy towards refugees is nothing of a surprise. At one point or another, governmental stance was bound to replace civic response towards the refugees, however reliable and humane the latter may have been upon the initial civic recognition of the refugees' plight. While this may tempt many to distinguish between the non-colonized West and postcolonial societies in their handling of their respective refugee population, such distinction is increasingly becoming less clear, if not irrelevant, with the change in the racial, cultural and religious composition of the refugee groups.

Three general trends in the policing of refugee populations by the state can easily be identified:

The policy of encampment. Although welcomed by the local population in the beginning, the Rohingya refugees in Bangladesh, when they came from Myanmar, were quickly brought under governmental control. There is now a total official restriction on the movement of the camp refugees. No refugee can go out of the camp without the approval of camp officials, which is seldom entertained. Anyone caught outside the camp without permission faces harsh treatment, including beating from the police. The case is no different elsewhere, whether in South India, the Middle East or Africa. There too, refugee camps are zones of incarceration, and the refugees are treated like criminals, punished for the 'crime' of leaving their places of origin and crossing borders into foreign territory.

Then there is the policy of disowning responsibility. Bangladesh, for instance, would be interested in seeing the continued presence of the UNHCR and the refugees in the country, not for any humanitarian reason but simply for the sake of profiting from their presence. The US Committee for Refugees once noted:

> Despite Dhaka's claim that caring for the Rohingya is an economic burden, Bangladesh has borne little of the cost of caring for the refugees. With the exception of $2.5 million that Bangladesh spent on relief prior to the UNHCR involvement, UNHCR, donor governments, and NGOs have paid for almost all of the relief operation. If anything, the UNHCR relief operation has led to a net financial gain for the Bangladesh' government and its citizens, as it has increased employment.

Corruption adds to the profit, contributing thereby to the birth of lobbies, not necessarily at the highest level but, more significantly, at the middle and lower levels, well disposed to the continued presence of the UNHCR and the refugees. The middle and the lower functionaries of both governmental and non-governmental organizations are powerful enough to create conditions for putting a halt to unprofitable changes and reproducing the post-refugee status quo.

This has other related dimensions as well, some going beyond direct financial benefits. Indeed, in the case of Rwandan refugees in Zaire, *The State of the World's Refugees 2000*, a UNHCR publication, said:

For the shaky government of Kinshasa, the refugees were a potential proxy force, useful to help reassert control of the eastern provinces. For President Mobutu Sese Seko, the refugees issue deflected attention from his government's mismanagement of the country and thereby offered a chance to regain the international stature he had lost since the end of the Cold War.

The plight of the refugees under such circumstances can hardly be exaggerated. Often, governmental agencies and militarized forces loyal to them in refugee camps have benefited from the benevolence and support of the humanitarian agencies, including the UNHCR.

Finally, there is the policy of repatriation. Despite the unwillingness on the part of the majority of the Rohingya refugees to return home for reasons of insecurity in Myanmar, by 1997 the UNHCR, with the direct consent of the government of Bangladesh repatriated, amid criticism of involuntary repatriation, all but some 21,000 refugees. Earlier, in August 1995, in the backdrop of UNHCR's resumption of repatriation efforts, the Zairean government tried to forcibly send back the Rwandan refugees by closing down the camps. In one instance, some 15,000 refugees were put on rented trucks and forcibly returned to Rwanda. India also tried to do something similar with the Chakma refugees when it drastically reduced the supply of food rations, so as to compel the refugees to leave the camps and return to Bangladesh. Examples of this kind are on the rise every year and in regions around the world.

To make matters worse, there has been a subtle change in the UNHCR policy of voluntary repatriation. This refers to the change in the UNHCR policy, from one of 'individual interviewing' before scrutinizing personal candidacy for repatriation to the promotion of repatriation through 'mass registration'. Critics have already questioned the principle of voluntary participation in such schemes. As a recent UNHCR publication noted:

The traditional principle that all refugees should be given the opportunity of a voluntary return, on the basis of individual informed choices, was difficult to put into practice. The reality was that most of the refugees had been coerced into exile by their leaders. Many of them were more like hostages than refugees. This was a different type of human displacement, in which the concept of voluntary return, and the very meaning of the word 'refugee', had been twisted into new and complex realities, which could not easily be tackled through traditional approaches.

We may suppose the time has come for redefining the concept of refugee, keeping in perspective the increasing policing of refugees and the plight of the millions of Budu Mias and Sakeenas. Maybe the UNHCR should come up with a new poster that would read, 'Einstein was a refugee and so are Budu Mia and Sakeena: treat them equally.'

Further Reading

UNHCR. 2000. *The State of the World's Refugees 2000: Fifty Years of Humanitarian Action*. London: Oxford University Press.

Roads

C. Douglas Lummis

All strategic roads were built by tyrants—for the Romans, the Prussians, or the French. They go straight across the country. All other roads wind like processions and waste everybody's time.

—*Adolf Hitler*

Before the Roman came to Rye or out to Severn strode,
The rolling English drunkard made the rolling English road.

—*G.K. Chesterton*

Paths and Roads

Paths exist in nature. Wild animals make them, as well as human beings. In crossing a valley or traversing a mountain pass, there is a route one naturally follows, and a natural place for the foot to fall. Walkers who leave the marked trail often discover they have fallen upon a trail made by animals. A human culture without fixed routes is barely imaginable. Even on sandy deserts, where passage leaves no lasting trace, there are routes between water sources; even on the open sea there are sea-lanes between ports.

Paths have a tendency to become public space, which becomes stronger with roads. As the term 'road construction' suggests, we tend to use 'road' to refer to routes that are not simply worn by travel but are artificially constructed and maintained, which further suggests some connection with a public authority. We will return to this point.

The Road in Culture

What would literature and poetry be without the symbol of the road? In the ancient epics of Gilgamesh and Odysseus, in the Monkey King's Journey to the West, in the Progress of Bunyan's Pilgrim, in Basho's wanderings down the Narrow Road, in Noyes's 'ribbon of moonlight / Over the purple moor', in the Road Not Taken by Frost, the road as a signifier forms the very axis along which some of our greatest literary works move.

The words 'road' and 'way' are two of the richest sources of metaphor in the English language. The Oxford English Dictionary lists forty definitions of the latter, mostly metaphorical, extending over nine pages. How impoverished our moral discourse would be without this image. The road to ruin; the road paved with good intentions; 'I am the way' (Jesus); 'The way [tao] that can be talked about is not the true way' (Lao Tzu); Way to go! (American slang).

The Road in Law

Black's Law Dictionary defines 'road' as 'an open way or public passage', and 'public road' as 'a road or way established and adopted by the proper authorities for the use of the general public, and over which every person has a right to pass . . .' The road (private roads aside) is a locus of rights; membership in the 'general public' is the only credential you need to be able to walk on it.

The 'proper authorities' may also assume the duty to maintain law and order on the road. The highway, 'being travelled on by the public in general, was early in English history brought under the protection of the King's Peace' (Webster), primarily to protect travellers from 'gentlemen of the road', that is, highwaymen.

Military Roads

The word 'way' comes from the Middle English *wey*, 'to carry', while the word 'road' comes from the Old English *rad*, 'to ride'. We can be sure it was mostly people carrying and people riding who travelled down the ancient trading roads—the Royal Road from the Mediterranean Sea to the Persian Gulf, the Amber Road from Denmark to Italy, the Silk Road from Shanghai to Cadiz.

The word 'road' is also related to the word 'raid'; one of its early definitions was 'an armed expedition', and the usefulness of a road system to an army is obvious. It was after his conquest of China in 221 BC that Emperor Ch'in Shih Huang-ti ordered the standardization of cart tracks as part of his programme for bringing the country under his permanent domination. In the century just before that, the Romans began the construction that eventually covered their empire with 80,000 kilometres of highways (the English word 'highway' comes from the fact that the Roman roads in Britain were raised) down which they could send their strike forces to rebellious regions with what in those days counted as lightning speed ('All roads lead to Rome' was only the reverse of that coin).

The Adjustment of the Road to the Machine

We will skip over the history of roads, and take up the story at the point where certain events in the West begin to affect the whole world. In the 1830s and '40s the steam locomotive was developed, which needed an entirely new kind of road, one with steel tracks on it: the railroad.

Beginning in the industrialized countries, and then in their colonies and a few other countries that could afford it, the 'proper authorities' shifted their attention to the construction of railroads, and roads for the use of people without train tickets went into an era of neglect. But this began to change again towards the end of the nineteenth century with the development of another mechanized vehicle that required a still different kind of road: the automobile.

From the very beginning it was recognized that the automobile was not appropriately designed for the existing roads; originally it was required to obey a speed limit of 6 kilometres an hour, and someone had to trot along in front waving a red warning flag. The solution, then and now, has not been to build vehicles appropriate to the roads, but roads appropriate to the vehicles.

With this, the nature of roads began to change. The auto lanes ceased to be public passages 'over which every person has a right to pass'. Now there was a property qualification: to go out there you had to have a car. Of course, walkers had always been driven aside by wagons and carriages, but now the danger was of a different order: the automobile does not share the horse's aversion to trampling on people. All sorts of things were invented allegedly to make driving safer, but in fact to get the speed limit raised: traffic lights, one-way streets, divided arterials, overpasses for walkers, signs that say PEDS WAIT ON CURB and traffic police. Patterns of residential architectures were revised to provide for (at least one) car in the basement, and cities were reconstructed not only to give the automobile free access everywhere, but also to relocate residential, shopping and employment areas at such distances that one (almost) cannot survive without an automobile. Has there ever been another case in human history where a civilization laboured so mightily to restructure itself so as to transform a privately manufactured luxury into a necessity?

The Superhighway

Construction on the high-speed autostradas was begun in Italy in 1924, two years after Mussolini came into power, but most sources agree that the first 'true' superhighway was the German Autobahn built under the Nazis. But the architectural spirit that gave birth to this new form of construction, a spirit that Norman Mailer once called Mussolini Modern, was not limited to totalitarian states. In the US both the Pennsylvania Turnpike and the Merritt Parkway (Connecticut) were completed before 1941, and after the Second World War there began a freeway construction boom in all countries of the world that could afford it—and also in many that could not.

This explosion of highway construction did not come about as the result of the fair operation of the free market. To cite an example that has become legendary, in 1938 the city of Los Angeles had the world's largest streetcar system. General Motors (GM), in combination with Standard Oil and Firestone Tire, bought it, shut it down and tore out the tracks. Los Angeles was reconstructed as the world's premier automobile metropolis. Natural outcomes of such reconstruction were the drive-in restaurant, the drive-in movie, the hot-rod, the three-car garage, the seventeen-car accident, the traffic jam and smog—all broadcast lovingly to the world via Hollywood. Today, two-thirds of the land space of Los Angeles is devoted to the operation and storage of cars. GM and its associates went on to buy up rail and streetcar lines all over the US and close them down in order to make way for its product.

But if the automobile manufacturers destroyed the rail and streetcar lines, they did not build the highways to replace them. Imagine how expensive the automobile would be if manufacturers had to build and maintain the roads their commodity operates on. But, with the exception of a few toll roads, it is governments that pay. Sometimes they pay with money from gasoline and automobile taxes, but not always. To take another striking example from the US: in 1956 the US Congress recognized the military value of good roads, and authorized the construction of the National System of Interstate Highways. This pet project of President Eisenhower, which was initially funded at $25 billion and eventually cost twice that, was at that time the largest public works project ever undertaken by the hand of man. (Part of this project was carried out in the area where I lived then. The goal was to replace the crooked road from San Francisco to the Carquinez Bridge with a perfectly straight one by cutting off the tops of a row of Pacific Coast Range Mountains and shoving the earth into the valleys between. It was rumoured to have involved more earth-moving than the Panama Canal.)

The result was something like a 65,000-kilometre airstrip, with gentle curves and many stretches dead straight, no steep grades, no bumps, no slow-moving vehicles, no stop lights or crosswalks or obstacles of any kind, just the car and the concrete, roaring twenty-four hours a day. Its effect on the environment has been catastrophic. Vast amounts of wilderness land have been bulldozed under by it. Where it is guarded by chain-link fence, it interdicts the migration routes of wild animals; where it is not, it is an animal slaughterhouse. It emits white noise and black gases. It bears little resemblance to what was once called a road, and movement down it bears little resemblance to what was once called travel. Unlike a road it is not a 'place' through which one moves, but a non-place; it has entrances and exits, but no 'wayside', no 'way stations', nothing 'by the way'. If your car stops on it, you must proceed immediately to an emergency telephone and get yourself rescued as quickly as possible.

Today the Car Wars have by no means ended. The big manufacturers are labouring to sell their products in the vast markets of Asia, Africa and Latin America. To do this they must transform those regions into automobile culture, a process that has advanced quite far in some countries. In particular, they need more highways built. Of course, they will not build them themselves; they will get it done with Official Development Assistance (ODA) loans, which later become debt. Using these methods, they hope to stay profitable for years to come.

Closing Parable

It is said that if you built a forty-eight-lane highway around the earth at the equator and put all the world's 350 million automobiles on it, they would be jammed together bumper to bumper. To give these cars enough space to move at a reasonable rate would require at least four times as much space, which gives us a 192-lane highway. Now imagine the 193rd lane being built at a pace rapid enough to accommodate all the new cars as they come off the assembly lines of all the world's manufacturers. Surely it will be racing forward at a dizzying speed and, before we know it, will snake up behind us to begin the 194th lap. The reader may wish to know what is to be done with such a thought. Perhaps it may come in handy some night when he or she is short of nightmares.

Further Reading

Kay, Jane Holtz. 1997. *Asphalt Nation: How the Automobile Took Over America and How We Can Take It Back.* Berkeley, Los Angeles, London: University of California Press.

Mantle, Jonathan. 1995. *Car Wars: Fifty Years of Backstabbing, Infighting and Industrial Espionage in the Global Market.* New York: Arcade.

Wall, Derek. 1999. *Earth First! and the Anti-roads Movement: Radical Environmentalism and Comparative Social Movements.* London and New York: Routledge.

Sacred Groves

Frédérique Apffel-Marglin

In the 1880s, the first Inspector-General of Forests in India, Sir Dietrich Brandis, was lamenting the disappearance of something he referred to as 'sacred groves'. By the way this phrase is being used today in the discourse of ecology, it seems to refer to patches of uncut primal forest in which a deity recognized by the local population is supposed to dwell. Such patches are reported to exist both in tribal and peasant contexts in many parts of the world.

One might wonder how the man responsible for introducing scientific forestry to the subcontinent came to wax nostalgic about the disappearance of these patches. Scientific forestry emerged in Prussia and Saxony towards the end of the eighteenth century as a state-sponsored activity designed to insure state revenue and a sustained yield of the commercially valuable species. A century later, in India, the newly formed Forestry Department was placed under the Revenue Department in most provinces and the Forest Service came to be regarded as a purely commercial concern. This administrative arrangement and the regulations that came with it (the Indian Forest Act of 1878) are basically still in force in India today. In other words, scientific forestry is a thoroughly profane, utilitarian manner of viewing and engaging with forests guided by three watchwords (to use James Scott's words) of 'minimum diversity', the 'balance sheet' and 'sustained yield'—the very opposite of anything the words 'sacred groves' might conjure up.

Are we to imagine Sir Dietrich being seized at the end of his career with remorse for the result of what he had created, namely an accelerated rate of deforestation? Did his sorrow at the demise of 'sacred groves' bespeak a desire to transform the Forestry Service into devotees of the domain of trees? Perhaps he thought that the natives who lived in the forest did not worship it in the right way. That would certainly explain why he devised legislation to keep them out of it. The natives by all accounts did not seem to understand the three watchwords of scientific forestry and must have been a serious handicap to the state's efforts to implement them.

Sir Dietrich the scientist was heir to the separation between fact and value, the head and the heart, religion and science. These fateful separations were established during the scientific revolution some 200 years earlier and had, by then, long been transmogrified into the way things simply are, into Reality. Reality had become bifurcated into the profane and the sacred, into the natural and the supernatural, into matter and spirit. Scientific forestry clearly belongs to the first half of these divisions, where trees are only profane matter. So the sacred or the spiritual did not vanish; they simply were relocated. In the subcontinent, they were located 'elsewhere' in certain aspects of reality and not in others. Forests in general could not qualify as 'sacred' since they were a source of livelihood for many natives, and the utilitarian had also become sharply demarcated from the sacred and become quasi-synonymous with the profane. So Sir Dietrich could with a clear conscience demarcate great swathes of forest as government preserves and banish from them the natives and their non-scientific, irrational uses of it. However, where the natives did not cut down the trees for their livelihood, this act was valid according to the notions of progress in the modern imagination. Where the natives also worshipped the trees, it was evidence of a clear case of sacrality. Thus, the sacred grove becomes the elsewhere of the government reserve forest.

Sir Dietrich's nostalgia about vanishing 'sacred groves' echoes the sentiments of the likes of William Wordsworth, Edmund Burke, William Gilpin and John Ruskin in Europe, and of Henry

David Thoreau and John Muir in the US. Like them, it locates the sacred in nature elsewhere from where nature is used for human livelihood. The doctrine of the sublime articulated by several of these thinkers referred to the wilderness, to areas of nature untouched, unsullied by human hands. God was to be found on mountain tops, chasms, waterfalls and the like. The first wildland park in the US was Yosemite, created in 1864, followed in short order by Yellowstone, Grand Canyon, Rainier and Zion. These wildlands, as the names themselves reveal, are virgin territory in the imaginary of most Americans. Their sacredness has everything to do with their virginity. It was certainly most convenient for the emergence of this particular myth that the creation of the first park corresponded with the last of the wars the US government fought with the native people of the North American continent. With the final defeat of the Native Americans, the US herded them into reservations and out of what became National Parks. As William Cronon (1995:79) points out: 'To this day the Blackfeet continue to be accused of "poaching" on the lands of the Glacier National Park that originally belonged to them and that were ceded by treaty only with the proviso that they be permitted to hunt there.' The sacred, after all, must be kept separate from the profane; it would just not do to have those boundaries transgressed even for reasons of survival.

The lofty elsewheres of the Euro-American imaginary were, by the second half of the nineteenth century, sorely needed. After all it must have become increasingly difficult to contact the sublime heights of God's presence while gasping for air in smog-filled urban centres. This has hardly changed today. We still desperately need these nature preserves, for how can we be filled with awe standing in front of rectilinear row after rectilinear row of the same variety of genetically engineered corn, as far as the eye can see, while we breathe in the acrid smell of pesticide fumes? So, out of our characteristic generosity of heart, we have shown the rest of the world how to preserve pristine nature and exported our nature park idea. And, of course, along with nature preserves also comes the necessary force to make sure the pesky natives living in these zones are persuaded, coaxed, commanded, compelled voluntarily or by force to evacuate.

Happily, today we have left behind the childish romanticism of our early nineteenth-century infatuation with nature's sublimity. Rhapsodizing over lofty mountains or sparkling streams is no longer in fashion. Today naturalists are qualified scientists, and they are serious. Seriousness is indeed called for. At the dawn of the third millennium, the non-human world finds itself under great strain. In particular, the awareness of the immense and growing loss of species has given a different image to nature preserves. Scientists are now calling for biological preserves to save biodiversity. To stem the tide of destruction seems to necessitate turning to the heart to energize our crusades for the conservation of biodiversity. E.O. Wilson speaks of his biophilia, 'love of life' in all forms. Somehow to drape the sentiments in the same Greek words used for most scientific works creates sufficient distance from gushing romanticism.

The discursive terminology may have changed, but not much else. The love, the respect, the nurturance, the awe, is still elsewhere, whether formulated unabashedly or coolly. The logic of elsewheres, whether sacred groves, national parks or biological preserves, allows us to continue to 'exploit natural resources' in the profane domain of utilitarian pursuits. After all, the economy must keep on growing. For were it to stop, catastrophe would strike us all. So perforce the preservation of nature has to occur elsewhere.

The love of life pertains to such elsewheres as a person's home—this haven in a heartless world—to churches, synagogues and other religious institutions where, mostly once a week, such sentiments are duly aired, to our varied leisure spaces, and to the varieties of nature preserves. But in the realms where the profane, utilitarian pursuit of a livelihood takes place—our workplaces—the love of life is a childish sentimentality. For do we not know for a fact—taught to us by the great white fathers of modernity—that it is universal human nature to pursue one's individual self-interest? The Great Victorious Market Economy would grind to a halt were the pursuit of livelihood based on the love of life.

The notion of a universal human nature has fared poorly at the hands of the postmodernist critique. It is beginning to look suspiciously like the particular nature of modern Euro-American man, moulded by his institutions and his ideas. And it turns out that the peasants or tribals worshipping the uncut trees in a patch of primal forest also worship the soil of their fields, the water of their rivers or of the sea, the seeds which they plant, the crop they harvest and preserve in sacred storage spaces, the bullocks that plough furrows in their fields, among other things. The uncut patches of primal forests cannot be seen as essentially sacred only because it is not being used. Rather, they spatially encode the alternations between fallow and productive periods, which in the time dimension beats the cosmic rhythm of regeneration. All craftspeople in India worship the tools of their craft: the loom, the potter's wheel, the scribe's stylus, the painter's brushes, and so forth. But in the literature, somehow, one does not hear of sacred seeds, soil, loom or bullocks. Worship and the pursuit of a livelihood are not antithetical in India, nor are they in the Andes, and probably not in most non-modern worlds.

The pursuit of a livelihood in these non-modern worlds seems to be based on foregrounding a recognition that our lives depend not only on the lives of other human beings but also on the collectivity of non-human beings that make up the rest of the world. Life emerges from constant exchanges between these two collectivities. The love of life is not quarantined to appropriate sacred or non-utilitarian spaces. Only a severe narrowing of perspective can yield the notion that what drives humans and the rest of nature is ruthless competition and the survival of the fittest. Such a constricted perspective leads to an us-versus-them stance which can only lead to further conflict. It has certainly led to an astounding violence towards the more-than-human world.

Furthermore, many of these exchanges are free: the exhalation of plants, sunlight, mother's milk. These are the gifts of life pouring forth spontaneously. As Marcel Mauss told us a long time ago, the gift is at the heart of non-modern societies. The gift characterizes exchanges between all the collectivities, human and more-than-human. The circulation of the gift is what keeps making life possible. Love of life, respect, gratitude, awe and responsibility are not located in elsewheres, away from people's pursuit of a livelihood. They are intertwined with it. As long as love of life is quarantined in various elsewheres and kept out of our mundane pursuits of a livelihood, the more-than-human world will be endangered.

We could begin a step in the right direction by changing our modes of thinking and teaching. It is time to publicly recognize that the modern boundary between the sacred and the utilitarian was invented in seventeenth-century Western Europe to solve religio-political problems of the day, and is not in itself a dictate for the future. There is no doubt that we urgently need to redraw these boundaries, if the earth and all the life forms it nurtures are to survive, and thrive.

Further Reading

Cronon, William. 1995. 'The Trouble with Wilderness: Or Getting Back to the Wrong Nature?' In W. Cronon, ed., *Uncommon Ground: Toward Reinventing Nature*. New York: Norton.

Gadgil, Madhav, and Ramachandra Guha. 1995. *Ecology and Equity: The Use and Abuse of Nature in Contemporary India*. London: Routledge; Delhi: Penguin Books.

Scott, James. 1998. *Seeing Like a State*. New Haven & London: Yale University Press.

Sanctions

Vinay Lal

It is truly an ironic solidarity that bound India and Pakistan together in the aftermath of nuclear tests by both nations in May 1998. Both countries were placed by the United States under sanctions that automatically came into effect under the terms of the Nuclear Proliferation Prevention Act, a price to be paid for gatecrashing into the white man's estate. Pakistan and India can be united at least in comradely expressions of suffering. Earlier that year, the US Senate also voted, by an overwhelming majority, to subject to sanctions those foreign enterprises found violating the Iran Missile Proliferation Sanctions Act, which aims to keep missile technology out of Iran's hands. The House of Representatives, not to be outdone, then passed a bill that would subject to sanctions countries where religious minorities are persecuted. Nor are these the only sanctions that the United States has imposed or threatened to impose unilaterally: as the President's Export Council noted in 1997, seventy-five countries, home to nearly 50 per cent of the world's population, were to be held accountable to American lawmakers, a largely troglodyte breed of mentally challenged jingoists and rapacious businessmen.

With the two largest countries of the Indian subcontinent, where well over 1.1 billion people reside, until recently under sanctions, the US might well be advised to enumerate those countries, short as that list is, which it deems worthy of its approbation. After the formation of the United Nations in 1945, and the resolution taken by member states to attempt to resolve conflicts between themselves through means other than war, sanctions were bound to assume an important place in world governance. However, many early attempts at imposing sanctions, such as against the apartheid regime of South Africa, were resolutely and successfully opposed by the US. The General Assembly of the United Nations, where the preponderant majority supported a systematic enforcement of sanctions to precipitate (in the words of the African National Congress leader Albert Luthuli) 'the end of the hateful system of apartheid', could do no more than implore the Security Council, which alone under articles 41-42 of Chapter VII of the UN Charter had the power to enforce sanctions, to make a just use of its mandate.

Time and again the three Western powers of the Security Council vetoed resolutions pressing for sanctions, but by the late 1970s the tide of international opinion could no longer be resisted, and even the US Congress passed, over President Reagan's veto, the Comprehensive Anti-apartheid Act. It was not until the fall of the Soviet Union, when American global hegemony could be exercised unimpeded, that an undiminished enthusiasm for sanctions began to be witnessed among members of the American foreign policy establishment. As of January 1988, sanctions mandated by the Security Council were in place only against South Africa; at the end of 1994, the number had risen to seven countries. Though the US purports to speak and act in the name of the 'international community', the halo of multilateralism that is spun around sanctions can barely disguise the fact that between 1945 and 1990 the US had to act with no support from any other nation on two-thirds of the over 100 occasions when sanctions were imposed.

Since mid 1990, the most rigorous sanctions ever known to have been inflicted on one nation have been in place against Iraq. No one doubted that after Iraq's invasion and occupation of Kuwait it was incumbent upon the world community to show its strong disapproval of Saddam Hussein's irredentist designs by enforcing comprehensive sanctions against Iraq. Resolution 661 of the UN Security Council urged all member states to adhere to a strict embargo on all trade with Iraq. The resolution exempted from the embargo 'supplies intended strictly for medical purposes, and in humanitarian circumstances, foodstuffs'. The Sanctions Committee was set up to monitor compliance with the resolution, but the militant obduracy of the Americans, reflected for instance in their rather perverse interpretation of the 'dual-use' provision, which stipulates that items of civilian use (such as ambulances) that could conceivably be used for military purposes will not be made available to the Iraqis, has had the effect of decimating Iraq socially and economically.

Even before the commencement of hostilities between Iraq and the American-led international force, the sanctions had severely wounded Iraq's economy. Proponents of sanctions, who opposed armed intervention, argued that Iraq had already been greatly debilitated and that the rigorous maintenance of sanctions was bound to produce Iraq's submission; but the United States and its allies, less persuaded that sanctions would render Iraq compliant, successfully pushed for a decisive military engagement. Yet the sanctions which were then seen as incapable of rendering Iraq compliant were retained and even strengthened. More than ten years later, the sanctions against Iraq have not been lifted, owing— as the US argues—to Iraq's abrogation of its numerous obligations under international law, principally its alleged failure to destroy all stocks of biological, chemical and nuclear weapons.

Before sanctions were first enforced, Iraq unquestionably had among the highest standards of living in the Arab world, a flourishing and prosperous middle class, and a formidable social welfare system that provided enviable material security to ordinary citizens. First, a campaign of sustained bombing was to relegate Iraq, in the words of an official UN fact-finding team, to the 'pre-industrial' age; then the sanctions were to push Iraq into the ranks of the underdeveloped nations. Iraq now has among the highest rates in the world of maternal and infant mortality; its hospitals are in a state of absolute disrepair; an astronomical increase in diseases and mental illnesses has been documented; and malnutrition, which had all but disappeared from Iraq before

1990, is estimated to afflict the vast majority of Iraqis. A report released in 1997 by UNICEF described one million children in Iraq under the age of five as being chronically malnourished; more recent data indicates that as many as 5000 children may be dying every month from shortage of medicines and inadequate medical treatment. The single largest cause of death is dehydration from diarrhoea: tap water is no longer treated, as chlorine is unavailable. One year after sanctions first went into effect, the real monthly earnings for unskilled laborers in Iraq had declined by nearly 95 per cent. Before 1990, one dinar fetched three American dollars; today 2300 dinars buy one dollar.

Surprisingly, there has been precious little debate, whether in the US (where it is most required) or elsewhere, on the moral meanings and cultural histories of sanctions, though perhaps it is characteristic of the state of American democracy that on the most fundamental issues there is almost never any discussion, much less dissent. Almost the only concern that is routinely voiced is that sanctions can be harmful to American businesses, leading both to loss of often hard-earned markets for American goods and decline in jobs, and then-President Bill Clinton at one point expressed consternation that sanctions were beginning to constrain him in the conduct of foreign policy. However, sanctions do not necessarily deter countries from pursuing a course of action that the 'international community'—generally an euphemism for Western powers and often for the US alone—considers undesirable. This is becoming increasingly clear, as the American response to the nuclear tests by India and Pakistan so amply demonstrates. Indeed, the destruction of ancient Buddha statues at Bamiyan in Afghanistan by the Taliban regime, which had been slammed with a new set of crippling sanctions just prior to this act of extreme cultural violence, suggests that arbitrary sanctions may even provoke some nations into committing outrageous actions. Surely, however, such actions ought not to be the only grounds for questioning the recourse to sanctions as blunt instruments of coercion?

Though sanctions are often represented as a non-violent and the least objectionable way of attempting to make recalcitrant states conform to acceptable standards of conduct, they are characteristic of late modernity in simultaneously pointing the way to genocide while appearing to be relatively benign. Sanctions often substitute for political negotiations and agreements a legalism and moral high-handedness that is only another form of brutal coercion. Though the institution of war justly faces increasing opprobrium, and the democracies (such as they are, in their present shrivelled and impoverished form) appear to have abjured the use of violence against other democracies, we cannot be complacent in the comfortable and erroneous belief that other modes of regulating conflicts, such as the imposition of mandatory sanctions, constitute a necessarily more civilized and humane endeavour to produce peace and relative equality among the nations of the world.

Towards the latter end of the nineteenth century, let us recall, Western imperial powers increasingly employed the 'punitive expedition' to regulate what they considered to be the errant conduct of their colonized subjects. But the punitive expedition was a form of what George Orwell described as 'pacification', itself grotesquely derived from the Latin word for peace, and it served to remind the natives that the sheer might of the colonial state could descend upon them at any moment. What the punitive expedition was to Britain, the foremost colonial power then, sanctions are to the US, the dominant world power today: chastisement has ever been the political idiom of the Anglo-American world order. Of course, the wielders of sanctions do not see themselves as possible objects of chastisement: who can dare to deploy sanctions against the US when it engages in conduct that the rest of the world recognizes as lawless, or defies, as it did when it was convicted of waging an undeclared war against Nicaragua, the opinion of the 'international community' as embodied in the decisions of the World Court and other like bodies?

There is no effective protection from actions authorized by the Security Council. This represents an extraordinary problem of international governance, making a mockery of the notion of the 'rule of law' and introducing the relatively new notion of legal terrorism. 'In the Western world,' states the jurist Hans Kochler, 'hardly a single expert on international law has seriously dealt with the problematic nature of the human rights offences caused by the sanctions policy of the Security Council.' There is almost nothing to warrant the belief that the wide and systematic use of sanctions will serve the dual ends of ensuring a just world order and help to make societies that are targeted by sanctions more open. Similarly, there is compelling evidence to suggest that such wide and seriously abusive use of sanctions exacerbates political repression within targeted nations and also paves the way for greater inequities between nations, eroding both the 'rule of law' and respect for the international system. As the sanctions regime against Iraq and other countries that the United States deems to be renegade or 'outlaw' states continues to be in force, it remains indubitably clear that the American ambition to remain supremely hegemonic will exact a punishing price from unsuspecting victims, sending them to a death by inches. No one should forget that Madeleine Albright, when asked whether the sanctions could be justified in view of the mass starvation and death of Iraqi children, replied without a moment's hesitation, 'We think the price is worth it.' Depravity has many names.

Further Reading

Arnove, Anthony, ed. 2000. *Iraq under Siege: The Deadly Impact of Sanctions and War*. London: Pluto Press.

Kochler, Hans. 1995. *The United Nations Sanctions Policy and International Law*. Penang, Malaysia: Just World Trust.

Weiss, Thomas G., et al. 1997. *Political Gain and Civilian Pain: Humanitarian Impacts of Economic Sanctions*. Lanham, Maryland: Rowman & Littlefield.

Scarcity

Lakshman Yapa

Until the nineteenth century, according to H. Achterhuis, the noun 'scarcity' meant something temporary—an episode of shortage or a period of insufficiency of supply. This remained the principal usage until the late nineteenth century, when neoclassical economics made scarcity its foundational postulate. Economists say that scarcity occurs when the supply of a commodity cannot sustain the demand for it. Indeed, elementary textbooks define economics as the science that teaches how to allocate scarce resources over unlimited wants. This discourse represents unlimited wants as a human constant and limited resources as a state of nature. If scarcity arises naturally it must reside in the material world, thus allowing economics to view scarcity as an object of scientific study. Arguing against this conventional position, a poststructural view makes the following general claims. First, the concept of scarcity is socially and discursively constructed, formed within a discursive material formation. The scarcity of goods is created in a nexus of coequal relations—technical, social, cultural, political, ecological, academic, and so on. Lastly, to reconceptualize the term scarcity, one must move beyond the commodity to its 'end-use'.

According to the famous economist Lionel Robbins (quoted in Xenos 1989), the scarcity of means to satisfy given ends is an almost ubiquitous condition of human behaviour. Here then is the unity of the subject of economic science. The forms assumed by human behaviour in disposing of scarce means. From economics, the term becomes commonly assumed as a concept signifying a general condition, that is, not 'a scarcity of something' or 'a time of scarcity' but, simply and naturally, scarcity (Xenos 1989).

The notion of scarcity goes to the heart of what is called the economic problem. Echoing what seems common sense, Stonier and Hague's (1964) classic textbook in economics puts the matter thus:

> It is assumed that the fundamental feature of the economic world, the feature which gives rise to economic problems at all, is that goods are scarce. Very few things in the world, with the exception of air, water, and sunshine, are available in unlimited amounts. If there were no scarcity and no need for goods to be shared out among individuals, there would be no economic system and no economics. Economics is fundamentally a study of scarcity and of the problems to which scarcity gives rise.

A more recent economics textbook by Riddell, Shackelford and Stamos (1987) introduces the chapter on scarcity using the title of a popular song by the Rolling Stones—Scarcity: 'You Can't Always Get What You Want'. According to the authors, scarcity is a fundamental fact of economic life because human wants are unlimited and the available resources for satisfying them are scarce. 'Physical resources are of a fixed level. There are just so many people who can labour. There is just so much wheat, corn, coal, gas, bauxite, copper, etc.'

Scarcity is the basis of the economist's laws of demand and supply. Consumers have unlimited wants and they demand more of a commodity at a lower price, other things being equal. Resources are scarce, so more of a good is supplied only at a higher price, other things being equal. The scarcity of a good is not just about supply; a good is scarce relative to the unlimited demand for it. Therefore, scarcity arises because of our limited ability to satisfy the unlimited demand for a good. As plausible as it seems, this way of understanding scarcity does not lead to a useful resolution of such problems as poverty because, as I will argue, unlimited wants and limited resources are not objective conditions: they are socially and discursively constructed.

We can understand this claim more clearly from a semiotic perspective. Any commodity can be viewed as a semiotic sign, and as such will consist of three parts: a word (signifier), a concept (signified) and an object. The theory of signs teaches us that it is not possible to go directly from a word to an object, because that path must always go through a mediating concept. This would not be an issue if concepts were unique, but they are not. For every single word/object pair there are a large number of mediating concepts. Since conversation can focus on only one or a few of these concepts, the commodity we reflect upon, discuss and consume is discursively constructed. The word and the concept form the realm of discourse, while the object and the concept form the realm of material. Therefore, every commodity is a discursive material entity. Complex formations such as scarcity, poverty and development are large systems of interconnected signs, and can be viewed as discursive material formations. Since there is no one-to-one correspondence between a word and an object, the meaning of a commodity such as a car is not confined to 'a vehicle to get from point A to point B'. The car is implicated in many other meanings originating in various fields, such as pollution, success, glamour and sex. After locating the commodity in a nexus of such relations, the many meanings (or concepts) attached to it, can be organized into nodes—technical, social, cultural, ecological, political, academic, and so on. The scarcity of a commodity is discursively constructed at these nodes of the nexus of relations.

To understand the constructivist nature of scarcity, it is necessary to move beyond the commodity to a concept called 'end-use analysis', an idea which was popularized during the energy crisis of the 1970s by writers and social critics such as Barry Commoner and Jeremy Rifkin. The logic of end-use analysis first arose in the field of energy studies and thermodynamics. The second law of thermodynamics states that high-quality energy in the world around us is being constantly degraded to low-quality energy.

Degraded energy exists in the form of diffused heat and cannot be reverted to a high-quality state. The rate at which such degradation takes place is called the rate of entropy.

Consider different ways of heating a home. In one approach the heating needs are supplied by electricity. This can be called a 'high entropy approach' because home heating through electricity leads to large quantities of waste heat. Moreover, the end-use in this case, namely home heating, requires only a low-grade source. Using electricity to heat a home is an example of 'thermodynamic mismatch', or what has been more colourfully described as 'cutting butter with a chainsaw'. The end-use of heating a home can be achieved through various 'low entropy approaches' such as passive solar devices, insulation, heat pumps and wood stoves. End-use analysis recognizes that different energy sources have different types of energy quality, and different types of end-uses can use different types of energy quality. The intent of energy end-use analysis is to match specific end-uses to the appropriate source of energy. Using high-energy sources for low-energy end-uses are forms of socially constructed scarcity because it creates an unnecessary demand for valuable high energy. The logic of energy end-use analysis can be easily adapted to construct a more general notion of social construction of scarcity.

We can begin with the economist's conventional idea of a commodity and then invoke the concept of the 'end-use' of that commodity. For example, the end-use of a furnace may be heating a home, and the end-use of an automobile may be the journey-to-work. Let us assume that the end-use associated with a particular commodity (s_*) can be satisfied in several alternate or complementary ways as shown by the different elements in the set $s = \{s_1, s_2, \ldots, s_*, \ldots, s_k\}$. For example, imagine s to be the set of alternative modes of intracity transport where s_* refers to the use of automobiles. For the sake of argument, assume the existence of mechanisms in society that restrict the availability of some elements of the set s except s_*. As the history of urban transportation shows, the automobile has been the favoured mode, while alternatives such as public transport, car-pooling, cycling and walking have received less emphasis, thus increasing demand for automobiles, and for supportive infrastructure. As another example, consider the demand for nitrogenous chemical fertilizer in a Third World country. Next, consider the complementary and alternative ways for obtaining nitrogenous fertilizer: anaerobic decomposition of organic waste, interplanting with leguminous crops, crop rotation and composting. One can argue that the increased demand for chemical fertilizer (or its relative scarcity) is partly a function of the non-availability of such alternatives. The net effect of making alternatives unavailable would be to increase the demand for particular commodities such as automobiles and chemical fertilizer. Thus the contraction of different sources or ways in which a particular end-use of a commodity can be met creates scarcity.

Another related mechanism increasing the demand for the commodity (s_x) occurs when its use develops beyond the original end-use. For example, the function of an automobile can go beyond the journey to work, and even of transport itself. Automobiles are implicated in multiple meanings as symbols of success, status, fun, freedom, sex, glamour, virility, and so on. This further increases the demand for automobiles. In other words, the demand for automobiles cannot be explained solely in terms of its use value as a means of transport. To use the language of semiotics, the automobile assumes a range of 'signifieds' that go well beyond those signifying transport.

Scarcity is created by expanding the demand for a commodity, which is done by contracting alternative sources of supply, and by expanding the use of that commodity beyond the original end-use. Not all nodes are particularly relevant for discussing how scarcity is created for a particular commodity. Prominent examples include the cultural significance of the automobile as a symbol of glamour; the demand created for automobiles through model changes and planned obsolescence; the marketing of seeds that are genetically designed not to reproduce; the promotion of infant formula in the Third World at the expense of breast milk; the marginalization of biogas technology because of state disinterest or cultural prejudice; and the neglect of the study of indigenous knowledge systems in influential university departments of agriculture. To understand the social construction of scarcity, we need to reconstruct the commodity's history, its principal end-uses, alternative ways of meeting that end-use and the reasons the demand for that commodity has expanded beyond its original end-use. Contrary to the claims of the economists, unlimited wants and limited resources are not self-evident objective conditions inherent in the material world; rather, they are socially and discursively constructed, and therefore equally available for deconstruction and reconstruction, hopefully with a more humane perspective.

Further Reading

Achterhuis, H. 1993. Scarcity and sustainability. In *Global Ecology: A New Arena of Political Conflict*, edited by W. Sachs. London: Zed Books.

Riddell, T., J. Shackelford, and S. Stamos. 1987. *Economics: A Tool for Understanding Society*. Reading, Massachusetts: Addison-Wesley.

Rifkin, J. 1980. *Entropy: A New World View*. New York: Bantam.

Stonier, A.W., and D.C. Hague. 1964. *A Textbook of Economic Theory*. London: Longmans.

Xenos, N. 1989. *Scarcity and Modernity*. New York: Routledge.

Singapore

C. J. W.-L. Wee

Postcolonial Singapore has become an Asian poster child (if a somewhat humourless one) of globalization, having transcended its 1960s Third World status to today being touted as part of the 'East Asian Miracle' in 1993 by the World Bank. This tiny city state of about 3.2 million (in 2002, four million including non-Singaporeans) achieved this status via a state-imposed paradigm of modernization. Its small size allowed the People's Action Party (PAP) government to force a great deal of society and most of Singapore's productive and reproductive articulations under the PAP's control. Japan's neo-mercantilism—if not its nationalism—also offered an example of how late development could be achieved.

The PAP government, in power since 1959, has worked at conditioning the island's complex plural society for the overwhelming purpose of rationalist development. The various Chinese (the largest ethnic group), Malay (or other ethnic groups which subscribed to Islam), Indian (mainly Tamilian) and 'Eurasian' communities made for a complex and sometimes incendiary ethnic mix. There had been communal riots in September 1964, started during the celebration of the Prophet Muhammad's birthday, and also the persistent suspicion until the late 1970s that Chinese-culture champions were either communalists or communists (or possibly communist sympathizers).

From the 1960s onwards, society was urbanized and traditional social organization was replaced with economically rational forms based on function and efficiency. The Anglicized, bourgeois leadership was scornful of 'retrograde' Asian cultural identities and traditions. The city state now represents a dynamic and, in many ways, an iconic authoritarian and multicultural utopianism adapted from the West. In this model, cultural difference and historical and racialist 'irrationalities' were suppressed, homogenized or sanitized for the purity of capitalist modernity's truths, so as to catch up with its erstwhile colonizers.

Singapore's immediate economy has its origins in the mid 1960s. South-East Asia's post-war instability—the communist action known as the Malayan Emergency, North Vietnamese communism, the Indonesian confrontation with Malaysia and Singapore's ejection from Malaysia in 1965—led the PAP state to attracting foreign direct investment (FDI) from the advanced West and Japan, to catalyse development. This positive attitude to multinational capital was in stark contrast with much of the postcolonial world's attitude regarding what then was called 'neocolonialism'. In the midst of the cold war, the city state located itself definitively within First World capitalist modernity.

Development from the 1960s to the 1990s might be described as a 'disciplinary modernization'. By the late 1960s, the government had effectively brought to heel the leftist political opposition which, when still part of the PAP, had ensured the party's early electoral victories. The government also limited the procedural and other mechanisms that would allow for strong participation and expression of the plurality of socio-political and ethnic forces. The result was a partial welfare state (adapted from the British colonial home model) that provided public subsidies in services and housing and invested social relations in their entirety. It became a capitalist society that contradictorily—in ideological terms—but self-consciously practised interventionism within its boundaries but supported liberal free trade outside it.

Capitalism itself is a cultural form (or forms), and for it to be embedded in ways amenable to multinational companies, more proletarians had to be formed out of farmers in the *kampungs* (Malay for villages), a professionalized managerial class created, consumerism encouraged, and so forth. The rationalizing modernity that was enforced was in keeping with the universalistic teleological thinking of the 1960s, and the cultural logic of capital that underlay modernization theory. One key policy initiative was a tremendous emphasis on the teaching of the English language—though taught as if it was culturally 'neutral'—so as to link the new nation with the international economy, given the demise of a possible Malaysian common market. 'Culture' became a residual category to be revamped or instrumentalized as part of the radical reconstruction of subjectivity itself for the economy.

The PAP government's deployment of the 'modern' should be contextualized within the once-commanding dream of what the modern world should undergo: endless renovation. It is now hard to think that anyone could believe that the slate could be cleaned and the new inscribed without any resistance. While many critics consider the PAP state 'conservative'—even 'reactionary'—for its pro-capitalist but illiberal politico-cultural orientation, the way the 'modern' has been adapted might be better described as 'radical'.

South-East Asian instability, Singapore's size and the 'Chinese' identity the region resents resulted in a persistent 'survivalist' theme in the PAP's representation of the city state at home and overseas. Tight discipline under a centralized bureaucracy, the party insisted, had to be maintained in the interests of political and economic survival. It has been argued that by repeatedly focusing anxiety on the island state's vulnerability, the state's originating agency is periodically ratified and its access to the instruments of power for national protection continually consolidated.

How sovereign was the postcolonial city state within the politico-economic ambit of what might be described as the 'globalizing West' (as it may be called) of which Singapore wanted to be a part? The answer seems to be that while agency did matter, choice was circumscribed by the larger context of multinational capitalism—by the at-least-incipient governmentality of the 'West' disseminated into the 'globe'.

When decolonization occurred, there had been at the same time a gradual decentring of production in the advanced economies.

That entailed the spread, across the world, of disciplinary forms of production that comprised Fordist wage regimes, Taylorist methods of the organization of labour and a welfare state that would be modernizing and paternalistic. High wages and the accompanying state assistance were the workers' rewards for accepting disciplinary modernization. Singapore was part of this development. Fortuitous circumstances (the island's geographical location at a crossroads; its early entrance to the field; its small size) helped make it more successful than other aspirants to become a paternalistic-protective, Fordist-Taylorized factory-society.

The 1997–2000 Asian economic crisis triggered by the devaluation of the Thai baht has led to the city state trying to internalize the perceived Outside of multinational capitalism even more thoroughly. While part of the Association of South-East Asian Nations (ASEAN) waffles over the proposed ASEAN Free Trade Area (AFTA), Singapore has since the crisis pursued bilateral trade arrangements with the US, Europe and Japan to 'leave' the region, as it were.

The Asian crisis thus leaves the PAP with the question 'Whither the protective-interventionist state?' that the West once allowed. The emergence of a multicentric world order that had North American and European zones and an Asian-Pacific zone had by the 1980s allowed the aggressive representation of an indigenous/ local relationship between culture and capitalist modernity. However, the 'Asian values' discourse of the 1980s–1990s—one which Singapore's senior minister Lee Kuan Yew, Malaysia's Mahathir Mohamad and Hong Kong's Tung Chee Hwa were among the foremost champions of—that at times belligerently self-represented a 'neo-traditional' Asian (and not Asianized) modernity and cultural identity, as the Other of the West's tainted, individualist modernity, had subsided by the mid 1990s, save for qualified pronouncements by Lee, an advocate of Confucian values. That discourse was an ideological fantasy of difference, one that apparently contested a capitalism that the PAP itself has taken continually to be universal.

Within its own borders, the PAP has hastened (cautious) economic deregulation. There needs to exist less conformist subjectivities and a vibrant sociocultural life. This, the government hopes, will result in a 'creative' and therefore less stifled productive population that will become an autonomous mass with intelligent productivity. Obviously, these hopes are at odds with the favoured disciplinary modalities of rule. The fear remains that intelligent productivity may lead to a less controllable democratic culture; and yet the ongoing reinvention of Singapore, the government itself argues, depends on the very creation of the autonomous forces of productive cooperation supposed to be the sine qua non of the New Economy. They will not or, possibly, cannot recognize that more than ever, their earlier assumptions of polarized oppositions between political economy and culture, the material and the discursive, are obsolete.

By and large, the city state remains a humourless morality lesson as an economic success story, as a paternalistic and pragmatic modernity, and as a managed and generally benign multicultural society—one achieved through measures to peacefully separate the various communities (even if now complicated by the events of 11 September 2001).

Singapore also, as a consequence of the elevation of petit-bourgeois values, became a 'cultural desert', well-known abroad as a land of shopping centres. 'High culture' was not generally encouraged, and idealism itself—even in education—seemed a weakness rather than a virtue. Historical amnesia, the inevitable by-product of the modernization process, is prominent and surpasses, one suspects, the level of dehistoricization in Euro-American societies: the 'Now' of mass consumption dominates. In many ways, this radical experiment in modernizing a small-scale Asian locality is a unique one. As with Japan, where, beneath the assertions of the 'unique Japan' hypothesis of modernization, the West has become a part of their 'Asian-ness', Singapore too, despite its small size, has internalized the West. English is now an Asian language, if still an uncertain 'mother' tongue.

Post-Asian crisis Singapore also desires to become a truly Global City. Before the crisis, in 1992, it announced, with that distinct PAP commitment to social engineering, that Singapore should be a Global City for the Arts, for a Global City cannot be a philistine one. Certainly, productive cultural energy exists: the theatre and visual arts scenes since the 1980s grapple with such concerns as globalization, memory and the significance of cultural and ethnic heritage—dealing with issues suppressed since independence. However, the PAP itself has not transcended its instrumentalist approach to 'culture'.

Time magazine proclaimed on 19 July 1999: 'Singapore Swings' and now 'Lightens Up'; it cautioned though, that the island was 'Changing, [but had] not [completely] changed.' The government, despite this qualification, seemed satisfied with the story. To the question as to whether there is a contradiction between 'the strong political line' and a 'younger and . . . more creative generation', Lee Hsien Loong—a deputy prime minister and the elder son of Lee Kuan Yew—replied: 'Our job is to try and to represent a middle ground . . .'

Singapore is unlikely in the middle term to become a first-rank global city. Not only is it small, too much of its diversity has been homogenized. Nevertheless, it is a place remarkable for directly implementing a modernization process that was less violent than it was historically in the West, for entrenching a certain respect for differences in ethnicity and religion, and for notably increasing equity in economic opportunities. The cultural, social and political costs that were paid, though, are real enough. It seems that the very nature of its 'success' makes the city anathema to Western liberals: Can such a modernity truly be achieved and also sustained without a full political modernity of democratic freedoms? That question remains to be answered. Further, as Singapore increasingly strengthens its 'hub' location for multinational capitalist flows, the following question will become pressing: Can such a delocalized and dehistoricized site really be a society possessing 'national identity' dimensions? Who will 'truly' belong in Singapore?

Further Reading

Chua, Beng-Huat. 1995. *Communitarian Ideology and Democracy in Singapore*. London: Routledge.

Heng, Geraldine, and Janadas Devan. 1992. State fatherhood: The politics of sexuality, nationalism, and race in Singapore. In *Nationalisms and Sexualities*. Edited by Andrew Parker et al. New York: Routledge.

Wee, C.J.W.-L. 2002. National identity, the arts, and the global city. In *Singapore in the New Millennium: Challenges Facing the City-State*. Edited by Derek da Cunha. Singapore: Institute of Southeast Asian Studies.

Spin Doctors

Raminder Kaur

Why pamper life's complexities
when the leather runs smooth on the passenger seat?

—from *This charming man* by The Smiths

Spinning in politics has come a long way from the pristine pursuits of Mahatma Gandhi. In the contemporary world, puritanism has been replaced by performative pizzazz, as plays on words and images are strung together by the doctors of spin. Never before had it reached such gargantuan proportions as it did for the US presidential battle between the Democratic candidate Al Gore and the Republican candidate George Bush. The 'truth' of the matter is more of a concern for apex courts, less so for the carnival of politicians, lawyers, media officers, publicity managers and campaign representatives essentially out to sway opinion and, most importantly, win votes. But rumour circulates fast as to how far even the courts are part of these cycles of spin. It is as if the sociologist Erving Goffman's backspaces have come out of the closet, taken centre stage and produced a pantomime of the senses, enveloping our realities: enthused panto cries of 'behind you' meet the eerie realization that the protagonists are perhaps all hollow one-dimensional people. In this vortex of reality and illusion, intention and performance, meaning implodes into a possible meaninglessness. Jean Baudrillard's rhetorical investigation 'Did the Gulf War take place?' takes on a wider resonance. It is not the event in actuality so much as the simulacrum of appearing to be genuine and sympathetic, of seeming to be efficient and reliable, of successfully looking the part. Image is added to the arsenal of words in another development of Karl von Clausewitz's nineteenth-century adage, where spin becomes war by other means. The hyper-real—whether we like it or not—ravishes our palates but, to the discerning, cannot fail to leave but a nasty taste in the mouth. For while successful spinmongering hides the evidence in a hall of mirrors, we cannot but smell the presence of invidious plotting and scheming.

So who are these merchants of spin? They range from image consultants, advertising giants, public liaison personnel, press officers to media-savvy politicians themselves. It takes a certain kind of politician—the relatively young, fairly good-looking, usually charismatic Bill Clinton and Tony Blair, for instance—to succeed in our times. It also takes a certain kind of spin doctoring to work effectively. Springing from the wand of advertisement, the spin wizards excel in sound bites, headline rhetoric and memorable phrases. 'Slogan' is too harsh a term for such utterances, and 'propaganda' is the phraseology of an old school realpolitik. Language has always been important in encapsulating the mood of the moment in politics: 'Friends, Romans, countrymen, lend me your ears,' or 'We have made a tryst with destiny', for instance; but, as Norman Fairclough argues in *Language, Politics and Government*, nowadays such occasions have become events in themselves, channels for mass consumption representing the 'mediatization' of politics and government. Political leaders become transformed into media personalities and it is the spin doctor's main job to accomplish this with seamless ease, concentrating on their communicative styles, language, bodily performance, dress and even hairstyle. According to Fairclough, a successful leader's communicative style is not simply what makes him or her attractive to voters in a general way—it conveys certain values which can powerfully enhance the political 'message'. Presentation becomes a crucial part of the process of policy formation. Spin doctors aim to cater to a common denominator, but this is catering in slick packaging according to the dictates of business corporatism. What it might lack in content it aims to make up for in terms of repetition. Normalization is attained through mass bombardment rather than the gradual accommodation of what seems like a fitting view.

Like so many other phrases, 'spin doctor' is a modern American import. Crucially, for it to work, it needs to be refashioned to suit local tastes. However, despite its latter-day provenance, its origins are shrouded in mystery, perhaps not uncharacteristically. We might assume it came from cricket parlance, but if that was the case, why the US? A more likely provenance is from the game of pool, where 'spin' is used to direct the balls on the table. An earlier avatar of the spin doctor might have been the king's adviser, the minister, perhaps even the court jester. But, paralleling Michel Foucault's observations to some degree, this para-sovereign entity has itself unravelled into a discursive armature constituted by an industry of experts. There is no one expert, only a number of dispersed representatives playing with and against each other in their obsession to provide a more compelling story.

However, this seems to be a failed enterprise from the outset, for in the heart of the spin doctor's malady lies an inherent irony, an aporia—that for all the might of the position, the agent must not be seen to be at work. As is the heart of most discourses of power, spin must lie invisible. Spin doctors are the cogs that turn the faces. They make things work without wanting to appear as manipulative, pulling strings, or even featuring in the picture—a sleight of hand, where magic might well appear as downright dirty trickery for some and appear as brilliance for others. Often spin doctors work behind a frontsperson. But occasionally, they can be one and the same person, as is argued to be the case with Britain's New Labour politician Peter Mandelson. But one diehard rule of thumb applies: spin doctors must never become a story in themselves.

The fruit of spin is, in the anthropologist Michael Taussig's words, 'a public secret'. Ironically, it is at the point of breakdown, of near-death where the 'real' story creeps out from behind the surface and disrupts the surface, that spin can be momentarily identified. Not quite truth, nor a blatant lie, spin is slippery, ambiguous, equivocal. Spin doctor can become a term of abuse, likened to witch doctors who are exposed as dabbling in the black arts, sinister conspirators lurking in the shadows. But then, just as with 'shrink', the seemingly pejorative term for psychiatrist, it can also be a term of admiration and perhaps even aspiration.

The media's exposure of stories as 'spin' amounts to stone-throwing in glass houses, for were it not for this enterprise, the profession itself would become redundant to a significant extent. There are as many spinners in the media as there are in the corridors of state politics. Citizen Kane is about to move to another house of power, resulting in a tug-of-war where the carpet is being pulled away from underneath the hack by the spin doctor. But the hack will not lie low. His/her duty is to expose news from the corridors of power as 'the real spin' and, true to their fourth-estate self-deceit, the press resists being beaten into obeisance by public relations initiative.

Undoubtedly, the spin industry has been given the fillip by the extraordinary boom in print media, audio, video, Internet and other forms of cable and satellite communication, particularly in the late twentieth century. We only need to turn to one of the Meccas of media—the US—to see the emergence of the need for spin-doctoring. The year: 1960. The event: Kennedy and Nixon battling it out for presidency on a televised debate. Nixon looks staunch and sweats buckets. Nixon loses the elections, a momentary death, on reflection attributed to bad public relations. That led to the birth of an industry of analysts and public liaison officers to manage the image and message sent out by the medium. The press officers for both parties were never, at that time, described as spin doctors. Dealing with the media was an activity essentially supplementary to politics. But by the 1980s, talking to the media became an almost independent initiative. It was around this period that the culture of spin-doctoring began to crystallize. Press officers became as familiar as politicians. Advertisements for communications advisers and experts in media relations became as frequent as those for clerks and administrators.

In Britain, the Conservative Party's campaign for the 1979 general elections entailed the unprecedented commissioning of the advertising giants Saatchi & Saatchi. Their catchphrase 'Labour is not Working' did a great part of the work for them. But ironically it was 1990s Labour that got spin to work for them the most— not the hard core of Old Labour, but the soft shell, yet hard sell, of New Labour. Post-1997 New Labour under the leadership of Tony Blair took it to its acme, employing sixty-nine special advisers and spin doctors as compared with the eight who had worked for the previous Conservative prime minister, John Major. However spin can become an uncontrollable beast. Eventually, in the public eye Blair became synonymous with spin, losing the faith of thousands—an issue that came to a head with New Labour's obsession to control the outcomes of the London Mayoral/Assembly elections in 2000. In this case the beneficiary of spin, Frank Dobson, collapsed under the heat before the old-guard profile of Ken Livingstone. The moral of the story: spin can have a nasty sting in the tail.

Furthermore, it is hazardous to assume that media necessarily precipitates spin doctors. The wider context of legal, historical and social factors needs also to be taken into account. We need only cast an eye at the Indian subcontinent, for instance. Post-1991 has seen the proliferation of satellite and cable media to add to the world's largest film industry, yet spin has only had a marginal effect on political conduct. Politics might have been mediatized through the use of religious icons and signifiers such as Ram and the Janmabhoomi mandir, but it is a different kind of spin, if it can be called that at all, from the Euro-American variety. The problems of Orientalism notwithstanding, South Asian spin here seems to be more entrenched in religio-ethical discourses. It is not a tension played within seemingly rational and transparent politics that is relevant here, but the significance of religion and traditional precedent as an ethicizing trope. Media-savvy youth in India might bemoan the 'uncool' appearance of their political leadership, subscribing as they do to a more Western style of presentation. But these guardians of tradition plough on, shouting their slogans, wearing their stay-pressed dhotis or, for the Congressite, the Nehru suit. How to make the politicians appear more media friendly is a constant preoccupation of media practitioners. But these aardvarks hold on to an older use of the media—one that lies as supplementary to conduct and practice. One where bowing down to the media is frowned upon, where the media is still a dirty word.

More broadly, spin is founded on an age-old practice. It is almost a sanctioned kind of gossip that not only promotes but also aspires to destroy. Did Bill Clinton really penetrate? Did Cherie Blair only accidentally give birth? Whether they did or not, no matter—the spin doctors are there to provide the answers.

So is it money or spin that makes the world go round? Are there any spaces that are not affected by the onslaught of mediatized politics? Anyone that is not affected by the doctors of spin? Mother Teresa? Nelson Mandela? The Pope perhaps? A subjective debate, but one that, nevertheless, alludes to the idea that people considered righteous do not need to resort to spin. They are beyond it, not behind it. Different contours apply in the demarcation of spin. In a world of representative politics, the search for some notion of purity and simplicity might even become more pronounced. Despite the whirling dervishes of spin, we still hanker after some notion of truth and unyielding certitude. Perhaps spin need not be as contagious as it is today. But when it is, it certainly cannot and should not be underestimated in terms of its capacity for perversion, distortion and downright falsehood.

Further Reading

Fairclough, Norman. 2000. *Language, Politics and Government*. London: Routledge.

State

R.L. Kumar

Some years ago, a diamond merchant in Bangalore was rudely woken up in the middle of the night. Opening the door, he was accosted by a group of four policemen and one man in civilian clothes. Waving plastic IDs in his face, the leader of the pack growled that they were from the Central Bureau of Investigation (CBI) and were there to search his house for evidence of suspected tax evasion and hoarding illegally acquired foreign exchange. The merchant took one look at the very officious van with blue and red swirling lights, sirens and all, and gave in without a murmur. He admitted to minor crimes and misdemeanours, and a mutually beneficial deal was agreed upon. A substantial sum of money changed hands and the CBI officers agreed to drop charges. On the way out, the policemen had to pass through the garage where they saw a couple of empty cooking-gas cylinders. One of the policemen stopped to pick up the cylinders, loaded them into the van and the squad sped away.

All would have gone well except for this small act of greed. The poor policeman who tried to 'jump the line' of those citizens waiting long periods for a cooking-gas connection gave the game away. When the merchant realized that the policemen had run away with his cooking-gas cylinders, he suspected something was amiss. Officers of the CBI don't steal cooking-gas cylinders! A quick check with the local precinct revealed that the van was just an ordinary patrol car out to deter petty thieves in the neighbourhood, and the policemen a gang of underpaid and overworked law enforcers masquerading as CBI officers. The merchant raised an alarm and the phoney super-sleuths were apprehended soon after.

I want to read this parable as a tragicomic tale of the twentieth century, about the making of nation-states and its abstract theoretical subject, the citizen, in non-Western societies.

The Nation-State-in-Waiting

Bangalore has the dubious distinction of being the software capital of the 'developing' world. Home to many Indian and some international software giants, it is a city under siege. Living with a municipal government close to bankruptcy, and a state government getting there soon, a measure of the culture of the state can be gauged by the ecstatic and hysterical reception routinely accorded to sundry software scions. It has even been suggested by some sections of the media that if a shadow cabinet comprising the heads of a handful of software firms ran the state, it would be in better health. Democracy, they say, is better served by handing over public assets to private corporations. By democracy, the worthies in the media mean, of course, smooth autobahns and expressways, trains running on time, unlimited electricity, international airports and imported cars.

With the city 'on the move', the crime graph is also rapidly ascending. The city fathers decided that a little of American-style crime prevention was in order. Enter the software firms, multinationals and banks to sponsor a squad of roving patrol cars. As an exercise in public relations, the sponsors' names were brightly and boldly exhibited on the body of the patrol vans. Everybody was happy—until the cooking-gas cylinder robbery.

The gas cylinder is not just a consumerist fantasy; it is a symbol of citizenship itself, something like what an electric connection was in the beginning of the twentieth century. A subject of intensely regulated state policy, it is a heavily capital-intensive technology meeting a fairly basic need, bestowing status in a society where an overwhelming majority depend on biomass fuel.

In the mid twentieth century in India, electricity was sold by providing attractive incentives to consumers. Door-to-door mobilization was implemented to convert the few existing electric connections into 'All Electric' ones, encouraging the use of high-consumption gadgets. Heroic narratives of famous men and women in India are usually annotated with stories of them studying under street lights because they could not afford this new luxury. Now in most of urban India, cooking-gas connections have long waiting periods, which sometimes stretch as long as even a year or more. Energy economists frequently marvel at the 'progress' we are achieving where cooking gas is getting to be cheaper than firewood, never mind that firewood is expensive simply because extensive biomass depletion has made even this most traditional and accessible of energy sources, which millions depend on, unaffordable. On the other hand, the magic marvel of electrification is today a failed enterprise. Most urban consumers can hardly afford it and hence resort to illegal tapping, and rural consumers are lucky if they 'see' this electric 'light' for more than a few hours a day. Today electricity, electrification and electric production are synonymous with graft, mismanagement and political intrigue. It is likely that a similar fate awaits other forms of capital-intensive fuel like petroleum and natural gas. (For example see 'Unnatural alliance', *India Today*, 23 April 2001.)

In this sense electricity is at the heart of the urban industrial vision. Non-Western societies have invariably pushed the technologies of urban industry from above as an exercise in nation-building, usually at the expense of their rural hinterlands. Industries located in rural areas enjoyed and continue to enjoy tremendous subsidies in the form of tax exemptions, cheap power, rail connections, cheap water and a free hand at polluting their environs. This is the stuff that nation-building, in societies like India, is made of: desperate consumerism, rapacious policies of resource exploitation, corporate public relations masquerading as law enforcement and strident demands for protecting democracy from dissenting/protesting subjects who are usually the victims of such nation-building. Today, the early optimism of nation-building and citizen-making look not only impossible to achieve but somehow impossible to live with too.

The Citizen-in-Waiting

As children, we were taught about the war between Alexander the Great and King Porus on the Indus plains as a morality tale. We were told that Alexander so admired the moral integrity and valour of Porus that he gladly 'returned' the kingdom he had just won. I would like to think that these ancient wars were not just about warfare—they were also about ideas of statecraft and governance, which are lost to us. The Greek historian Arrian, who accompanied Alexander on his extensive campaigns, marvels in *Indica* that Indian farmers were so respected that they were left alone even when a great war raged all around them. Where history textbooks dramatically illustrate the vanquishing of one dynasty or state by another, by expanding or contracting boundaries on the map, the thousands of villages around the borders politely moved out of the path of marauding, invading, retreating armies and then moved back to resume their lives. Contrast this with the kind of border warfare we live with today: the 'great wall of Texas' built to keep Mexican immigrants out; the Berlin wall of yesteryears—symbolic of a madness called nuclear deterrence; the borders within South Asia which in some cases run right through homes and farmlands. Boundaries and borders of modern nation-states deprive whole communities of people of their autonomy. These people on the 'borders' are the collateral victims (Pentagonese for civilian casualties) of a war called the maintenance of national security, waged in times of peace.

The justification for doctrines of national security—derived from nineteenth-century European ideas of state, among other things—institutionalized and exported world over the idea of a rational citizen. This ideal type of the 'citizen' located in his ideal habitat, that is, 'civil society', is the single greatest cause of a kind of deculturation that political and economic systems in the non-Western world are caught in. The history of the twentieth century could be seen largely as a history of the erasure of other culturally distinct traditions of political and economic subjecthood. This 'catching up' with the West, as it is often described, has an important fallout in the production of the 'citizen' and his 'habitat' in non-Western societies. This is the making of the so-called 'middle classes' and their urbanization. It is not an accident, for instance, that working-class struggles in India owe their origin less to the industrial working classes (as it more or less did in the West) but more to those classes of 'workers' created directly by state employment. After all, until recently, in most of these societies the nation-state was the biggest employer. Counter-movements to the state, therefore, usually worked with a utopia of building a hard nation-state implicitly defining the scope and limits of dissent of those movements that run counter to the state and capital itself. The near-total internalization of the idea of a hierarchy of civilizations that nineteenth-century European consciousness deployed worldwide consecrated the modern nation-state as the final stage in the realization of human potential, made possible by the hero of this 'march of history', the 'citizen in his habitat'.

But has this endeavour to legitimize/universalize the 'citizen in his habitat' been successful? Partly, yes. Thanks to global mass media, expanding democratic participation in formal politics and the university knowledge system, there is a fantastic expansion and proliferation of the discourse on rights. The idea of rights and duties, as the universal grammar of the 'citizen's' life, has eclipsed other culturally distinct notions of justice, obligation and entitlement. (For a superb elaboration of this, see Clifford Geertz's work on the notions of dharma and adat in 'Fact and law in comparative perspective', in *Local Knowledge*.) The modern nation-state has emerged as the favourite political arrangement of most ethnic, religious or linguistic communities in search of their own distinct destiny. But it is most often an embarrassing version of the original.

Another parable might make this point clearer. A certain major of the Indian Army is an unhappy man. Charged with the task of training recruits, he tries to ensure that his 'boys' are whipped into becoming lean, mean, fighting machines. But come furlough time, our new soldiers go back to their distant villages and come back always looking well fed and a trifle prosperous. Frustrated, the major investigated this consistent attempt to undo his rigorous training. He discovered that whenever the soldiers went back home, their families, aghast at the way the lads had lost weight and looked emaciated, insisted on feeding them well and ensured that the nice little paunch and the well-fed look came back.

Such is the stuff military history and nation-building are made of. In the most crucial instance of producing the perfect citizen or even the perfect crime, human realities defeat the agendas of the state—not unlike the policeman stealing the cooking-gas cylinder.

While the proliferation of various kinds of rights since the 1980s is a reminder that the nation-state has now emerged as the biggest violator of the rights of its subjects, popular movements against the state have repeatedly sought to refine and extend the rights of 'citizens'. Rarely pausing to question the politics of 'nation-building' and 'citizen-making', they too often find themselves co-opted into this process. Every nation-state in the last three decades has equipped itself with gigantic bureaucracies dealing with labour, women and the environment, the three major counter-movements of the twentieth century. I believe that the implicit and explicit rejection of other forms of state and other arts of governance culturally distinct from the modern nation-state explains this co-option. Perhaps a return to the values and reasons of state and statecraft, even suitably updated, of a Porus or Alexander, might provide insights into humane governance and into humane warfare too.

Further Reading

Arrian. 1893. *The Anabasis of Alexander, together with the Indica.* Translated by E.J. Chinnock. London: George Bell and Sons.

Geertz, Clifford. 1983. Fact and law in comparative perspective. In *Local Knowledge: Further Essays in Interpretive Anthropology.* New York: Basic Books.

Stones

Teshome Gabriel

Don't mistake the finger pointing at the moon for the moon
itself.

—Buddhist proverb

It is common knowledge that stones do not lend themselves to
speech; but because stones are mute, it does not mean that they
do not speak; they actually do, only they speak in a language that
we do not recognize, that we do not know. The question then is:
Can we translate their silences into our language? Stones, as tools,
have long been associated with early technologies, from weapons
to buildings to games. They have also been associated with
writing, and with painting, providing early humans with surfaces
to write upon and screens on which to create the first images.
Stones are also the tablets on which spiritual messages were
transmitted. Stones carry within them not just a material
composition but also a virtual one, a sense of what can be
actualized.

There are other links that we can visualize in stones as well,
though more disjunctive or perhaps mysterious ones: with the
elemental forces they signify, as seals for political and religious
matters, and for decorative and aesthetic purposes. The physicality
of stones might be seen as an impulse to rethink the concrete and
to re-imagine the empirical. What is being suggested here is that
stones may serve as bridges to ideas, concepts, knowledge, locations.

They give rise to what we might call a poetics of life. Stones are often seen as the most substantial of forms, yet their metaphorical bearing emphasizes their fluidity. Poets have known throughout time that elemental factors must be heard and addressed. The Egyptian poet Zion El Abdin Fouad, in his poem entitled 'Belted in oppression: A new song for Cairo', writes:

> Are the roads getting white hair?
> Or is it me who has grown old alone . . .
> The river of age is running, escaping into the alleys . . .
> I flood sand and stone.

Stones rubbed together create sparks and fire. The connection of stones to the senses is evident in that stones are often kissed, from the Blarney stone to prelates' rings to pilgrims' rituals. Stones constantly make noises, whether in action with the wind, with water, with animals or with human beings. Considered more broadly, molten lava can be seen as the stone's 'in-between'—a state in which the fluidity inherent in the stone comes to life. In lava, stone is transformed from a symbol of being to a signifier of becoming: it changes the shape of the planet, demarcates powerful changes taking place below the surface. It therefore opens the space for a new hermeneutics of stone reading.

Here, the solidity of space can be reconsidered in terms of movement and mobility. Movement is not just a spatial displacement or a matter of sequence or of a linear history. While stones are generally associated with immobility, those that tend to remain still are in fact the ones that move the most throughout history. By not moving at all, they move in other directions, in other dimensions, in their own curious and often ironic way. Pyramids would seem to be the most immobile of things, yet they have been all over the world; there is no place in the world that does not carry archival memories of pyramids, no people for whom the pyramid does not signify something of deep cultural importance. One can argue that the same forces are at work in the Wailing Wall of Jerusalem and the Great Wall of China, and the Kaaba of Mecca. Stones, like sacred relics, travel and induce us to do likewise; they move us emotionally, spiritually and in many other ways.

Another form of travel would be that of the stone objects, marbles and obelisks that were carted off to Europe and America by colonial powers and installed in their own locations as part of a different cultural heritage. These objects have been narrativized by European poets and statesmen who assumed the mantle of guardianship for these objects. The stone objects that have been sequestered under European control are supposed to convey a grand historical narrative that leads to their present circumstances, but in this context they actually say something quite different. Here, we must listen to the narratives that lie buried within these stones, including narratives of dispossession and displacement and resistance. If we listen carefully to these stones' subdued eloquence, what they convey is no more and no less than their forced isolation, their imprisonment, their silencing. They cannot now move or change or speak as they would have otherwise.

Despite appearances to the contrary, stones are always in constant movement, whether they serve as paving stones or appear in the hands of Palestinian youth or are placed in the mouths of nomads in order to slake their dryness as they travel through the desert. Stones also have a powerful connection with water, providing the banks and shaping the trajectories of rivers and streams around the world, as well as forming beaches in many places.

We look to the impermanence of the world's cities as ruins in the making. We are left with an impending legacy of memories of structures that appear to be sturdy, but which are in the process of becoming ruins. This certainly gives a sense of the transitory nature of many of the civilizational forces at work in the world and tends to propel us into a different mode of thinking about what constitutes the narratives of 'nations' and, for that matter, narratives of 'narrations'.

In demolishing the twin stone statues of the Bamiyan Buddhas in Afghanistan, the Taliban sought to destroy the symbol of peace that the statues celebrated. Yet, the symbols remained and will remain in the imaginations of the world. Ironically, news has surfaced that a much larger statue of a reclining Buddha lies buried beneath the earth very close to the site of the destroyed statues. No doubt, the earth will continue to bear witness to other stories, other secrets, other memories.

Sir Richard Burton, who translated the *Tales of the Arabian Nights*, is buried within a Bedouin tent carved out of stone in London. For Sir Richard, this stone resting place signals an ironic end of his wanderings around Arabia. Multiplying these ironies, the Zimbabwean poet Musaemura Zimunya addresses Sir Richard as well as himself in the following epitaph:

And behold these stones,
The visible end of silence,
And when I lie in my grave
When the epitaph is forgotten
Stone and bone will speak
Reach out to you in no sound
So mysteries will weave in your mind
When I'm gone.

Stones have often been boundary markers, establishing the early parameters of territories and states. Borderlands are themselves landmarks where the cycle of so many beginnings and endings have been played out. Across the world today, borders are figured as sites of opposition, played out in war and death. Yet, borders are never just lines of concrete between opposing forces, however fortified they become. Surely we need to think of borders as areas of dynamic cultural interaction, zones where groups come together and share their differences, rather than continuing to see these spaces as realms of slaughter. We must let the silence of the ancient stones speak, not simply of a narrative of opposition but to and for the malleability and floating nature of contemporary borders.

The things we tend to dismiss or overlook are the things that speak the present. The ones that are most boisterous and loud are the ones that mask history. We want to go beyond the appearance of the polished, of the powerful. This way allows us to see beyond the screen of a supposedly mute and unchanging solidity, beyond the silence of the present. To do so is to see and hear an alternative form of narrative, one that listens more attentively to the silences and sees more carefully the seemingly empty spaces that make up our existence. Survival necessitates a different relationship to the elements and to those elemental things that are based on our daily interactions, on quotidian existence. Stones are not elements that belong to a permanent and unchanging history that leads, like marble steps, to the present. They are elements that are always changing, just as the present itself is always changing.

Thinking-through-stone reminds us of the continual crisis of the present, of its impermanence, and ours. We are constantly on the edge of living—on the borderline of a present—that we never seem able to cross. We are under the ominous threat of survival. The discovery of carved-out rocks, labyrinthine tunnels, tombs and caves is regarded as markers of the unknown 'other', and ancient civilizations are almost always seen as chiselled in stone. Thus, we are enmeshed, as if in stone, in the many aspects that make up the history of the present. The present is generally seen as a projection of the future, or as an outcome of the past. But it is not the case that when the present is finished, it is no longer there. If we understand the present as constantly existing, then the future is in the present, and the past also is in the present. The stone, as the element that is always present in all forms, and always changing, represents this persistence of the present, much more than it does the supposed permanence of past.

Who then speaks for the present? It is the stone itself, which recalls who participated in its carving, who carried it to a certain place, who kissed it, cooked with it and killed with it. These Sisyphean labourers, the humblest of us all, carve the stones, inscribe the letters that shape and form our lives and deaths. These etceteras of histories, who build bridges and roads, engrave portraits and statues, erect the stones that mark graves, listen and react to the idioms of the language of stone. Those who labour without authorship attached to their names have left us a virtual dictionary that retains indelible marks and fingerprints of the memories of stone. Stones, as repositories of eloquent mysteries, affirm our various modes of being and the process of our becoming part of the wisdom of our forbears.

As Mahmud Darwish, the Palestinian poet, meditates:

> We will hear the voices of our ancestors in the winds
> We will listen to their pulses in the blossoms of the trees
> This holy earth is our grandmother, stone by stone.

Just as our ancestors, in their stone spaces, regarded the sacred history of our universe, stones call on us to participate in a mysterious sense of wonder at the interwoven nature of existence and becoming. Stones, then, are far more than materials that we use to construct our bridges and temples and mausoleums.

Stones are the epitome of that which crosses over, even though they seem to remain ever the same. Stones mark the passages between phenomena, between life and death, material and spiritual. Consider the image of a child who picks up a pebble and tosses it into a pond and delights at the motion of the stone and the disruption it causes on the placid surface of the water. This primary sense of play and its attendant notions of awe and joy, in the magic of being, are what we are attempting to evoke here. There exist spiritual forces embedded in our cultural inheritances that require us to recast the unthought of stone into the ripples of meaning.

In short, 'stones' are 'ideas'—in the crude paving of our thoughts. Stones are the unwritten upon which spark the infinite and rewritten soliloquies of meaning. They are like chants that carry prayerful inscriptions and texts that are continually at play.

Sugar

Ashis Nandy

In the early 1990s, Kalpnath Rai, then minister of food in India, banned the production of gur (molasses, treacle or jaggery) in India, perhaps the first country in the world to do so. All sugar cane would be diverted to the production of sugar, he declared, to meet the shortage and the rising price of sugar in the country. In the long run that edict turned out to be temporary, but this was probably the first time someone had dared to take on gur, to officially mark the final decline of an important, if not dominant, dietary tradition that was at least two millennia old in India. It was a tradition that was already dead or moribund in most other countries of the world.

The attack on gur was not new and Rai and the Indian state, not being particularly imaginative, only followed conventional wisdom. The process they unleashed has been now endorsed by the quickening pace of globalization of the world economy. Only the multinational corporations and the industrialization of agriculture have begun to do, less crudely but more efficiently, what India's food minister in effect wanted. We can be pretty sure that gur will be effectively finished as a normal part of everyday diet in much of Asia and Africa. Gur will not be banned; it will be, in fact, celebrated as a healthier product and will be available in stylish restaurants and cafes as an alternative to sugar for the knowledgeable and the cultivated. It too will be produced by the large sugar factories as a costlier gourmet additive to food. Its fate in this respect will be the same as that of the kimono.

In the meanwhile, sugar will displace gur in the everyday life of ordinary people and gur to them will become an esoterica. Sugar is a cash crop that fetches higher price, stores better and is an industrial product. It can be also used for producing high-priced alcohol and the global food industry loves to put it in as many industrial food products as it can think of—from ketchups and potato chips to breads and jams. According to laboratory tests done by the Consumer's Association of Penang, the results of which have gone unchallenged in any court of law, each bottle of Coca-Cola contains about six and a half teaspoons of sugar and each bottle of Pepsi-Cola the equivalent of a little less than six spoons of sugar. Naturally, sugar-making is seen as a form of development and international bodies like the World Bank have always been partial towards it, often investing millions of dollars in the growth of sugar industry.

The production of gur, on the other hand, is a lowbrow, non-polluting cottage industry and family skill. It is seen as a surviving custom that has little to contribute to a country's growth rate. One indicator of this way of thinking is that, for the last so many years, when farmers get loans for producing sugar cane in India, they cannot use their crop to produce gur—they have to produce sugar.

White, crystalline, refined sugar is a relatively new entrant in the world scene. The older civilizations did not use it, though some of them almost certainly knew how to make it. It became a part of the West's staple diet only in the seventeenth and eighteenth centuries. Its production got a boost after the African slave trade began and brought cheap labour to the cultivation of sugar cane in the Americas, particularly North America. Even after slavery was abolished in the British colonies in the Americas, in some places in the Caribbean islands farmers cultivating other crops were often forced at gunpoint to cultivate sugar cane.

With the expanding production of sugar and a dramatic fall in its price, the popularity of sugar in Europe increased, not merely among the European elite but also among the hoi polloi. Something that was sweet, pure and white could not but be good for health, the argument presumably went. By 1815, per capita sugar consumption in Britain, at the time the most industrialized country in the world, had risen to 33 kilograms a year. However, it was still a far cry from the present average of over 55 kilograms per person in the highly developed countries.

Sugar consolidated its position as the main sweetener and drove out jaggery from the diets of most of the Asian and African societies only in the twentieth century. In parts of India jaggery was used in tea until quite recently. Even in the so-called advanced societies of the West, the consumption of sugar had reached pathological levels only in the last century. For instance, despite the growing popularity of various sugar substitutes and growing health consciousness, each day the average American still consumes a gargantuan amount of sugar, to equal which he would have had to daily eat roughly 30 kilograms of beetroot in the days before the popularization of refined sugar.

The human body is not designed to bear such a massive assault. According to some accounts, such rates of consumption leads to a quick 'high' in blood sugar level, followed by the pancreas trying to feverishly break it down by secreting insulin and thus creating an artificial 'low'. According to Dag Poleszynski, who worked on the subject for years, low blood sugar level produces a severe state of stress, giving rise to 'emotional instability in the form of depression, anxiety, irritability' and, predictably, a craving for more sugar. He believes that to some extent, the high rates of mental illness and the spread of various forms of drug addiction in the West could be traced to the mindless consumption of sugar. Others hold the body's inability to cope with huge fluctuations in blood sugar responsible for fatigue, nervousness, inability to handle alcohol, lack of concentration and allergies.

In much of West Europe and North America the mortality patterns are now quite similar. A little more than half the casualties are due to cardiovascular diseases and a little more than one-third die of various forms of cancer. (The pattern should not be very different for South and South-East Asia's Westernized elite, for available data suggest that the incidence of heart diseases is much higher among Indian immigrants than among natives in the First World.) Of these, the cardiovascular ailments have been linked directly to overconsumption of sugar; some forms of cancer have been linked to sugar more indirectly, through the changes in dietary habits that have accompanied the popularization of sugar. Apart from the well-known side effects of sugar such as obesity and diabetes, its overuse has also been linked to a variety of social pathologies, including non-specific violence. A high intake of sugar is not merely a marker of modernization—it seems that it also paves the way to self-destruction.

In the meanwhile, as with the other pathologies of modernity, the problems created by sugar have encouraged the corporate world to generate, and then cater to, a new set of needs. The markets are now flooded with all kinds of remedies designed to cope with the ill effects of sugar. They range from a variety of sugar substitutes to a large number of drugs that are advertised as certain protection against overindulgence in sugar. For example, the same companies that produce sugar, which damages teeth, often have a stake in companies that produce fluoride toothpastes designed to redress the situation. The same companies that specialize in producing customized pesticides for sugar cane also produce low-calorie sugar substitutes. And so on. The medical establishment also is all too willing to discuss the hazards of eating sugar and the problems created by obesity. But nobody, or almost nobody, dares to suggest that the production of sugar need not be encouraged.

The Atlantic slave trade was one of the most tragic and violent chapters in human history; it is a story of unbelievable human cruelty towards fellow-humans. By some estimates, about one-third of all captured slaves perished in transit during the passage from Africa to the Americas. Shackled below deck, in dark, airless holds, they died like flies from epidemics and unbelievable brutalization, and no dignity was granted to them even in death. Their bodies were disposed of the way rotten food was often jettisoned during long sea voyages. The spread of slavery owed much to the demand for cheap labour in the sugar plantations in the new world, though tobacco and cotton farming too played their roles.

The story of tobacco in human history, chronicled often enough, seems about to end; that of sugar shows no sign of doing so. Moreover, the second story has, for some inexplicable reason, attracted few chroniclers. Yet, as James Ridgeway sums it up: 'No agricultural crop has brought such misery to the world as sugar. Sugar has ruined land from one end of the earth to the other.'

The cultivation, production and popularization of sugar and tobacco—which owed so much to the slave trade—is now repaying that blood debt with interest. My guess is that, if one takes into account both direct and indirect victimization, including the abridgement of life and the degradation of its quality, the number of people killed by sugar and tobacco during the last 200 years may well turn out to be larger than the number of Africans killed on the way to America's sugar plantations.

There is more than poetic justice in this. It is an articulation of the harsh fact that oppression and domination, in the long run, may prove as disastrous to the oppressors as to the victims. In the short run, however, this may not be much of a consolation to the defeated cultures. All they can do is to marvel at the fact that what the white plantation owners and promoters of sugar did at gunpoint about two centuries ago, a new generation of policy elite in Asia, Africa and South America, encouraged by the World Bank and the development fraternity, are trying to do by pushing files.

Further Reading

Ridgeway, James. 1994. *The Haiti Files: Decoding the Crisis.* Washington, DC: Essential Books.

Narratives of Colonialism, Sugar, Java and the Dutch. In Horizons in Post-Colonial Studies Series. Pal Ahluwalia and Bill Ashcroft (Editors).

Third Ways

Trent Schroyer

The invention of 'third ways' in the twentieth century accommodates the dark side of capitalism by simulation of the social worlds that it destroys. To give this term a substantive meaning, we have to retrieve alternatives that existed before the conflict of economic liberalism (capitalism) and revolutionary liberalism (Marxist socialism) in Western history and throughout the world.

Contemporary 'Third Ways'

The efforts to create New Democrats in the US and Tony Blair's New Labour in the UK were the most aggressive 'third way' projects in the last decade of the twentieth century. The US Democratic Leadership Council in 1996 claimed it begins with reforms concerning the family, crime, the decay of communities and humanitarian international interventionism, in ways that bring 'issues of the left' before the ordinary citizen. It postulates 'a politics without adversaries' that accepts the world for what it is!

New is the mixture of pushing economic dynamism with concerns for social solidarity and culture, while challenging entrepreneurial initiative to focus on the social. Less prominent European third ways are dissents from the shareholder model of capitalism promoted by the US and the UK. These projects deviate from the organizational infrastructures for a stakeholder model of capitalism to include affected people and communities.

Critics of 'third ways' have not viewed them as new ideas but as reactive accommodations of weakened welfare states to regain political credibility—in short, as hollow visions defining themselves negatively against left and right and having little real substance. Indeed, the track record shows that inequalities in wages and wealth have continued to widen, while health reform, arms control and the environment have continued to decline.

Enthusiasts rebut that the 'third way' is a political culture that combines market liberalism with a new progressivism that forms a political consensus at the centre. Using the metaphor of the three-legged stool, the third way is imaged as a stable, just and prosperous society where neither the state, the market nor the civil society is too dominant; each is able to restrain the others' power. Anthony Giddens argues in *The Third Way and Its Critics* that it is the best way of dealing with the 'twin revolutions of a globalizing world and a knowledge economy'. Hence Bill Clinton's new world order strategy, when he was President, was to create economic growth, which brings in greater need for information, which in turn activates the civic culture essential to jump-start democracy. Of course, this subordinates reform to the primacy of economic growth and makes any regeneration of democratic government dependent upon serving the corporate interests first.

Rediscovery of Trust and Civility Is 'Social Capital'

Whereas Marxists never found out 'how working-class consciousness is possible', third-way theorists claim to have rediscovered the secret of solidarity. Giddens thus advises us to fuse 'social capital' that creates mutually respectful, trusting relationships among citizens and workforces and facilitates optimal sharing of relevant information. Social capital is the key to the promotion of institutional confidence, and has a synergistic relation with human capital formation (that is, producing specialized knowledge workers) and productivity in increasingly knowledge-based and services-oriented economies. For third-way modernizers, like Clinton and Blair, social capital is the new mechanism for managing social reintegration and inclusion of excluded groups. Economic, social and civil entrepreneurs will compete and cooperate to bring services to excluded groups such as minorities, the poor, the elderly and the disadvantaged.

But can these mechanisms be extended to re-include those who have been marginalized by corporate globalization, such as the poor in sub-Saharan Africa or the indigenous people everywhere? Or are these merely social simulations that cannot replace irreversibly destroyed sociality in the fragmenting and deterritorializing commodifications of economic globalization?

Retrieving Other Paths Not Taken in Modern Western History

Karl Polanyi has remarked that after the 'great transformation' to modern liberal capitalism, people suffered cultural amnesia about the world that preceded it. The first insight about what to do with the people displaced by commercializing enclosures emerged amid Quakers, whose principle that the 'greatest resource is friendship' still remains central to equity-secured local credit systems today, such as the Grameen Bank in Bangladesh. John Bellars in 1696 proposed 'Colleges of Industry' where people could economically transact exchanges among themselves. The same principle was central to later schemes that resisted economic liberalism, from Robert Owen's Villages of Union, to Fouriers's Phalansteres, Proudhon's Banks of Exchange, Lois Blanc's Ateliers Nationaux and Lassalle's National Wertstatten.

In 1819 Robert Owen republished John Bellars's 120-year-old plan for setting up Colleges of Industry and used it to promote his own movement that was outvoted in the watershed 1830 elections, where the economic liberals were victorious and created the first 'free market' system. Owen claimed that he had rediscovered the 'nucleus of society' in his village communities. He recognized the lie of economic society—namely, that what appear to be economic solutions to poverty are not, because the problems and solutions are basically social. Bellars and Owen understood that purely economic interventions and ideologies could not satisfy the social nature of humans. As Karl Polanyi has written in *The Great Transformation*, 'The new market institutional system was the destruction of the traditional character of settled people . . . and their transmutation into a new type of people, migratory, nomadic, lacking in self-respect and discipline—crude, callous beings of whom both the labourer and the capitalist were an example.'

In this light, contemporary third ways are desperate attempts to square the circle of economic society by trying again to recreate the social in ways that are compatible with the primacy of the economic. Unfortunately, this is a difficult task where 'society' as viewed as the aggregate of individuals and the political as a management system for individual economic clients. Third ways end up being 'internal colonizations' of social communities in the name of building an entrepreneurial culture. Remembering alternative paths being worked out by those who create other frames for market society is more fruitful.

Third Ways from the Other West

A third way is implicit in what later economic historians called 'proto-industrial districts' where market livelihoods remained tied into craft traditions and their communities and municipalities. Resisting dislocations, they worked out 'embedded' cooperative solutions to changing economic circumstances, and created municipal social economies. Hence Proudhon, Terence Powderly and Herman Schulze-Delitzsch, all promoted systems of cooperatives supported by cooperative banks that sought to stabilize communities and municipalities in the face of interventions that promoted national market formations.

The 'progressive' views of Karl Marx, and the classical economists, rejected these craft models because they were tied to the particularities of trade fraternities and mutual-aid societies in municipal centres. In contrast, the craft production theorists (social economists) were convinced that competition and productive associations were complementary, and that flexible machinery could extend human skills. Michael Pirore and Charles Sable have argued in *The Second Industrial Divide* (1984) that the craft model of 'flexible specialization' must now be adopted since its imitations in Japan and Germany cannot be ignored. Flexible manufacturing, or economies of scope, is today seen as essential for niche marketing and made ever more possible by innovations of informational and small-scale technologies.

Analogously, the response of many city regions to the expansion of the market system was, and remains today, a shield to globalization and an affirmation of their own cultural practices and socio-economic arrangements. Thus the third-way path not taken was the creation of federated cooperative movements of producers, consumers and credit that enabled communities and municipalities to resist wider market dislocations.

A contemporary form of this alternative socio-economic integration has been documented by Robert Putnam who has shown that in northern Italy there are many networks of small, locally owed firms: local ownership is the key. In these contexts the political arrangements can be reversed to create a 'cosmopolitan localism', that is, where citizens are aware that communities can invest, contract, zone, tax, lobby and thus learn how bottom-up politics can influence the national polity.

The Way before We Needed a 'Third Way'

In 1949 the philosopher Martin Buber examined these movements in *Paths in Utopia* in order to develop principles for 'the organic reconstruction of society'. Buber's reflections point to the complex diversity in the social worlds that preceded capitalism, and suggest that their pluralistic vitality enabled them to resist the totalitarian tendencies inherent in the pre-revolutionary centralist state. This reflection is also valid wherever forced neo-liberal 'nation-building' destroys organic socio-political configurations that then evolve into dependencies and totalitarian regimes. In Western history these organic potentials for resistance by free associations were broken first by the French Revolution and then by the centralizing logic of the liberal state that dealt only with 'individuals' and succeeded in atomizing society. In the ideology of new-liberalism this is called creating an 'entrepreneurial culture'!

Buber's insights suggest that other organic 'third ways' may be possible wherever pluralistic cultures and local knowledge can be sustained. Unique blends of participatory, conventional, managerial governance arrangements may be appropriate for particular societies, and can only emerge through their own experience—no one 'democratic' blueprint fits all. Postmodern arguments that insist we should not think of liberty or freedom as a linear process from oppression are relevant here: the realities of power are more complex and require different approaches.

The Principle of Subsistence: A Planetary Third Way?

Ivan Illich has called the era of modernization 'a 500-year war against subsistence'. The evolution of the capital forces the creation of physical and social scarcity in ways that are not measured by the indicators of 'progress'. Illich's reflections imply that Westernizing modernization has ironically created an inversion of progress in that the common man has been forced into greater suffering and dependency in the name of eliminating the same.

Illich, like Polanyi, sees fear of scarcity as ironically forcing scarcity by destroying the physical and cultural environment of those who are to be emancipated by modernization. Documentation of the systematic destruction of the organic customary organizations of kinship, neighbourhood, profession and creed defines a different research programme—the history of scarcity instead of stages or 'logics' of development. In this frame, enclosures, including contemporary economic globalization, bring intentional destruction and deliberate disconnection from organic social arrangements. Effectively they are instrumental means of weakening the self-limiting cultural restraints that were, and are still today, essential for households and communities to secure both natural commons and agreed-upon social limits to growth.

Rather than be pushed into the game of catch-up development, communities and regions can become organized around 'sufficiency', or 'enoughness', and work out more self-reliant economies. In a world of overconsumption that has gone beyond the earth's capacity to provide ever-new materials, or absorb the wastes of industrial systems, innovative social logics of minimizing consumption are essential. Today this transition is made possible by innovative, flexible, specialized technologies and a growing convergence on the need for devolution to cosmopolitan localism. Here renewals of subsistence logics from many diverse cultures are alternative resources as well as contemporary sustainability experiments. A strategy of subsistence is implied in a wide range of efforts—from Gandhi's 'swaraj' (self-rule), to various socio-political grass-roots movements for decentralization and devolution, such as the contemporary Eco-village movement as shown by Veronika Bennholdt-Thomsen and Maria Mies in their book *The Subsistence Perspective* (1999).

Third-way alternatives to the progressive utopias of socialism and capitalism *have* gone beyond the modernizing mentality to recognize the wisdom of the organizing principle of the subsistence mentality.

Further Reading

Bennholdt-Thomsen, Veronika, and Maria Mies. 1999. *The Subsistence Perspective: Beyond the Globalised Economy*. London: Zed Books.

Giddens, Anthony. 2000. *The Third Way and Its Critics*. London: Polity Press.

Pirore, Michael, and Charles Sable. 1984. *The Second Industrial Divide*. New York: Basic Books.

Polanyi, Karl. 1944. *The Great Transformation: The Political and Economic Origins of Our Time*. Boston: Beacon.

Tourism

Paul Gonsalves

The stars mean different things to different people. For travellers
they are guides.

—from *The Little Prince* by
Antoine de Saint-Exupéry

Tourism: The Industry of the Future?

Mass tourism, the modern world's favoured form of leisure, is
among the world's biggest industries. It is one of few economic
enterprises that dictate that consumption take place on-site, bringing
consumers and producers face to face in hitherto unprecedented
ways, and alongside transformed conventional notions of the
marketplace.

Competing with trade in armaments and oil as the world's
largest economic activity, tourism is growing at an annual rate
exceeding 5 per cent, with the total number of tourists annually
approaching 600 million, accounting for an annual expenditure of
about US $500,000 million and employing close to 8 per cent of
the world's workforce. These trends are predicted to continue at
least until the year 2010, when the number of tourists is expected
to approach one billion a year.

Mass tourism today is a diverse industry with many niche
markets, having come a long way from its early modern history in

the 'social tourism' days of the nineteenth century. Practically everything and anything that can be sold to tourists is up for sale, as long as it brings in the moolah. Ecotourism, adventure tourism, sex tourism, gay/lesbian tourism, Aboriginal tourism, Tibetan Buddhism tourism, Save Willy tourism—you want it, you can have it. There is even a Bureau of Atomic Tourism dedicated to promoting tourism to former explosion and weapons sites. Outer space too has begun to be viewed as a legitimate zone for future tourists.

Not surprisingly, the industry has generated enormous and wide-ranging social interest. Activists criticize it for its 'impacts' on nature, culture, economy and society. Economists calculate its contribution to national income. Academics seek to unravel questions such as 'What is tourism?' and 'Who is a tourist?' Travel writing is big business, and even the medical profession has sprouted books such as *The Traveller's Good Health Guide*. Moreover, you can buy yourself a holiday today on the Internet. Movies like *Total Recall* are a precursor to VR, or virtual reality, tourism that could well be the next generation version of mass tourism.

Anthropologically, tourism is an archetype of centre-periphery relationships, and the tourist has been likened to the anthropologist in his quest for the other. He/she hopes that through encountering the other, he/she will eventually come to know him/her self. Yet another issue that baffles anthropologists is that of representation: numerous academic conferences, paid for by industry, endlessly ponder over whether the tourist can really know the other (or the self for that matter), and the meaning of such knowledge and what it represents. Anthropologists are the likely ultimate tourists!

For others, tourism is a form of religion, with attendant rites de passage, whereby the tourist enters an altered, unknown, state (or place), crossing a liminal threshold and returning to 'normality' at the end of the experience. During this period, social norms and mores are abandoned, allowing for 'abnormal' behaviour. Tourist brochures are full of paradisiacal imagery where 'you can let your hair down'. The behaviour of British beer louts in Ibiza and young Australians in Kuta, Bali, speaks for itself.

Third-World Tourism: Questionable Benefits

International tourism is growing most rapidly in the Third World, especially in the Asia-Pacific region. This rapid growth can have serious consequences for the area, and for tourism itself. Mass tourism has negatively impacted countries and regions which have developed tourism as a major economic sector, such as Thailand, Sri Lanka, the Philippines, Goa, Kashmir, Kenya, Hawaii, Jamaica, Costa Rica, and so on. Third World countries, especially those emerging from recent conflicts or newly independent, often see tourism as the only way to earn foreign exchange. This imperative overlooks social and ecological considerations.

The debate on tourism in the Third World is now nearly thirty years in the making, closely linked in its origins to the 'development debate' of the 1960s. Frantz Fanon, in his classic *The Wretched of the Earth*, characterized tourism as an 'European hedonocracy', where 'the national middle class will . . . take on the role of manager for Western enterprise, and . . . will in practice set up its country as the brothel of Europe'.

More recently, organizations such as the Ecumenical Coalition on Third World Tourism and Equations (Equitable Tourism Options) have played key roles in advancing these issues worldwide. The tourism industry and national governments have begun to take notice, and tourism is now part of the official agenda of several trade and official bodies across the globe.

In economic terms, tourism is an export industry, earning foreign exchange in order to pay for imports. However, tourism itself is heavily import-dependent, as tourists will often only pay for the familiar and known. The 'leakages' reduce gross foreign exchange earnings in some countries by as much as 75 per cent.

Tourism-driven urbanization means that once-pristine environments are turned into concrete jungles, and sewage and waste from massive hotel and resort complexes devastate marine and land ecology. Plastic, air and noise pollution are endemic. Cultural traditions are packaged for sale, their meanings often changed beyond recognition. While tourism has encouraged the rebirth of forgotten arts and crafts, these are often mass-produced by factory workers who have no inherent emotional connection with them.

No Pain, No Gain

Tourism is rooted in global inequality, with terms of trade defined by a powerful North over a much weaker Third World. Mass tourism has thus resulted in a synthesis of local elites with multilateral agencies and multinational companies.

The centres of power have become distanced from the arenas of action, which lie—literally and figuratively—on the periphery. Human rights are secondary to profit objectives: local residents have been displaced from their ancestral lands in order to make way for golf courses and luxury resorts. Rather than serve the interest of citizens, some governments have allowed child prostitution and forced labour to feed the tourism industry and its clients, colluding with the Mafia.

Economic arguments against tourism focus on issues such as it being a seasonal industry, volatile and sensitive to risk factors; it is also argued that tourism develops as a monoculture, as well as providing employment that is both servile and low paid. Tourism is seen as a new form of colonialism, replicating the white-master—black-servant regime.

The Other-izing inherent in tourism has meant that people and nature can be objectified, turned into commodities, their worth defined by profit. Human rights abuses, especially those of women, children, indigenous minorities and other marginalized groups, are widespread in tourism. Sex tourism has been instrumental in the spread of HIV/AIDS in many countries.

Not surprisingly, tourism and conflict are intertwined. There have been attacks on tourists and tourist facilities as far apart as Goa, Egypt, Yemen, Kenya, Hawaii, Fiji and the Philippines. Such conflict derives primarily from the comparative wealth of the tourists and the tourist industry, and is an expression of deprivation of the excluded masses.

Power and Place

The fundamental conflict in tourism is access to and control over resources—natural, economic and sociocultural. Hotels, golf courses and swimming pools deprive whole villages of access to water. Conflicts over land are primary in many parts of the world and closely related to the larger question of peoples' participation in development. Tourism has led to displacement of people from traditional lands, denial of means to livelihood and alienation from sacred sites.

On a family holiday to the Nilgiris (in southern India), we were on an early morning bus to Ooty, the main town. There was a snaking traffic jam on the hillside road, and I leaned out to see what the problem was. Coming towards us was a man with an oxcart, moving, well, at ox-pace. His cart was empty, and he was having difficulty dealing with his beast on the crowded, narrow path. Soon a traffic policeman turned up, and began belabouring the cart driver with his baton. He pushed the man and his cart off the road, on to the narrow ledge separating them from a 150-metre drop downhill.

Pondering over this scene later, I realized that this man was probably returning home after delivering produce to the markets and hotels of Ooty—produce that would eventually find its way to the tables of tourists. His labour supplied our leisure. And yet, in the abjectly twisted logic of tourism, the person at the bottom of the tourist chain is not just the most poorly paid but ends up paying for his presence.

Simply a Question of Modernity?

Sociocultural disruption and dysfunction continue to take place in many parts of the world which are experiencing the painful transition to modernization. The tourism industry has already acknowledged the need to bear the costs of environmental destruction. But the underlying issue is whether tourism is an appropriate form of development, or indeed the only path to development as suggested by its proponents such as the World

Tourism Organisation and the World Travel and Tourism Council. Statements like 'tourism is essential for peace and international understanding' conceal the reality that tourism is fundamentally a short-term industry, that it uses (or abuses) resources intensively and has a low-skills and growth orientation in terms of human resource development. Moreover, since it competes for resources with local communities, should not local needs be prioritized over that of tourists?

Tourism is a form of integration into the global market economy, linked to the free movement of capital. The inclusion of tourism in the new General Agreement on Trade in Services has serious implications for the countries of the Third World, which are no longer allowed to build up indigenous capacities and strengths.

Ecologically there has been much discussion on the issue of emissions and the ozone layer. This is a Northern obsession, making ground-level issues of ecological survival in the Third World appear insignificant. Many communities in the Third World see nature as part of a living symbiosis, interdependent with human beings, where the destruction of one also destroys the other. In the North, such views are pagan, belonging to an ancient forgotten past, with no relevance to today's debates.

A materialistic *Weltanschauung* that sees nature as a resource to be controlled and managed using ruthless interventionist mechanisms allows the destruction of natural habitats. It is not surprising, then, that as an extension of this world view, technology is seen as the only way to deal with the problems arising from the tourism industry's excessive abuse of nature.

Similar misplaced notions shaped landscapes in Asia and Africa during the colonial era. In *Imagined Communities*, Benedict Anderson speaks of nature and human beings categorized for the purpose of efficient and orderly management. Issues of tourism—conflicts over cattle-grazing by the Masai in the national parks in Tanzania and Kenya, for example—are rooted in this colonial history. Modern-day civil servants and managers have absorbed the values and world views of past rulers.

Is There a Future for Tourism?

Tourism is drawn into the discourses of nationalism and so-called fundamentalism creeping across the globe today. As geographical boundaries are redefined, so too are questions of identity, culture and related rights, issues central to the tourism debate. Not surprisingly, tourism is emerging as a tool for expressing those identities and rights, with the express intent of advancing new interpretations of peoples and their origins while other interpretations are obscured. The very transience of the tourist's visit ensures a flattened, relatively two-dimensional image of the countries or communities visited.

The terrorist attacks on the World Trade Center and the Pentagon on 11 September 2001 have not only redefined suicide bombing, but air travel itself, the engine—or vehicle, more accurately—on which modern tourism is dependent. The future of tourism is thus an open question. When passenger planes are turned into weapons of destruction, how shall we travel long-haul?

Moreover, with identities being defined in ever narrower terms, are not all tourists potential terrorists?

Will Afghanistan be the favoured tourism destination of future? Will the Bamiyan Buddhas be rebuilt?

Further Reading

Anderson, Benedict. 1991. *Imagined Communities*. London: Verso.

Utopia

Peter Wollen

Utopia has always been an imaginary place—a city, a land or an environment which offers the promise of a different life in a different future. It has both a political dimension (the organization of an ideal society) and an artistic dimension (an act of imagination and creative thought). These two aspects of the utopian vision—political and artistic—can be superimposed in many ways, but there is always a residual tension between them. Politics is the realm of realism (planning for a possible future) but utopianism is characterized as fantasy (hopes and dreams of an imaginary future). This tension was already expressed in Frederick Engels's *Socialism: Utopian and Scientific*, published in 1883. Engels respected the great nineteenth-century utopian thinkers and activists—Claude Saint-Simon, Robert Owen, Charles Fourier—but also regarded them as unrealistic, because of their failure to accept that socialism could be reached only through class struggle and the seizure of state power.

Yet today's decline in utopian thinking has resulted principally from the disenchantment that followed the ignominious collapse of the Soviet Union. In communist countries, the proletariat was forced to work long Stakhanovite hours and spent little time on enjoyable leisure activities. The Soviet Union ultimately descended into dystopian horror and, by doing so, it contributed greatly to discrediting the whole concept of utopianism. Indeed, the word 'utopian' has come to mean 'doomed to failure'. Yet, in reality, the

Soviet leadership had never been utopian. They stuck faithfully to Engels's critique of utopian thought. In the 1970s Molotov, Stalin's closest comrade, angrily dismissed an interviewer's question with the observation, 'This is worse than Khrushchevism, this is utopianism.' The love-hate relationship between Marxism and utopianism ended by discrediting both. At its worst it produced the dystopias of the Gulag, the Khmer Rouge or North Korea.

In this context, we need to look again at the distant origins of utopianism, beginning with Thomas More and going on to encompass the great nineteenth-century utopians, who never were orthodox Marxists. In the twentieth century, utopianism was pursued by deviant Marxists (André Breton and Ernst Bloch, for example) and radical idealists such as Mahatma Gandhi and C.L.R. James. Since the 1960s, as the political climate changed, women have become a major source of utopian writing—Shulamith Firestone, Ursula LeGuin, Joanna Russ, Margaret Atwood—and utopian thought has flourished mainly within the cultures of feminism, ecology and the arts. The foundations of utopian thinking have changed enormously since Thomas More published his very first book on this theme, *Utopia*, in Latin. It is clear that utopias reflect the historical and cultural contexts in which they are written, however fanciful they may be. More, after all, wrote his book in the context of Tudor England and his Utopia was clearly influenced by the traveller's-tale writings of the age of exploration. It also owed a great deal to long-established monastic traditions.

More's *Utopia* contains a detailed description of the island of Utopia itself, as recounted by Raphael Hythloday, a Portuguese sailor who visited it after traveling to the Americas on one of Amerigo Vespucci's transatlantic voyages. It centres principally on the capital city of Amaurote, the largest of the island's cities, which Hythloday describes as looking very much like London, except that it is full of communal gardens, cultivated in the space behind the rows of houses. They contain grapevines and 'all manner of fruit, herbs and flowers', so pleasant, abundant and finely kept that they surpass any others the protagonist has seen on any of his previous travels. The houses, each three storeys high, fireproof and damp-proof, with glass windows, are all public property. Anyone could go in and out of them whenever they choose, 'for there is nothing within the houses that is private or any man's own'.

Utopian clothes are all of one design, and each Utopian works a six-hour day at various crafts or tasks, such as weaving or road-mending, with a three-hour shift before lunch and another three hours after lunch, followed by a two-hour siesta. For the rest of the day both men and women attend lectures, spend time on hobbies, repair or improve their homes, play board games, talk together and listen to music. They eat in communal restaurants where they also spend time working in the kitchens. The women do the communal cooking and then convicted criminals do the washing up and other dirty jobs. Every citizen also spends a period outside the city, farming. Now and again the magistrates, elected by a senate of wise elder citizens, reduce the communal work load because there is nothing more that needs doing. Those who still need anything simply go to the communal storehouse and help themselves.

More's Utopia is significant for three reasons. First, it is set in a kind of garden city. Second, it is highly organized and scheduled. Third, it is proto-communist in that there was no private property but public service is expected of all. These themes reoccur in most subsequent descriptions of Utopia, although there are significant exceptions. In the 1830s, for instance, Fourier outlined the plan for his 'phalanstery', an ideal community built to house a minimum of 1620 people in a single massive building, even larger than the royal palace at Versailles, containing workshops, schoolrooms, studies, libraries, ballrooms, meeting rooms, dining rooms, kitchens, stables, etc., linked by covered arcades. All would work for a basic wage at a variety of different jobs, primarily agricultural. Those who did difficult or unpleasant work would get the highest pay. Marriage would be abolished. In the phalanstery, there would be free love and communal child-care. Fourier believed that the passions were intrinsic to our humanity, and that repressing them created more problems than it solved. He acquired an enthusiastic following among individual socialists, thinkers and artists, intrigued by his theory of 'passionate attraction', his eccentricity and commitment to self-sustaining communities.

William Morris moved even further from More's model of the utopian city than Fourier. In his 1890 *News from Nowhere*, the narrator, William Guest, wakes up in London and unexpectedly finds himself in a landscape which he can't recall. He boards a boat which sets off upriver, passing beneath a beautiful bridge reminding him of the old Ponte Vecchio in Florence. 'It was built, or at least opened, in 2003,' the boatman tells him. 'The date shut my mouth as if a key had been turned in a padlock fixed to my lips,' Guest recalls, 'for I saw that something inexplicable had happened'. He has been transported into AD 2034, where he finds a very changed version of London, almost as if he had travelled back in time back to the fourteenth century. Since the great house clearing of 1955, he is told, there have been far fewer buildings than before, and everywhere there are now flower gardens and allotments and woodlands and orchards and children giving away fruit out of baskets.

There is no industrial production at all—everything is hand-crafted and the workers he passes in his horse-drawn wagon are volunteers, laughing and joking as they mend the road with pick-axes, a heap of their silken and gold-embroidered garments piled up by the roadside. The slums have been cleared, an event celebrated every May Day with games and feasting and the singing of revolutionary songs by the prettiest girls. Parliament has been turned into a storehouse for manure, since Londoners no longer need an elaborate system of government—their society is entirely self-regulating. Education takes place at home—printers and bookbinders provide hand-bound volumes of poetry for reading and teaching. The arts are strongly encouraged. Crime is 'a mere spasmodic disease', to be treated by forgiveness and social pressure.

Morris's nostalgic Utopia was close to the antique concept of Arcadia, the rustic paradise. It also prefigures Ernest Callenbach's 1975 book, *Ecotopia*, which describes the secession of northern

California, Oregon and Washington from the United States. The standard of living in Ecotopia is lower than in the rest of North America, but life is lived in complete contentment and harmony with nature. Society is organized on a stable-state basis, recycling is enforced and ecologically offensive products have been eliminated. Houses are built of wood and, whenever one is built, new trees must be planted. Automobiles have been abolished. Transport is by bicycle, electric taxi, minibus or on foot. Women receive equal pay and hold key political positions. Free love is taken for granted and education unregulated. Most victimless crimes have been taken off the books, although severe prison sentences are still given for rare cases of robbery or assault. The gross national product has been allowed to drop in order to provide more leisure time, small businesses are encouraged, energy use is regulated and conservation is enforced. Productivity remains high despite the limited working hours.

The twentieth century's greatest theorist of Utopia, Ernst Bloch, argues, following Freud, the unconscious mind is the repository of 'what has been', images oriented towards past memories rather than towards the future, the 'not yet conscious' which is the essence of utopia. It is in our daydreams that this 'not yet conscious' makes itself known, daydreams that signify a future consciousness just beginning to emerge. Bloch relates utopianism to the fairy tale, which he describes as 'the oldest known form of utopian narrative', as when the brave little tailor conquers the ogres with cunning, that Chaplinesque weapon of the poor, and wins the beautiful princess, or arrives in the mythical land of Cockaigne, 'where the streams are flowing with the best Muscatel'. Tables that lay themselves, magic carpets, Aladdin's lamp, all evoke utopian longings. Bloch argues that the great utopian writers all conveyed an orientation towards the future. They spoke out 'on behalf of the coming bearers of society and for the particular tendency to come'. For Bloch, another key concept is 'hope'. Rather than being trapped within past or present, we must throw ourselves forward into the hoped-for future, a time of 'becoming' rather than 'being'.

In *What Is Globalization?* Ulrich Beck calls for a new kind of global future. He welcomes in particular the possibility of what he calls 'a utopian ecological democracy', whose citizens, linked through global communications but located in their own particular contexts, can 'debate the consequences of technological and economic development *before* the key decisions are made; which places the burden of proof concerning future risks and dangers upon those who might cause them, and no longer upon those potentially or actually harmed or endangered by them'. Beck's utopianism is future-oriented, as signified by his italicization of *before*, his emphasis on future risk and potential damage. Here we have a time-based utopia, in contrast to the spatial utopias of More and his successors. Beck's emphasis is both global and local—what he calls 'glocal'—combining the dream of a cosmopolitan democracy with a localized vision.

Krishan Kumar observes that 'with the invention of Utopia we cross the divide between ancient and modern history'—a history whose modernity is marked by Hythloday's discoveries as a mariner at the very time the globe was first circumnavigated. Today we have embarked on yet another voyage—a headlong journey into globalization. In this new context, we must expect new utopias which are 'glocalized' as Beck suggests. As we become ever more deeply immersed in the dystopian wave of globalization, with its instant legacy of corporate enrichment, combined with collapse of the 'social' or 'welfare' state, civil wars, terrorism, homelessness, fanaticism, poverty and migration, the revival of a cosmopolitan utopianism becomes all the more urgent. Dream on!

Weapons of Mass Destruction

Itty Abraham

As best as I can tell, the first detected use of weapons of mass destruction (WMD) is recorded in the Old Testament, a text revered by the Judaeo-Christian-Islamic religions, when, in a fit of anger, Yahweh sends seven plagues to Egypt. Most of these weapons fall under present-day categories of biological and chemical weapons, and some are indeterminate; together they wipe out a great deal of the kingdom's livestock, productive lands and elite manpower. Hinduism too, not to be outdone by the other major religions, has its share of major weapons systems. Here the gods tend to appear as gatekeepers to the holy arsenal, providing warriors and sages with devastating weapons calibrated to the extent of their religious sacrifices. However, these tend to be single-issue weapons, their efficacy dissipated after their first, usually unplanned, use. Dare we then assume there may be a clash of civilizations implicit even in the memory of these weapons?

It would be easier to answer this question if we knew exactly what WMD are. The term itself is relatively new, a child of the fevered abstractions that swirled between Cambridge, Massachusetts, and Washington, DC in the 1950s. As time went on, WMD went out of semantic favour, resurfacing only in the aftermath of the cold war and the rise of new threats to American military power. Now it seems, in a historically analogous moment of global anxiety, WMD is back. Every Eastern cult leader, tinpot dictator, shadowy Islamic terrorist and reformulated communist may have one, be close to having one or simply thinking of having one, according to unnamed high official sources close to the American administration.

Given the obvious bias in its everyday overuse, it is easy to dismiss WMD as just another loaded term-of-the-day, subject to the usual myopias of race, nation and capital. To take the term apart is to see its barriers to entry. The 'weapon' part of WMD can be a missile warhead loaded with toxic chemicals, a syringe full of killer anthrax, a Petri dish of incurable viruses; but what is it not? Weapons are not the regular toxic spills from nuclear reactors, not the dumping of waste chemicals in local rivers, not tuberculosis bacteria that have become immune to repeated over-prescriptions of antibiotics, not the strange afflictions of environmental disease, mental illness and other murky modern-day illnesses that escape the probe of medical instruments and electronic diagnostics, and certainly not the seeds that are programmed to commit suicide in a single harvest cycle. The 'mass' refers to an undifferentiated people that translate into the body of the nation, a Western, powerful body that has a lot to lose, a homogenous group of ingenues that needs to be protected at all costs from the aforementioned threats. The mass is never the millions who die from a lack of the most basic things needed for material survival, the farmers who commit suicide because their debts have mounted beyond their ability to ever pay them back in this lifetime, the boy soldiers of countless wars of attrition taking place because of the wanton disregard for limits in the making of wealth, the young children who are hauled into seedy brothels in order to satisfy the demands of diseased sybarites. 'Destruction' seems unambiguous, but, as we can see, selective.

Given this ambiguity—the selective meanings that dominate the public use of this term—we must ask how it is possible to keep these meanings apart. For example, what distinguishes the release of a cloud of toxic gas from a Union Carbide plant in Bhopal, killing thousands and crippling hundreds of thousands more, from Saddam Hussein's alleged use of poison gas against the Kurdish minority of Iraq? Both actions killed scores of people, but only one is typically classified as the use of WMD. Why? The answer, it appears, lies in the deliberateness of the act, the degree of awareness of the intended effects, the wantonness of the act of destruction. Hence, since Saddam Hussein's use of chemical weapons against the Kurds was done in the full awareness of what he was trying to achieve, that is, the en masse destruction of the Kurds, Union Carbide's action falls into the category of an 'industrial accident'. The cause of the 'accident' cannot be identified with any one actor, whether the designer of the plant, the employees, the owners or the state government of Madhya Pradesh. Calling the gas leak at Bhopal and the consequent death of thousands an 'accident' makes the event akin to a natural disaster, a so-called act of God, not the use of a weapon of mass destruction. Ultimately, this distinction is only possible because of a particular understanding of the nature of 'accident'. Is this distinction meaningful?

When we speak of an accident, we usually imply an event that cannot be predicted, that happens as a result of complex factors whose relation to each other cannot be known completely before an 'accident' occurs. A 'true' accident cannot be known in advance, else it would not be an accident. There are 'good' accidents of course, the chance meeting with a friend on the street, discovering a new food that turns out to be a cure for a long-standing illness, and so on. But in the context of modern technology, the realm of 'good' accidents ends once we leave behind the phase of scientific research and industrial development. Large-scale complex modern technologies, whether oil refineries, steel mills, air-traffic control systems or chemical factories, are all built to a scale that makes them impossible to 'know' completely. The omniscience we associate with the inventor of an artefact (the personal computer, for example) does not hold up in the case of these mega-technologies, both because no one person can master the complexity of the entire system and because the system itself is greater than the sum of its modular parts. In other words, because of the scale and complexity of the system, it is impossible to comprehend its totality. What can be known, or rather measured, is the output of certain key factors, inputs, variables or products. If the measured values of these factors lie within certain bounds, then all is considered well. If not, there is a potential crisis.

In this context, an accident is an extreme kind of crisis, which can be expressed in terms of the extent to which key variables exceed acceptable limits. A crisis is usually measured in term of variables expressing its absence, usually 'safety' or 'efficiency'. But what does a term like '99.9%' efficiency actually mean in practice? According to the popular US magazine INC, in terms of (US) standards, operating at a 99.9% level of perfection means the following—16,000 pieces of mail lost by the US Post Office every hour, two unsafe landings a day at Chicago's O'Hare airport, 500 incorrect surgical operations a week, 20,000 incorrect drug prescriptions a year, and 32,000 missed heartbeats per person annually. Few mega-technologies of the kind described above are nearly that reliable. 'Accidents', in other words, are a structural feature of mega-technologies. Accidents cannot be done away with without getting rid of the technology. The distinction cannot hold.

Deus ex Machina

One of popular culture's most vivid maxims is 'Guns don't kill, people do', the seductively reasonable slogan of the US National Rifle Association. The logic underlying this statement is familiar. Guns, whose only purpose is to kill living beings, are being discursively made into silent technical artefacts whose futures are determined by a single factor, the operator of the gun. Guns in the hands of the police and the patriotic citizen are good things, but not in the hands of the criminal or the terrorist. Likewise, with the weapon of mass destruction. What is critical is not the instrument or even its killing potential, but the mind of the person behind it. The ability to prevent weapons of mass destruction from proliferating across the globe then becomes the need to control those who might use these weapons for conscious purposes of mass destruction. We have shifted from the control of weapons to the control of those who might use them. The machine is made into a mute technical switch, a purely neutral object, and all attention must now be focussed on the operator himself and his thought processes. The strategy of focusing attention on the man behind the machine allows for the full play of cultural difference to be read in racial and civilizational terms. He is now the 'rogue leader' who must be stopped at all costs.

This is not new, but the contemporary logic of 'intervention' in the making (and stopping) of rogue leaders is. The triangulation of three fronts for intervention—the transnational media, the international humanitarian industry, and political-military power—produces an endless stream of rogue states led by rogue leaders who can be found in darkest Europe, sub-Saharan Africa, South Asia, North Korea and the always-popular Middle East. Weapons of mass destruction appear when the transnational media discovers a suitably recalcitrant, larger-than-life tyrant or rebel; the international humanitarian industry discovers the scores of victims that have been created by the actions of this tyrant or rebel; and, finally, the military-intelligence complex discovers in the tyrant signs of interest in weapons of mass destruction, ideally funded through rents from their near-monopoly on some precious metal or mineral. If only one of these three fronts are present, we get a momentary news event or a low-level humanitarian problem. If two are present, then the media joins the humanitarian industry and starts making a case for the importance of the event in relation to the well-being of 'international society'. If the conjuncture of politics is right, military-intelligence steps in and we have a full-fledged crisis, proclaimed on all three fronts. This was the case in the Gulf War, East Timor and Kosovo, but not in Rwanda or Kashmir. Weapons of mass destruction are a product of the clash of civilizations, the triangulation of interventionary fronts, not their cause.

Further Reading

Beck, Ulrich. 1992. *Risk Society: Towards a New Modernity.* Translated by Mark Ritter. London and Newbury Park, California: Sage Publications.

Chomsky, Noam. 1987. *The Chomsky Reader.* Edited by James Peck. New York: Pantheon Books.

Vaughan, Diane. 1996. *The Challenger Launch Decision: Risky Technology, Culture, and Deviance at NASA.* Chicago: University of Chicago Press.

West

A. Raghuramaraju

Modern cultural and political discourse binds a historically extended sense, dating back to the classical era, to the term 'West'. This concedes more antiquity to the term than is perhaps deserved. According to the OED, its use other than as an adverb—as a noun or as an adjective—is a 'later development' that gained currency during the Great War, although the immediate source of such usage 'has not been established'. The processes that culminated in the formation of homogeneous nation-states, together designated as *the West*, date back to the advent of modernity, even though the term itself came into vogue much later. In fact, this process of formation—actually an act of self-transformation, which undid in its wake its own diverse pre-modern basis—provides content to the term 'West'. Notwithstanding its modern use, which is roughly only three centuries old, the term is employed to definitively designate Western civilization, culture, society, philosophy, literature and music—cardinal aspects of which antedate the contemporary use of the term. The 'West' is coterminous with modernity, but not in the sense that some critics of the West and modernity insist.

Subsequently, the term acquires a clearer meaning when it impacts on the *outside* world as colonialism. Perhaps, in line with Buddhist epistemology, according to which knowledge consists of not only knowing what it *is* but also what it *is not*, the term in its outbound colonial journey becomes sharply conscious of what it is not. It is this epistemological need for identity consolidation, rather than the political programme of colonial expansion, that seems to necessitate the postulation of the 'other' as different from 'self': materialistic 'self' versus spiritual 'other'; non-despotic 'self' in relationship to the despotic 'other', and so on. These contrasts, mediated through constructs like 'Orient' and 'East', aided this consolidation by providing a broader consensus and wider use of the term. The postcolonial exaggeration that the West is known *only* through its 'other' derives from mistaking this shift in identity formation for the identity itself.

A look at the whole process yields some interesting insights. First, the pre-modern, inasmuch as it is destroyed in reality, is available to the modern self only in 'sociological imagination', that is, in an *imagination* that seeks an 'ideational desideratum' (à la Anthony Giddens). This search is conducted primarily in 'art, literature, language, and the cultural artefacts' (Susan Bordo). Perhaps, to critique 'the modern', from a vantage point that offers both hindsight and foresight, Michel Foucault seems to suggest the need to conflate 'pre-modern' and 'postmodern' as 'countermodernity'. This new domain, along with anthropology (study of inhabited spaces) and history (study of time), delimits the political programme of dissent to modernity in the West.

Second, this process of radical transformation within the West was not a smooth affair. It involved wholesale violence and oppression. The transformation from agrarian 'low culture' to 'high culture' of homogenized modern nation-states, according to Ernest Gellner, is not smooth, neither governed by sympathy nor by an understanding of what is being transformed. Foucault's work bears testimony to how modern knowledge systems disempowered their human subjects within the West.

Next, the project of modernity, consisting of a new form of universalism, instrumental rationality and autonomous abstract individualism, decultured the embedded individual and turned him into what the philosopher, René Descartes was to call *cogito*. Its universalism is premised on the emptying of differentiating cultural sediments. The social contract philosophers later stationed these cognitive nudes in an imaginary solitary island called 'the state of nature'. Subsequently, the modernized West extended the project outwards into other pre-modern realms, listing the jobs accomplished and those yet to be accomplished: its own past fell under the first category and that of the non-West under the second. It is not the case of an imperial culture transforming another, but one decultured world view, after emptying itself of its own cultural contents, attempting to universalize its project. It is a case of self-transformation *preceding* the transformation of the 'other'.

This inevitable structural dependency on the 'other' explains why, to use an observation made by Ashis Nandy, modernity/West 'as an ideology can thrive only in a society that is predominantly' non-modern. And, once 'a society begins to become' modern 'or once the people begin to feel that their society is being cleansed of religion and ideas of transcendence' the political status of modernity changes. The insecurity of the displaced, modern, atomized self seems to underlie its attempt to reach out in desperation to the 'other'. Shrouded in this desperation is both the fear of and contempt for the 'other'. This psychological state, to use Edward Said's words, vacillates between its 'contempt of what is familiar and its shivers of delight in—or fear of—novelty'.

Finally, an important feature of the West is the invariance in its intentionality. It has done to the non-West only what it has done, and is doing, to itself. The ideals of modernity were first lab-tested and experimented upon within the West before they were unleashed elsewhere. For instance, colonialism attempted to homogenize the intrinsic pluralism of Indian society by integrating diverse legal, economic and administrative systems of the 'natives' in an image of the British system. This helped crystallize the modern Indian nation and its nationalism, and while positive local laws were not annulled wholesale, their subservience to the overall laws of the colonial state was clearly enunciated, and this led to their gradual fading out. This whole project simply mimicked the earlier British process.

Modernity is Janus-faced; it both internalizes and thus incorporates the other, while also trespassing into the other. So it is necessary to preface our discussion of what the West did through colonialism to non-Western societies by the question 'What did modernity do to its own pre-modern societies?'

Despite these turbulent tensions, internal discontinuities and the recent origin of the term 'West,' many thinkers, for example Hegel (who used the term positively) or Spengler (even while declaring its decline), built a huge edifice called the 'West'. Paradoxically, even the staunchest critics of the West, like Edward Said, often fail to recognize its recent origin and its internal tensions, and author anti-climactic views wherein they credit their adversary, the West, with more strength than it actually has. This conceptual laxity has permeated deep into postcolonial discourse, leading to considerable misunderstanding and misinterpretation.

Though Said disregarded the internal project of modernity, the poet Aimé Césaire in his *Discourse on Colonialism* (1972) at least partly captures its nature and suggests that 'no one colonizes innocently . . . a nation which colonizes . . . a civilization which justifies colonization . . . is already a sick civilization, a civilization that is morally diseased . . .' Rather than sickness, it is the dynamics of the internal project of modernity that can better ground a postcolonial criticism of the 'West'. Nandy, whose position is closer to Mahatma Gandhi, aptly describes the psychological state of the colonizer when he says that he is 'not the conspiratorial dedicated oppressor that he is made out to be, but a self-destructive co-victim.' Here let us stretch the temporal phases of the phrase 'co-victim' a little. The oppressor does not become a 'co-victim' in the process of victimizing the 'other'. In fact, as already pointed out, victimizing the 'other' is preceded by or springs from self-victimization. Hence the need to replace the term 'co-victim', as it carries the sense of simultaneity instead of the sense of a sequence.

The 'West' has become, like the Kantian self, a source of knowledge, but something that cannot know itself. This, says the philosopher K.C. Bhattacharyya, might ultimately relapse the Kantian self either into agnosticism or to be merely postulated as a necessity of thought or as moral faith. To avoid this, it is necessary for this self to have self-knowledge. The West too needs to become aware of itself, particularly, of its recent origin and its modern form, and not claim antiquity. The antidote to the construction of the 'other' will thus be the deconstruction of itself through this act of looking within. Without this self-awareness, the West might gain political mileage, but it will face serious problems with regard to its own existence. It may be that the West, like the proverbial eye, needs a mirror to be able to carry out the task of looking at itself. For that, the only option is to turn the gaze from the non-West to the West's own pre-modern self. This realignment of gaze has to be in an epistemological and not moralistic sense; else the central point made above may be misread as the valorization of the pre-modern West. Such an epistemological exercise will reconfirm that the West is not a monolith.

These internal tensions between modernity and pre-modern plural social realities, the recent origin of the West, the invariance in its intentionality and the internal process of modernization preceding the external process of colonialism—all are important, particularly in the present context when the West or modernity claims to be 'everywhere.' Though everywhere, it is not all over: it is confined to certain pockets from where it continues to give a deceptive, spectral feeling of being everywhere. Within the present non-Western societies, it is possible to locate and identify its absences, pockets of resistance to it, as well as its ineffectiveness, along with, of course, its presences and success. Together they can provide a site to actively negotiate, neither a pure modernity/West nor even a pure non-West but a simultaneous combination of both. The possibility of simultaneity, which is available in the non-Western societies, is to be contrasted with their ordering, which is sequential within the West. This is also the occasion to recognize the West-centredness of Foucault's plea to conflate the pre-modern and the postmodern. This active negotiation between the modern and the pre-modern outside the West and not a tame surrender of the pre-modern to the modern within the West should significantly limit modernity's claim to being everywhere.

To conclude, the destruction of its own pre-modern self and

contrasting it with its own constructions such as the 'Orient' are the two historically significant resources that shaped the formation of the term 'West'. Given these dimensions of the term, it may be a worthwhile exercise to do some sorting of its various uses in the writings of modern thinkers such as Hegel, Spengler, Toynbee, Said and others to arrive at new insights and possibly identify the limitations of their historiography.

Further Reading

Bhattacharyya, Krishna Chandra. 1993. The concept of philosophy. In *Studies in Philosophy*. Delhi: Motilal Banarsidass.

Césaire, Aimé. 1972. *Discourse on Colonialism*. Translated by Joan Pinkham. London: Monthly Review Press.

Nandy, Ashis. 1999. The twilight of certitudes: Secularism, Hindu nationalism, and other masks of deculturation. *Alternatives* 22(2):157–76.

Said, Edward. 1979. *Orientalism*. New York: Vintage Books.

Yahoo

Ziauddin Sardar

In Jonathan Swift's *Gulliver's Travels* Yahoo is the name of an imaginary race of brutish creatures. In postmodern times, Yahoo is a race of flesh-and-blood boorish people who live their lives on the Internet. It is also the name of the most popular online navigational guide to the Web, and the name of a magazine that is the Bible of 'Internet life'. Yahoo could be said to personify as well as characterize the Net.

One of the main features of the Net is that it tends to do things in exponential terms. Yahoo, the directory service for Web pages, is a good example of this. It was started in April 1994 by David Filo and Jerry Yang, two electrical engineering graduates at Stanford University, to track their favourite sites on the Web. It grew exponentially in the first six months to become the unofficial starting place for exploring the Internet. When they went public, the two graduates become instant multimillionaires. Within a few years, Yahoo took over the world. That's the kind of pace that the Internet sets.

Another basic feature of the Net is its mythological nature. Yahoo sometimes stands for Yet Another Hierarchical Officious Oracle. In classical antiquity, the oracle as a mode of prophecy was an infallible guide to the future; it was a place where advice or prediction was sought by human beings from the gods. One of the world's leading suppliers of software for information management, with revenues approaching scores of billions, is also called Oracle. A software package for building e-business applications, popular with developers, is called Delphi. As we all know, the ancient Greeks believed that Delphi, where the oracle was located, was the centre of universe: Zeus himself sent two of his angels to the end of the earth—understood to be a flat disc— to determine its centre. The divine birds had met at Delphi. So mythology, and not just Greek mythology, is quite integral to the institutions, software and conceptual makeup of the Net. Indeed, mythology is the material of which the Net is woven.

When two essential features of the Net are combined together, we end with an accelerating mythology. The world of 0s and 1s, created in and by cyberspace, is a mythological utopia where communication is immediate and automatic, friendships emerge instantaneously and all information is available at the touch of a button. In this utopia, muzak comes out of our beds, medicine emerges from our data sockets, we live in intelligent houses, drive around in self-guiding smart cars and all of us publish our own books.

Cyberspace, like mythologies, is about redemption. It is the new god of secular salvation. Its priests are the managers of Intel, Xerox, Apple, Lotus and Microsoft—the people who dragged the computer out of their technological temples and on to our desks. Its prophets, sometimes described as 'techno-metaphysicians', search for more profound meaning in the information revolution. These yahoos talk reverentially about 'information society', 'third-wave technology', the 'fourth discontinuity' and other claptrap. They constantly prophesize about 'The Next Big Thing', and eagerly anticipate the arrival of the machine 'who' really thinks.

I have no problem with the assertion that computers will improve the way we work and play. But yahoos are not content with this. Computers, they tell us, will not only improve the way we think, they will actually turn us into better human beings and more sensitive, ethical communities. The Net articulates the unity towards which the world has been working ever since we tripped over technology. At last, we can realize our true spiritual potential, combining material quest with ethereal yearning, and thus further our evolution into a higher life form. Like Greek gods, the postmodern yahoos are lusty fellows. They lust for power, control, perpetually desire more and more, and also more of the carnal variety.

Computer enslavement begins with the lure, the promise of increasing and accelerating computer power and connectivity at decreasing costs. Once you are caught and invest heavily in the use of computers to perform crucial tasks, you become irreversibly committed. Systems have to be perennially upgraded; new software has to be constantly installed.

One of the great myths about computers is that they are getting cheaper and cheaper. What they are getting is more and more powerful. And the latest model, with the whirls, buzzes and the whistles—the one that *you* want—is not cheap. And what constitutes cheap anyway? The machine on your desktop is hardly cheap when what it costs can feed a whole family in Bangladesh for a full year. Computerization creates a whole new set of dependencies on hardware and software manufacturers. One is trapped in a 'pathological scramble' to keep up with the incredible rate of change.

An equally great myth is that computers lead to noticeable increases in productivity. In truth, administration and management systematically absorb all that ever-increasing power, while workers are not much better off in terms of autonomy, flexibility or greater control. Technical efficiency is just another name for increased control by management. Thanks to computers, management now knows exactly what the workers are doing, when they are doing it and with whom.

But who needs workers anyway? No matter what the yahoos tell us, the dominant cyber trend is towards destroying, and not creating, more jobs. This is nowhere more pronounced than in the sunrise high-tech enterprises. What early computers did to manual workers, the new computerized networks are now doing to white-collar personnel. Crafts and skills are evaporating fast. When intelligent machines arrive, knowledge workers too will receive their exit orders.

Cyberspace is the territory where delinquents and perverts, radical nihilists and terrorists roam freely and in exponentially large numbers. Some forty categories of undesirable activities—ranging from pornography, fraud, hacking, 'freaking', virus creation, promoting violence and cyber terrorism—have established themselves firmly on the Net. New web sites promoting fascist and extremists ideas spring up with mundane regularity, as do manuals for bomb making. More than 20,000 new hosts of pornographic sites are created daily. Child pornography, much of it from Eastern Europe, is the biggest growth industry. Eastern Europe also produces some of the best and most fanatical hackers who have the ability to bring down airport flight-management computers, power systems, hospital equipment and, not least, stock markets such as NASDAQ. Information put on a computer is seldom secure; molecular analysis of a hard disc can reveal much of what was 'deleted'. That innocent looking e-mail may be concealing text within text—what is known as the art of steganography. So that what appears to be a purchase order may actually be a command to carry out an assassination.

Complex networks like the Internet suffer from a serious weakness. A network is essentially a collection of nodes. The World Wide Web is a network of web pages joined together by hyperlinks; the Internet is the physical communication network linked together by routers. All a yahoo terrorist has to do to cause untold damage is to target the most connected routers or web sites. The average performance of the Internet is reduced by a factor of two if just 1 per cent of the most connected nodes are destroyed; and with only 4 per cent of crucial nodes down, the Internet looses its integrity, becoming fragmented into small disconnected domains. So, like Achilles, cyberspace has an exposed point of extreme vulnerability.

But we don't need yahoo terrorists to cause chaos. The Internet is taking us towards chaotic times naturally and in more ways than one. The first signs of this come from the financial markets and computerized trading, which seems closer to the promise of virtual reality than any other human activity. As computerized networks and powerful satellite communication links make markets accessible from almost anywhere on the globe, a new breed of 'paper entrepreneurs' increasingly displaces experienced traders. These are computer wizards who depend on their computers rather than upon any awareness of economic activity.

Surely, anyone with an intelligent head on their shoulders should be able to detect that there are serious problems with the computerized utopias towards which we are being hurled. The problem with the yahoos is that they are just too spaced out, too drunk on accelerating technology, too out of breath from organizing life at the speed of light, to be intelligent. William Gibson, who coined the term in his 1984 novel *Neuromancer*, described cyberspace as 'a consensual hallucination'. The yahoos are perpetually hallucinating; and their hallucinations have both historic and physical reasons.

The origins of cyberspace are to be found in the American war machine. Like Teflon and the mini hi-fi, it is a partially foreseen by-product of research whose sole purpose is to discover better and more efficient ways to kill. In the 1960s, a group of technologically twisted hippies slowly subverted the computer from its Armageddon arithmetic, brought the network out into the open and used it to chat and play games. Today, cyberspace bears all the hallmarks of its hippie subverts—from an obsession with pagan, psychedelic and New Age spirituality to sexual neurosis and perversion to plainly daft talk about free information, community and love.

Virtually all the myths about cyberspace have their origins in this history. One of cyberspace's frequently repeated aphorisms, attributed to the 'Whole Earth' guru Stuart Brand, declares that information wants to be free. So, like an ageing hippie, information is a libertarian entity. Yet nothing of value on the web is free. What appears to be free is only an invitation to entrapment, like the drug pedlar's initial fixes.

Similarly, we are constantly being told that cyberspace is linking us all together, bringing communities closer and producing communities where there were none. Wherever we go in our global village, we can tap into a cellular phone, get online with a personal digital assistant with built-in modem and satellite connection, and surf the web to our heart's content. But connection does not make a community. Nor does it actually lead to meaningful communication. The community that cyberspace generates is purely an illusion. The Net facilitates and encourages a separating-out into endlessly subdividing groups. It is populated largely by style-groups where people define themselves through their fantasies. When you look closely at the world of yahoos, you find discrete, isolated, sad, desperate individuals. You can jerk off using a computer, but you can't develop a meaningful relationship with it.

The real appeal of cyberspace is the fact that it offers a society dominated by individualism what that society desires most: a world designed to accommodate individual impulses. It is the ideal place for those incapable of saying hello to their neighbours, but ever ready to fire bursts of text detailing their fantasies to complete strangers in newsgroups, forums, chat rooms and countless sites (over a third of the Net) devoted to all variety of perversions. Building communities is hard work. It requires you to be out there interacting in the real, messy world, not sitting in front of a terminal talking to someone you have never met, nor likely to meet. On the other hand, exposure to the wider world via the Net appears to make people less satisfied with their personal lives and more aware of their limitations.

If one tries to form a relationship with a computer, one should not be surprised to know that it is not physically too healthy. Computer-induced hallucinations are now becoming common. The ever-growing cloud of 'data smog' subtracts from our quality of life, leading to stress, confusion and ignorance. Computer addicts everywhere are suffering a whole array of diseases described collectively as 'fragmentia'. These include increased cardiovascular stress, weakened vision, impaired judgement, confusion, frustration, decreased benevolence and overconfidence. One direct product of the information revolution is a brain imbalance called attention deficit disorder (ADD). This syndrome causes acute restlessness, boredom and distraction. Sufferers cannot focus on anything for more than a few seconds. We are, it seems, heading straight for an ADD epidemic.

ADD spells death for the book. The yahoos have all but written off the book. Reading any kind of book requires a sustained effort. You can't surf the book and jump perpetually from place to place the way you can on the World Wide Web. Moreover, now that we can all bundle our thoughts together using some desktop publishing package or some idiot-proof software for writing hypertext, and publish it on the Net, the book really is redundant. But the crap that saturates the Net makes the book more, and not less, important. The Net only encourages vanity publishing on a colossal scale. It's the domain of the unread semi-literate, clutching web pages, screaming about his undiscovered genius, and stalking cyberspace for victims.

In its extreme forms, computer-induced hallucination leads to the idea that the Internet represents the next stage of human evolution. Modes of communication have evolved in a linear fashion, from alphabets to monotheism, reaching their natural apex with cyberspace. So the next quantum leap, the next step up the evolutionary ladder, is the merging of cyberspace and physical space and the dissolution of humanity into virtual reality. Individual consciousness will be submerged in the Overmind of the Internet. Soon, in the not-so-distant future, we will be downloading our minds on to the Net and cruising the world as a digital signal. Virtual reality already makes this possible to some extent. So we should not be surprised when newspapers are published directly into our heads—side-stepping the problem of actually reading them—while poetry and literature can be experienced by all computer users directly in digitized forms.

Frankly, I would prefer that the yahoos be 'deleted', disappear in electronic blips, thus leaving the world to people with real imagination.

Notes on Contributors

Itty Abraham is the author of *The Making of the Indian Atomic Bomb* (London: Zed Press, 1998) and various articles on science and security. He lives in New York.

Imtiaz Ahmed is currently the chairperson of the Department of International Relations, University of Dhaka, and is also the executive director, Centre for Alternatives. He is the editor of *Theoretical Perspectives: A Journal of Social Sciences and Arts* (Dhaka) and co-editor of *South Asian Refugee Watch* (Colombo and Dhaka) and *Identity, Culture and Politics: An Afro-Asian Dialogue* (Dakar and Dhaka). His publications include *The Efficacy of the Nation-State in South Asia: A Post-Nationalist Critique* (Colombo: ICES, 1998).

Frédérique Apffel-Marglin is professor of anthropology at Smith College and collaborates with several grass-roots NGOs in Peru and Bolivia. She is the author and editor of seven books and many articles on religion, gender, critiques of science and development and biocultural diversity. Her most recent books are (co-edited) *Decolonizing Knowledge: From Development to Dialogue* (Oxford: Clarendon, 1996) and (with PRATEC) *The Spirit of Regeneration: Andean Culture Confronting Western Notions of Development* (Zed Books, 1998).

Charles Carnegie is associate professor of anthropology at Bates College where he also chairs the Program in African American Studies. He is a member of the editorial collective of the journal *Small Axe*, editor of *Afro-Caribbean Villages in Historical Perspective* and author of *Postnationalism Prefigured: Caribbean Borderlands* (Rutgers, 2003).

Ajaya Dixit chairs the largest technical NGO in Nepal (Nepal Water for Health) on a voluntary capacity and co-edits, with Dipak Gyawali, the interdisciplinary journal *Water Nepal*. His current works involve the study of local water management methods and the social response to water scarcity at local, regional and global levels. His latest book, *Basic Water Science*, brings together natural and social sciences of water.

Gustavo Esteva can be described as a nomadic storyteller, a deprofessionalized intellectual and a grass-roots activist. Among his many works in Spanish and English are *Zapatistas and Grassroots Postmodernism* (Zed Books, 1999). Former adviser of the Zapatistas, he is associated with many networks and social movements in Mexico and abroad. He lives in a small indigenous village in the south of Mexico, where he produces his own food, and participates in initiatives for cultural regeneration in hundreds of communities in Oaxaca and Chiapas. He writes a column in an important Mexican newspaper.

Teshome Gabriel has been associated with the University of California, Los Angeles, for over three decades and he is presently professor in the School of Film & Television. He has written widely on cinema, poetry and nomadism. A collection of his essays is forthcoming from Basil Blackwell. He is editor of *Emergences*, a journal for the study of media and composite cultures.

Paul Gonsalves was founder of Equations (Equitable Tourism Options), Bangalore, the first NGO to explore issues related to tourism in India. He worked later with the international NGO Ecumenical Coalition on Third World Tourism. In 1997, he was MacArthur Fellow, King's College, London. He has also researched and worked on contemporary geopolitical issues in the Mekong region and Indonesia.

Dipak Gyawali is currently Pragya (Academician) of the Royal Nepal Academy of Science and Technology (RONAST), co-editor of the biannual interdisciplinary journal *Water Nepal*, member of the New York Academy of Sciences and member of the Oxford Commission on Sustainable Consumption. By profession, he is a hydroelectric power engineer and a resource economist. His current activities are centred around local water management institutions, alternative hill transport systems and the social response to disasters. His most recent work is *Water in Nepal* (2001).

John Hutnyk teaches visual anthropology at Goldsmiths College, University of London. He is the co-editor (with Raminder Kaur) of *Travel Worlds: Journeys in Contemporary Cultural Politics* (Zed Books, 1999), and among his recent works is *Critique of Exotica* (Pluto Press, 2000). He is a frequent visitor to Kolkata.

Raminder Kaur teaches social anthropology at the University of Sussex. She is a script-writer for film/theatre, co-editor (with John Hutnyk) of *Travel Worlds: Journeys in Contemporary Cultural Politics* (Zed Books, 1999) and author of a study of the politics of the Ganpati festival, published by Oxford.

Manu Kothari and **Lopa Mehta** are physicians and have co-authored nine books, including *Living and Dying* (Marion Boyers) and *The Other Face of Cancer* (The Other India Press), and more than seventy articles on a wide range of medical subjects such as surgery, cancer, medical philosophy, anatomy and biology. They have been associated with KEM Hospital, Mumbai, for over two decades.

Vatsal Kothari is an internist and lecturer in internal medicine at the Seth GS Medical College & KEM Hospital, Mumbai.

Sankaran Krishna is professor of political science and director, Center for South Asian Studies, at the University of Hawaii at Manoa. He works on contemporary Indian politics and in international relations. He is the author of *Postcolonial Insecurities: India, Sri Lanka and the Question of Nationhood* (University of Minnesota Press, 1999).

R.L. Kumar is a self-taught and practising architect working at the Centre for Informal Education and Development Studies, Bangalore. He works with a building craftpersons' cooperative called Shramik and is a regular contributor to the journal of the Council of Architecture. His main concern is the theoretical elaboration and practical application of vernacular architectural traditions as a sustainable alternative to modern architecture.

Vinay Lal was educated, as much as he cared to be, at Johns Hopkins and the University of Chicago. He now teaches in the Department of History at the University of California, Los Angeles. Ahistoricity is one of the principal subjects of his most recent book, *The History of History: Politics and Scholarship in Modern India* (Delhi: Oxford, 2003).

C. Douglas Lummis studied politics at the University of California, Berkeley, in the 1960s and taught until recently in the Department of Political Science at Tsuda Juku College near Tokyo. He is the author of several books, including *Ruth Benedict, Radical Democracy* (Cornell University Press, 1996) and *Japan's Radical Constitution* (Tokyo: Shobunsha, 1987, in Japanese).

Philip McMichael is an Australian expatriate managing life in the Empire State of the USA, New York, as a professor of development sociology at Cornell University. He supports the slow food movement, which he believes is the essence of food sovereignty, and the condition for a post-imperial future. His books include *Settlers and the Agrarian Question* (1984) and *Development and Social Change: A Global Perspective* (2000). He has edited *The Global Restructuring of Agro-Food Systems* (1994) and *Food and Agrarian Orders in the World-Economy* (1995).

Sudesh Mishra has taught at universities in Fiji, Australia and Scotland. His books include *Preparing Faces: Modernism and Indian Poetry in English* (criticism), *Tandava* (poetry) and *Ferringhi* (play). He resides in Melbourne. His most recent book is *Diaspora and the Difficult Art of Dying* (Otago University Press, 2001).

Ashis Nandy was for many years senior fellow, Centre for the Study of Developing Societies, Delhi. He is the author of over fifteen books.

David Punter is a poet, critic and amateur gardener. His published books include *The Literature of Terror* (1980; second edition 1996), *The Hidden Script* (1985), *The Romantic Unconscious* (1989), *Gothic Pathologies* (1998), *Writing the Passions* (2000), and *Postcolonial Imaginings* (2000), as well as four volumes of poetry. He is currently working on a book to be called *Writing in the Twenty-First Century*, which looks at the global fate of postmodernity.

A. Raghuramaraju teaches philosophy at the University of Hyderabad, India. In addition he does farming for two months in a year in his village. He grazed sheep and cattle in the forest before he took academics seriously. His essays on nationalism, secularism, Gandhi and human rights have appeared in the *Economic and Political Weekly*, *Journal of the Indian Council of Philosophical Research* and various edited volumes. He also writes essays on Telugu literature in Telugu. *Indian Philosophy: Classical, Colonial and Contemporary* is forthcoming from Oxford (Delhi).

Majid Rahnema was minister for science and higher education in Iran before he joined the UN, first as UNDP Representative in Mali (1979–82), later as UNDP Special Advisor for Grassroots and NGO Matters (1982–85). He has also held other important posts within the UN system, such as UN Commissioner to Rwanda, Vice-President of the UN Economic and Social Council, and Member of the Executive Board of UNESCO. He has written extensively on sociocultural and international matters, and his books include *Learning to Be* (co-authored, Paris, 1972) and (edited) *The Post Development Reader* (London, 1997).

Sudhir Chella Rajan writes on politics, energy and the environment and is the author of *The Enigma of Automobility: Democratic Politics and Pollution Control* (University of Pittsburgh Press, 1996). He is a senior scientist at Tellus Institute, Boston, and is presently working on a study of poverty, environment and the claims of global citizenship.

Roby Rajan is professor at the School of Business, University of Wisconsin, Parkside. His articles and reviews have appeared in a variety of journals including *The International Economic Review, Operations Research, Empirical Economics, The Journal of Development Studies, Cato Journal, Alternatives, Rethinking Marxism, Emergences, and Futures.*

Barry Sanders is professor of English and the history of ideas at Pitzer, the Claremont Colleges, California. From 1985 to 1990, he occupied the Peter S. and Gloria Gold Chair. He is the author of nine books, including *ABC: The Alphabetization of the Popular Mind* (with Ivan Illich); *A Is For Ox: Violence, Electronic Media, and the Silencing of the Written Word*; *The Private Death of Public Discourse*; and *Sudden Glory: Laughter as Subversive History.*

Michael Sells is Emily Judson Baugh and John Marshall Gest Professor of Comparative Religions at Haverford College. He is the author of *The Bridge Betrayed: Religion and Genocide in Bosnia* (1994, 1996) and a web page dedicated to documenting war-crimes in the former Yugoslavia. He is also a founder of the non-profit organization Community of Bosnia that works to support a multireligious Bosnia-Herzegovina. Further information can be found at his home page http://www.haverford.edu/relg/sells/home.html.

C.J.W.-L. Wee teaches literature and cultural theory at the Nanyang Technological University, Singapore. His books include *Culture, Empire, and the Question of Being Modern* (2003) and (edited) *Local Cultures and the 'New Asia': The State, Culture, and Capitalism in Southeast Asia* (2002).

Peter Wollen is professor at the School of Film and Television at UCLA. He is a frequent contributor to the *London Review of Books* and the *New Left Review*. His books include *Signs and Meaning in the Cinema* (1972), *Raiding the Icebox: Reflections on Twentieth-Century Culture* (1993) and *Howard Hawks, American Artist* (1996).

Lakshman Yapa is an associate professor of geography at Pennsylvania State University. He teaches courses on economic geography, Third World development, urban poverty in the US, and computer-assisted regional analysis. His current research concerns theories of development and poststructural interventions in poverty. He has served as a consultant to US, UN and World Bank projects in Bolivia, Egypt, Eritrea, Sri Lanka, Malaysia, Thailand, Philippines and Indonesia.

Index